Government Spending Facts 2

Government Spending Facts 2

by Isabella Horry and
Michael Walker

THE FRASER INSTITUTE

The Fraser Institute
Vancouver, British Columbia, Canada

Printed in Canada.

Canadian Cataloguing in Publication Data

Horry, Isabella, 1963—
Government spending facts 2

Includes bibliographical references.
ISBN 0-88975-158-7

1. Government spending policy—Canada. 2. Canada—Appropriations and expenditures. I. Walker, Michael, 1945— II. Fraser Institute (Vancouver, B.C.). III. Title.
HJ7660.H67 1994 336.3'9'0971 C94-910685-2

Table of Contents

List of Figures and Tables

Figures:

Tables:

Chapter 6 Appendix Tables

Appendix C Tables

Appendix D Tables

Preface

UNDOUBTEDLY ONE OF THE MOST PRESSING economic issues of the 1990s is concern about the level of government expenditures. The ongoing deficits at the federal level as well as the failure of most provinces to balance their budgets, together with the rising burden of public debt interest costs will continue to focus public attention on the activities of government. The purpose of this book is to provide a compilation and analysis of government spending both currently and historically. This information will better enable Canadians to assess government activities and to place both current developments and the claims of government in perspective.

Almost invariably, when a Minister of government is approached on the subject of the "excessive" expenditure of his or her government, the response is, "Which expenditures should be cut? Give me some suggestions as to where we can cut expenditures." This is a fairly safe demand for politicians to make since most Canadians, including the politician, have very little information about how government currently spends the funds it absorbs from the private sector. This book and the ongoing project associated with it provide Canadians with comprehensive information about how the three levels of government spend taxpayers' money.

Chapter 1 presents expenditures of all levels of government on sixteen categories of expenditure, ranging from culture and recreation to the protection of persons and property. Chapter 2 analyzes the distribution of total government spending by province without regard to the level of government involved. Chapter 3 provides a compilation of the expenditures of the federal government by province and the opportunity to compare total federal expenditure in each of the provinces with the revenue that is raised in the province. Chapter 4 discusses the ways in which provinces spend their tax dollars and shows how spending priorities differ by province. Chapter 5 provides an indication of expenditures on public debt interest charges.

The final chapter presents a preliminary analysis of the extent to which Canadians at different income levels benefit from government expenditure.

The data upon which the book is based are for the most part compiled from Statistics Canada sources and aggregated according to methodology that is reported in the technical appendix. The compilations of provincial data have been circulated to the Ministers of Finance for each of the provinces to solicit their opinions regarding the accuracy of the data. With the exception of 2 provinces there were no responses indicating difficulty with the data. In those instances where difficulties were identified they have been rectified in the current data set. As near as can be ascertained, then, this book contains the most accurate and most up to date compilation of figures on the expenditures of the government that is available. The authors encourage readers to examine the data and the ways in which the data have been calculated, as reported in the appendix, and welcome any suggestions for improvement in the ways in which the data is compiled or presented.

Most of the content of this edition of Government Spending Facts, like the first edition, was written by us. However, we are pleased to acknowledge that in the writing of Chapter 6 we had the help and the insights of Professor Filip Palda of l'École Nationale d'Administration Publique. In particular, Filip helped us to add an intergenerational feature to the calculation of benefits and costs and to adjust certain benefit calculations. We are grateful and hope that we will lure him back to play a more significant role in the production of the next edition.

Isabella Horry
Michael Walker

September, 1994

About the Authors

Isabella D. Horry

Isabella Horry is a research economist with The Fraser Institute. She was born in Vancouver, Canada and attended the University of British Columbia. In 1985, she received a Bachelor of Arts in Economics and in 1987, a Master of Arts in Economics. She joined The Fraser Institute in 1988, and co-authored *Tax Facts 6* (1988) and *Tax Facts 7* (1990) with Sally Pipes and Michael Walker, *Government Spending Facts* (1991) with Michael Walker, and Tax Facts 8 (1992) with Filip Palda and Michael Walker.

Michael A. Walker

Michael Walker is Executive Director of the Fraser Institute. Born in Newfoundland in 1945, he received his B.A. (summa) at St. Francis Xavier University in 1966 and his Ph.D. in Economics at the University of Western Ontario in 1969. He worked in various research capacities at the Bank of Canada, Ottawa. Immediately prior to joining The Fraser Institute, Dr. Walker was Econometric Model Consultant to the Federal Department of Finance, Ottawa. Dr. Walker has also taught Monetary Economics and Statistics at the University of Western Ontario and at Carleton University.

Dr. Walker writes regularly for daily newspapers and financial periodicals. His articles have also appeared in technical journals, including the *Canadian Journal of Economics, Canadian Public Policy, Canadian Taxation*, and the *Canadian Tax Journal*. He is author, editor, and contributor to 26 books on economic matters.

Chapter 1: Government Spending in Canada

Government spending rising faster than incomes

TABLE 1.1 PRESENTS THE EXPENDITURES by all three levels of government on sixteen categories of expenditure for selected fiscal years from 1970/71 to 1990/91. It records the fact that in the interval from 1970/71 (referred to as 1970 from now on) to 1990, the aggregate level of government expenditure increased from $31.97 billion to $309.50 billion, an 868 percent increase over the twenty year period. During the same time, the gross domestic product (GDP) or the total amount of income produced in the country increased by only 653 percent. This means that a significant fraction of the growth in the spending of government over the past two decades has been accomplished by the government sector absorbing an increasing share of control over the spending power generated in the country.

This evolution in the share of GDP absorbed by the government sector can most clearly be seen in table 1.2, which reports the various expenditure categories as a percentage of the GDP in that year. In 1970, for example, total government expenditures were 35.9 cents out of every dollar earned in Canada; by 1990 they constituted 46.1 cents out of every dollar earned. The data for 1990 have been presented in a pie chart as

Table 1.1: Total Government Spending by Function (Millions of Dollars)

Function	1970	1975	1980	1985	1988	1990
Culture & Recreation	584	1,796	3,103	4,685	5,404	6,617
Education	5,869	10,167	17,476	27,352	31,729	35,329
Environment	557	1,879	3,157	4,194	5,337	6,884
Foreign Affairs and International Assistance	289	748	1,076	2,050	3,632	3,495
General Services	2,284	4,995	8,564	12,692	15,595	18,668
Health	4,272	9,006	15,962	27,726	35,488	41,570
Housing	78	624	1,521	2,527	2,515	3,115
Labour, Employment and Immigration	399	919	1,578	2,881	3,720	4,059
Other	341	1,496	2,996	5,628	4,997	5,092
Interest Payments	3,327	6,920	17,395	40,165	51,284	62,682
Protection of Persons and Property	3,068	5,702	10,267	17,919	20,826	23,557
Regional Planning and Development	197	576	808	1,145	1,356	1,601
Resource Conservation and Industrial Development	1,564	5,312	10,775	15,297	14,769	12,787
Research Establishments	395	527	1,137	1,311	1,348	1,780
Social Services*	5,944	15,496	26,720	46,461	54,441	67,128
Transportation and Communication	2,797	5,832	9,222	12,462	13,152	15,136
Total	31,965	71,995	131,757	224,495	265,593	309,500

*excludes Canada Pension Plan revenues and expenditures.
Source: Data from the Public Institutions Division of Statistics Canada and calculations by the authors.

Table 1.2: Total Government Spending as a Percentage of Gross Domestic Product (Percent)

Function	1970	1975	1980	1985	1988	1990
Culture and Recreation	0.7%	1.0%	1.0%	1.0%	0.9%	1.0%
Education	6.6%	5.9%	5.6%	5.7%	5.2%	5.3%
Environment	0.6%	1.1%	1.0%	0.9%	0.9%	1.0%
Foreign Affairs and International Assistance	0.3%	0.4%	0.3%	0.4%	0.6%	0.5%
General Services	2.6%	2.9%	2.8%	2.7%	2.6%	2.8%
Health	4.8%	5.3%	5.2%	5.8%	5.9%	6.2%
Housing	0.1%	0.4%	0.5%	0.5%	0.4%	0.5%
Labour, Employment and Immigration	0.4%	0.5%	0.5%	0.6%	0.6%	0.6%
Other	0.4%	0.9%	1.0%	1.2%	0.8%	0.8%
Interest Payments	3.7%	4.0%	5.6%	8.4%	8.5%	9.3%
Protection of Persons and Property	3.4%	3.3%	3.3%	3.7%	3.4%	3.5%
Regional Planning and Development	0.2%	0.3%	0.3%	0.2%	0.2%	0.2%
Resource Conservation and Industrial Development	1.8%	3.1%	3.5%	3.2%	2.4%	1.9%
Research Establishments	0.4%	0.3%	0.4%	0.3%	0.2%	0.3%
Social Services*	6.7%	9.0%	8.6%	9.7%	9.0%	10.0%
Transportation and Communication	3.1%	3.4%	3.0%	2.6%	2.2%	2.3%
Total	35.9%	42.0%	42.5%	47.0%	43.8%	46.1%

*excludes Canada Pension Plan revenues and expenditures.
Source: Data from the Public Institutions Division of Statistics Canada and calculations by the authors.

figure 1.1 and clearly show the split of the proverbial income pie between the private and public sectors.

Control versus spending in the public sector

Although the income pie comparison is frequently made, it is important to recognize that not all expenditures controlled by government actually result in final expenditure on goods and services by government. Money that is collected from taxpayers by government and transferred to other taxpayers in the form of transfer payments is actually spent by the final recipient of the transfer payment rather than by the government itself. So from the point of view of resource utilization, while the governments' share of the total income pie gives a sense of the extent to which government is able to control how that money was spent, it does not yield a correct impression about the extent to which government is absorbing or using up the resources in the economy.

Figure 1.1: Income Split Between Private and Public Sectors, 1990

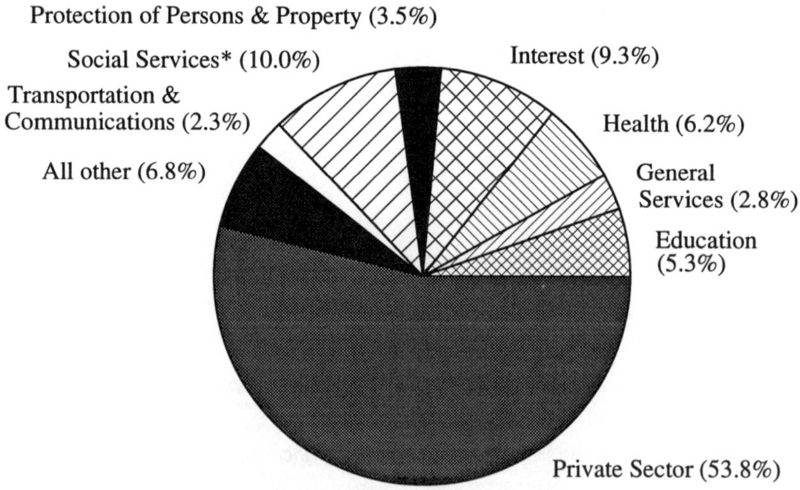

* *excludes Canada Pension Plan*

While this distinction may be regarded as entirely academic to the taxpayer who loses control over his or her income and has to surrender it to the government, it is nevertheless important to recognize that the difference exists. In 1990 governments were redistributing, through social programs, 10.0 percent of GDP, an increase from 6.7 percent in 1970.

The question from an analytical point of view is which definition of government spending provides the best and the most robust depiction of government sending: total government spending including transfers to persons or total government spending excluding transfers to persons? Our conclusion after some deliberation is that the total including transfers is the appropriate definition and the reasons for this choice can be illustrated by means of the following simple experiment. Suppose at the beginning of 1990 the federal government had employed all current recipients of unemployment insurance as consultants on how to live with a reduced level of income while at the same time abolishing the unemployment insurance program—citing as the reason the long standing problems with unemployment insurance which had been pointed out in Fraser Institute studies in 1978, 1985 and 1994.

If the definition of government spending had excluded transfer payments, the foregoing insubstantial change in government policy —nothing real happened, they just redefined the unemployment insurance program—would produce a very large apparent increase in government spending since the low income consultancy program would suddenly be "on the books," accounting for some 20 billion dollars worth of spending. Evidently, a definition of government spending which permits such arbitrary shifting of apparent spending is not a useful definition. Accordingly, we use the broader, inclusive definition of government spending to avoid this sort of problem. (Incidentally, the problem which plagues the definition of government spending in this context also causes problems for the interpretation of government's contribution to total final demand in the economy. While government's contribution to final demand includes its spending for consultants, it does not include its spending on transfer programs since these "only transfer spending power from one citizen to another and don't involve the government in actually purchasing final goods and services." A switch in government policy of the sort discussed above would therefore provide a very large apparent burst of growth in aggregate demand and the gross domestic product! It is highly doubtful that such measurements are useful and this raises the question as to whether the contribution of government to the gross domestic product is appropriately captured by the measurements currently in use.)

Spending priorities and how they change

While it is useful to examine government expenditure as a fraction of the total income in the country, it is also helpful to examine the structure of government expenditure itself, that is, how government allocates its total budget. Table 1.3 displays this data while figure 1.2 graphically displays the composition of total expenditure by all levels of government during 1990. The pie chart shows the division of government expenditure into its sixteen components or functional allocations.

Figure 1.2: Composition of Total Government Spending in 1990

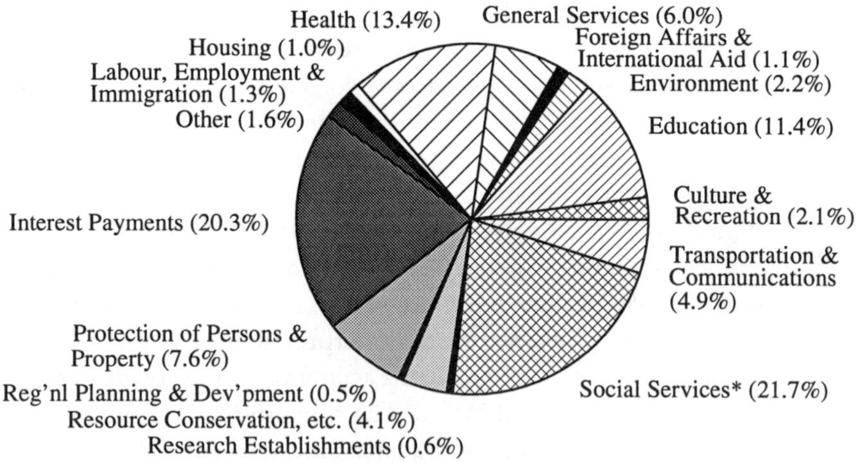

* *excludes Canada Pension Plan*

Table 1.3: Composition of Total Government Spending (Percent)

Function	1970	1975	1980	1985	1988	1990
Culture and Recreation	1.8%	2.5%	2.4%	2.1%	2.0%	2.1%
Education	18.4%	14.1%	13.3%	12.2%	11.9%	11.4%
Environment	1.7%	2.6%	2.4%	1.9%	2.0%	2.2%
Foreign Affairs and International Assistance	0.9%	1.0%	0.8%	0.9%	1.4%	1.1%
General Services	7.1%	6.9%	6.5%	5.7%	5.9%	6.0%
Health	13.4%	12.5%	12.1%	12.4%	13.4%	13.4%
Housing	0.2%	0.9%	1.2%	1.1%	0.9%	1.0%
Labour, Employment and Immigration	1.2%	1.3%	1.2%	1.3%	1.4%	1.3%
Other	1.1%	2.1%	2.3%	2.5%	1.9%	1.6%
Interest Payments	10.4%	9.6%	13.2%	17.9%	19.3%	20.3%
Protection of Persons and Property	9.6%	7.9%	7.8%	8.0%	7.8%	7.6%
Regional Planning and Development	0.6%	0.8%	0.6%	0.5%	0.5%	0.5%
Resource Conservation and Industrial Development	4.9%	7.4%	8.2%	6.8%	5.6%	4.1%
Research Establishments	1.2%	0.7%	0.9%	0.6%	0.5%	0.6%
Social Services*	18.6%	21.5%	20.3%	20.7%	20.5%	21.7%
Transportation and Communication	8.8%	8.1%	7.0%	5.6%	5.0%	4.9%
Total	100.0%	100.0%	100.0%	100.0%	100.0%	100.0%

*excludes Canada Pension Plan revenues and expenditures.

Figure 1.3 displays similar information to that contained in figure 1.2, but this figure compares the percentage composition obtained in 1990 with that obtained in 1970. There are some fascinating observations to be made. For example, in 1970 the top spending category was social services. It absorbed 18.6 percent of total government expenditure. Running a close second was education with 18.4 percent of the total spending. In 1990 social services was still the top spending category consuming 21.7 percent. However, education had fallen to fourth posi-

Figure 1.3: Composition of Total Government Spending in 1970 and 1990 (Percent)

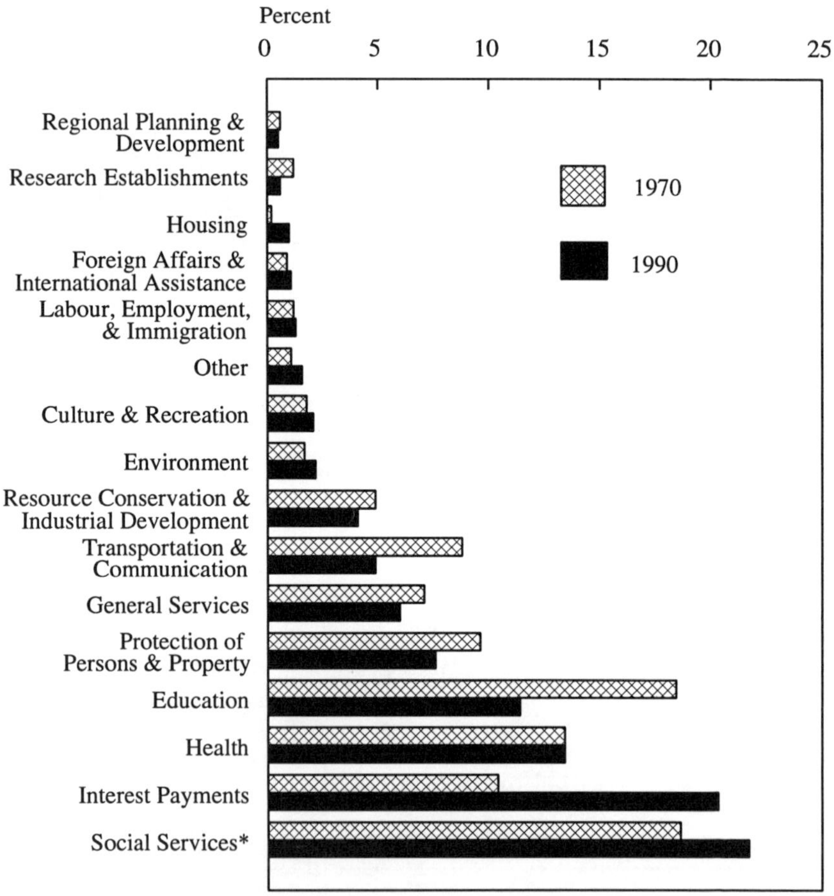

** excludes Canada Pension Plan*

tion overall. Governments at all levels were spending only 11.4 percent on education. Social services, it should be noted, refers to all transfer payments to persons including old age pensions, family allowances, unemployment insurance, welfare, et cetera (it excludes Canada Pension Plan and Quebec Pension Plan payments).

The other dramatic change in the composition of total government expenditure over the last two decades has been the evolution of interest costs. Whereas in 1970 total interest payments by all levels of government amounted to only 10.4 cents out of the total expenditure dollar, by 1990 it amounted to 20.3 cents. Against this background of dramatic change, expenditures on health care, for example, were relatively stable. In both 1970 and 1990 aggregate health care expenditures amounted to 13.4 percent of total government spending. Transportation and communication attracted a much smaller percentage of total expenditure in 1990 than they did in 1970, amounting to only 4.9 percent of the total compared to 8.8 percent of the total in 1970. Protection of persons and property, which is essentially the expenditure on the armed forces and police forces, declined from 9.6 percent of total government expenditure in 1970 to 7.6 percent in 1990.

Table 1.4: Spending on education per student in 1986 dollars

	Elementary & secondary	Post-secondary
1970	2,191	10,898
1975	2,642	12,011
1980	3,332	11,742
1985	3,625	11,409
1988	3,813	9,487
1990	3,770	9,190

Since the greater portion of spending on education goes to elementary and secondary education, the decline in spending on education can be explained by the decline in the number of school age children as a fraction of the total population. Between 1970 and 1990, enrolment in elementary and secondary schools fell from 5.9 million to 5.1 million. At the same time, enrolment in post-secondary institutions doubled; the number of full-time students rose from 0.5 million to 0.9 million and part-time students went from 0.2 million to 0.5 million. Table 1.4 details spending on education per student in real (or constant) dollars. (Expressing all of the years in terms of 1986 dollars raises the dollar amounts before 1986 and reduces the values after that date. Expressing the values in terms of constant dollars of 1986 purchasing power effectively removes the impact of inflation from the values).

The explosion of expenditures on interest payments is a direct result of the failure by governments at all levels to balance their budgets from 1975 onward. The accumulation of those deficits is reflected in the rising interest costs. From 9.6 percent of total expenditure in 1975, interest costs jumped to 13.2 percent in 1980 and had more than doubled as a share of total expenditure to 20.3 percent in 1990.

Interest payments distort the picture

The presence of rising interest costs within the budgetary framework distorts to some extent the impression one should have about the way in which governments have been allocating the resources they have available to them. Once the debt has been incurred, interest costs are not an optional expense and government has no choice regarding the spending allocated to this budget item. Therefore, it may be more revealing to look at expenditures excluding interest costs to get an assessment of how governments used the discretion available to them to allocate expenditures during the last two decades.

When interest costs are excluded, as in table 1.5, a somewhat different impression of government spending emerges than that gleaned from looking at expenditure including interest. Expenditures on health care increase as a fraction of total spending excluding interest. The decline in education expenditures is not as marked, but the increase in social security spending is much more dramatic than it appears from

Table 1.5: Composition of Total Government Spending Net of Interest Payments (Percent)

Function	1970	1975	1980	1985	1988	1990
Culture and Recreation	2.0%	2.8%	2.7%	2.5%	2.5%	2.7%
Education	20.5%	15.6%	15.3%	14.8%	14.8%	14.3%
Environment	1.9%	2.9%	2.8%	2.3%	2.5%	2.8%
Foreign Affairs and International Assistance	1.0%	1.1%	0.9%	1.1%	1.7%	1.4%
General Services	8.0%	7.7%	7.5%	6.9%	7.3%	7.6%
Health	14.9%	13.8%	14.0%	15.0%	16.6%	16.8%
Housing	0.3%	1.0%	1.3%	1.4%	1.2%	1.3%
Labour, Employment and Immigration	1.4%	1.4%	1.4%	1.6%	1.7%	1.6%
Other	1.2%	2.3%	2.6%	3.1%	2.3%	2.1%
Protection of Persons and Property	10.7%	8.8%	9.0%	9.7%	9.7%	9.5%
Regional Planning and Development	0.7%	0.9%	0.7%	0.6%	0.6%	0.6%
Resource Conservation and Industrial Development	5.5%	8.2%	9.4%	8.3%	6.9%	5.2%
Research Establishments	1.4%	0.8%	1.0%	0.7%	0.6%	0.7%
Social Services*	20.8%	23.8%	23.4%	25.2%	25.4%	27.2%
Transportation and Communication	9.8%	9.0%	8.1%	6.8%	6.1%	6.1%
Total	100.0%	100.0%	100.0%	100.0%	100.0%	100.0%

*excludes Canada Pension Plan revenues and expenditures.

Table 1.6: Total Government Spending Per Capita (Dollars)

Function	1970	1975	1980	1985	1988	1990
Culture and Recreation	27	79	129	186	209	249
Education	276	448	727	1,087	1,225	1,328
Environment	26	83	131	167	206	259
Foreign Affairs and International Assistance	14	33	45	81	140	131
General Services	107	220	356	504	602	702
Health	201	397	664	1,102	1,370	1,562
Housing	4	27	63	100	97	117
Labour, Employment and Immigration	19	40	66	114	144	153
Other	16	66	125	224	193	191
Interest Payments	156	305	724	1,596	1,979	2,356
Protection of Persons and Property	144	251	427	712	804	885
Regional Planning and Development	9	25	34	45	52	60
Resource Conservation and Industrial Development	73	234	448	608	570	481
Research Establishments	19	23	47	52	52	67
Social Services*	279	683	1,111	1,846	2,101	2,523
Transportation and Communication	131	257	384	495	508	569
Total	1,501	3,172	5,480	8,921	10,251	11,631

*excludes Canada Pension Plan revenues and expenditures.

Table 1.7: Total Government Spending Per Capita in Real Dollars (in 1986 Dollars)

Function	1970	1975	1980	1985	1988	1990
Culture and Recreation	88	179	192	194	192	208
Education	889	1,013	1,082	1,132	1,128	1,111
Environment	84	187	195	174	190	216
Foreign Affairs and International Assistance	44	75	67	85	129	110
General Services	346	498	530	525	554	587
Health	647	898	988	1,148	1,261	1,307
Housing	12	62	94	105	89	98
Labour, Employment and Immigration	60	92	98	119	132	128
Other	52	149	185	233	178	160
Interest Payments	504	690	1,077	1,663	1,823	1,971
Protection of Persons and Property	465	568	635	742	740	741
Regional Planning and Development	30	57	50	47	48	50
Resource Conservation and Industrial Development	237	529	667	633	525	402
Research Establishments	60	53	70	54	48	56
Social Services*	900	1,545	1,654	1,923	1,935	2,111
Transportation and Communication	424	581	571	516	467	476
Total	4,842	7,176	8,155	9,292	9,439	9,733

*excludes Canada Pension Plan revenues and expenditures.

looking at the data including interest payments. These calculations also provide an indication of how government would be likely to allocate any savings in interest expenditures achieved by the elimination of ongoing deficits and the eventual retirement of government debt.

Program spending per capita

Tables 1.6 and 1.7 provide a more meaningful compilation of the expenditure data by putting these calculations in per capita terms. Table 1.7, in addition, adjusts the expenditure for the purely inflationary increases in expenditures over the period. In 1990 total spending of all levels of government in Canada was $11,631 per Canadian, an increase from $1,501 in 1970 (see table 1.6). Much of the increase in that total amount is due to inflation (see table 1.7). In real (inflation-adjusted) terms, the 1990 figure is $9,733 per capita, as opposed to the 1970 level of $4,842. While smaller than the increase in the raw figures, the real increase still represented a doubling over the period. In other words, in the period 1970 to 1990, adjusting for inflation, governments have doubled the amount they spend per capita.

Health care, interest, and social security costs climb

The magnitude of the increases in expenditure categories such as interest on the public debt is clearly shown in table 1.6. In 1970 this amounted to only $156 per capita but by 1990 it had climbed to $2,356 per capita. Total health care expenditures were $1,562 per capita in 1990 or an aggregate amount of $6,248 for a family of four. That expenditure, however, is overshadowed by the social services outlays which amounted to $2,523 per Canadian.

An examination of table 1.7 and the inflation-adjusted percentage changes in spending since 1970 reveals a number of interesting observations. As expected, the expenditures on interest on the public debt have risen the most dramatically. The category "other," a miscellaneous catch-all for government functions not specifically allocated, increased by 210 percent since 1970 and is perhaps a reflection of the increasing incursion of governments into areas which historically were not thought to be their natural domains.

It is also somewhat surprising to discover that notwithstanding the recent importance of research and development, the total expenditure by governments on research establishments has actually declined by 15 percent in real terms since 1970. Interestingly, there has been almost no change in the transportation and communications expenditures of governments. Given the apparent increase in concern about law and order issues, it is noticeable that expenditures on protection, policing, and public security have increased less rapidly than have other major categories of expenditure.

In reviewing the expenditure breakdowns in table 1.6, it is interesting to contemplate where, if one were an all-powerful manipulator of the finances of the various levels of government, one would make changes in the expenditure profile to change the overall outcome. For example, in 1990 the total expenditures of $11,631 per capita reflected a deficit of $1,314 per capita. To balance the budgets of the different levels of government, overall expenditures would have to be reduced by $34,962 million[1] or by $1,314 per capita. If there were to be a reduction in that amount per capita, this would eliminate the deficit of $34,962 million and would balance the budgets of the different levels of government. There would still remain the problem of apportioning the total spending cuts by level of government, but identifying the overall focus of the cuts would be a good start.

You may find it interesting to review the expenditure categories and make a note of the areas of overall government expenditure that you might cut in order to reduce the national deficit. In the following chapters, we will explore the expenditures of the federal, provincial/territorial, and municipal governments and it will then be possible to see which level of government would have to cut its expenditures and by what amounts.

---

1 This is the deficit on an FMS (Financial Management System) basis.

Chapter 2: Total All-Government Spending in the Provinces

IN THE LAST CHAPTER WE PROVIDED data on the total spending by all levels of government on the various functions that governments perform. In this chapter, it is our intent to consider the total expenditure of government on a province-by-province basis (including the Yukon and North West Territories combined). Since expenditures are an indication of the level of government activity, the data compiled here provide an opportunity to make some interesting comparative analyses of government presence in each of the provinces.

Tables 2.1, 2.2, 2.3, and 2.4 outline provincial allocation of total expenditure by government. It should be noted that in each case the dollar amount spent includes all levels of government: federal, provincial/territorial, and municipal. In 1990 governments at all levels spent $309 billion, up from $32 billion in 1970. As already noted, this both boosted the share of the government sector in the national income and substantially increased the aggregate real tax burden associated with government spending. The relationship between spending and taxes is the subject of analysis in chapters 3 and 6.

Table 2.1: Total Government Spending by Province (Millions of Dollars)

Province	1970	1975	1980	1985	1988	1990
Newfoundland	636	1,749	2,971	5,440	5,727	6,517
Prince Edward Island	175	407	666	1,109	1,352	1,543
Nova Scotia	1,325	3,120	5,922	8,906	10,006	11,074
New Brunswick	891	2,179	4,289	5,919	7,408	8,467
Quebec	8,008	18,413	35,174	55,465	64,744	74,985
Ontario	12,381	25,891	44,134	78,450	98,173	119,149
Manitoba	1,430	3,124	5,404	9,384	11,294	12,413
Saskatchewan	1,336	3,070	5,445	9,874	11,279	11,225
Alberta	2,669	6,029	13,217	24,342	26,954	28,560
British Columbia	2,947	7,650	13,828	22,939	26,698	33,352
Territories	167	364	708	2,667	1,960	2,214
Canada	31,965	71,995	131,757	224,495	265,593	309,500

Sixty-three percent of government spending is in Ontario and Quebec

As might be expected, the distribution of total government expenditure within the country follows generally the distribution of population and income. Thus, for example, we find in Table 2.2 that 0.5 percent of all government expenditure in Canada is conducted in Prince Edward Island, and that 38.5 percent is conducted in Ontario and 24.2 percent in Quebec. Between them, Ontario and Quebec account for 62.7 percent of total government spending. These two provinces, together with Alberta and British Columbia, account for fully 83 percent of the national total. This more or less natural distribution is placed in more relevant perspective by relating expenditure levels to the population levels in the provinces and calculating the per capita provincial distribution of government spending.

Table 2.2: Distribution Of Government Spending Across Canada (Percent)

Province	1970	1975	1980	1985	1988	1990
Newfoundland	2.0%	2.4%	2.3%	2.4%	2.2%	2.1%
Prince Edward Island	0.5%	0.6%	0.5%	0.5%	0.5%	0.5%
Nova Scotia	4.1%	4.3%	4.5%	4.0%	3.8%	3.6%
New Brunswick	2.8%	3.0%	3.3%	2.6%	2.8%	2.7%
Quebec	25.1%	25.6%	26.7%	24.7%	24.4%	24.2%
Ontario	38.7%	36.0%	33.5%	34.9%	37.0%	38.5%
Manitoba	4.5%	4.3%	4.1%	4.2%	4.3%	4.0%
Saskatchewan	4.2%	4.3%	4.1%	4.4%	4.2%	3.6%
Alberta	8.3%	8.4%	10.0%	10.8%	10.1%	9.2%
British Columbia	9.2%	10.6%	10.5%	10.2%	10.1%	10.8%
Territories	0.5%	0.5%	0.5%	1.2%	0.7%	0.7%
Canada	100.0%	100.0%	100.0%	100.0%	100.0%	100.0%

The territories have the highest per capita government spending

The territories, at $27,707, have the highest per capita spending by all levels of government (see table 2.3). The province that has the least amount of government expenditure per capita is British Columbia, at $10,647, and the province that has the most is Nova Scotia, at $12,372. The impression gained from the per capita expenditures in current dollars is not to any great degree changed by observing the inflation-adjusted figures in table 2.4. British Columbia is still the lowest spending province with $9,054 in 1986 dollar terms, compared with $10,530 per capita in the case of Nova Scotia and $24,114 per capita in the case of the territories.

Table 2.3: Total Government Spending Per Capita (Dollars)

Province	1970	1975	1980	1985	1988	1990
Newfoundland	1,230	3,184	5,254	9,519	10,068	11,379
Prince Edward Island	1,594	3,479	5,423	8,801	10,520	11,808
Nova Scotia	1,694	3,807	7,008	10,225	11,346	12,372
New Brunswick	1,422	3,276	6,167	8,338	10,371	11,721
Quebec	1,332	2,980	5,508	8,514	9,749	11,079
Ontario	1,640	3,168	5,150	8,710	10,410	12,221
Manitoba	1,455	3,082	5,273	8,820	10,418	11,399
Saskatchewan	1,420	3,383	5,675	9,792	11,129	11,258
Alberta	1,673	3,390	6,174	10,365	11,284	11,548
British Columbia	1,385	3,144	5,187	7,992	8,958	10,647
Territories	3,332	5,818	10,565	35,370	25,317	27,707
Canada	1,501	3,172	5,480	8,921	10,251	11,631

Variations in provincial spending per capita

Tables 2.5 and 2.6 together collect the expenditure by function by province for the year 1990. It is immediately apparent from examining these data that there are considerable variations amongst the provinces in almost every category of expenditure, particularly in the major expenditure categories such as education, health, and social security.

Education expenditures ranged from $1,164 per capita in Prince Edward Island to $1,461 in British Columbia and $2,901 in the territories. Health care expenditures ranged from a low of $1,194 per capita in Prince Edward Island to $1,673 in British Columbia and $3,393 per capita in the territories. Social security expenditures are lowest in Alberta at $2,052 and highest in Newfoundland at $3,632. There also are, surprisingly enough, wide variations in the amount of interest payments made by all levels of government in each of the provinces.

Table 2.4: Total Government Spending Per Capita In Real Dollars (in 1986 Dollars)

Province	1970	1975	1980	1985	1988	1990
Newfoundland	4,240	7,301	7,829	9,793	9,562	9,999
Prince Edward Island	4,945	7,566	7,815	8,980	9,795	10,084
Nova Scotia	5,328	8,498	10,276	10,552	10,604	10,530
New Brunswick	4,624	7,340	9,177	8,631	9,738	10,052
Quebec	4,311	6,802	8,295	8,916	9,002	9,413
Ontario	5,265	7,154	7,733	9,092	9,463	10,017
Manitoba	4,622	6,849	7,675	9,206	9,593	9,587
Saskatchewan	4,372	7,484	8,154	10,064	10,154	9,421
Alberta	5,238	7,517	8,923	10,719	10,565	9,812
British Columbia	4,410	6,937	7,627	8,231	8,396	9,054
Territories	11,623	14,224	16,994	36,741	23,884	24,114
Canada	4,842	7,176	8,155	9,292	9,439	9,733

The distributions of expenditures in table 2.6 have to be interpreted with some caution since they reflect decisions made by three levels of government. An additional source of potential difficulty with the figures is that varying levels of expenditure on health care, for example, do not necessarily imply differences in the distribution of health care service or supply. It may, for example, be less costly on a per capita basis to provide health care in Ontario, a highly urbanized population, than it would be in a province like Newfoundland, which has a very dispersed population. There are, in other words, economies of scale in the production of government services and the more tightly compacted the population, the more pronounced those economies of scale can be expected to be. In general, the measurement of the effectiveness of these expenditures and the level of service corresponding to them requires more information than is being considered in this study.

Table 2.5: Total Government Spending by Function, 1990 (Millions of Dollars)

Function	Nfld	PEI	NS	NB	Que	Ont	Man	Sask	Alta	BC	Terr.	Cda
Culture and Recreation	97	29	206	125	1,401	2,450	363	288	782	794	81	6,617
Education	794	152	1,096	875	8,276	13,232	1,425	1,310	3,361	4,576	232	35,329
Environment	110	16	188	94	2,117	2,593	245	208	610	652	51	6,884
Foreign Affairs and International Assistance	75	17	118	95	889	1,281	143	131	325	411	10	3,495
General Services	389	118	832	509	5,483	6,175	703	708	1,509	1,887	354	18,668
Health	769	156	1,336	1,013	9,157	16,259	1,748	1,646	3,973	5,241	271	41,570
Housing	63	19	96	69	965	998	108	205	381	173	38	3,115
Labour	74	23	247	104	1,214	1,417	155	99	368	318	38	4,059
Other	99	26	154	143	1,268	2,119	124	137	496	434	93	5,092
Interest Payments	873	195	1,720	1,091	13,518	31,350	2,316	1,605	4,318	5,496	201	62,682
Protection of Persons and Property	406	124	1,506	1,247	4,788	9,515	1,001	541	1,933	2,350	146	23,557

Table 2.5: Total Government Spending by Function, 1990 (Millions of Dollars)

Function	Nfld	PEI	NS	NB	Que	Ont	Man	Sask	Alta	BC	Terr.	Cda
Regional Planning and Development	24	4	55	35	324	587	114	31	183	169	76	1,601
Resource Conservation and Industrial Development	253	106	379	290	2,247	2,728	634	1,596	3,164	1,167	224	12,787
Research Establishments	27	4	54	42	487	604	52	66	211	229	4	1,780
Social Services*	2,080	448	2,534	2,209	18,795	23,246	2,672	2,052	5,076	7,801	216	67,128
Transportation & Communi-cations	383	107	553	525	4,056	4,595	610	602	1,870	1,655	180	15,136
Total	**6,517**	**1,543**	**11,074**	**8,467**	**74,985**	**119,149**	**12,413**	**11,225**	**28,560**	**33,352**	**2,214**	**309,500**
Canada Pension Plan	206	56	497	340	42	5,335	570	502	946	1,694	11	10,199
Total + CPP	6,723	1,599	11,571	8,807	75,027	124,484	12,983	11,727	29,506	35,046	2,225	319,699

* excludes Canada Pension Plan revenues and expenditures.

Table 2.6: Total Government Spending Per Capita, 1990 (Dollars)

Function	Nfld	PEI	NS	NB	Que	Ont	Man	Sask	Alta	BC	Terr.	Cda
Culture and Recreation	169	224	231	173	207	251	333	289	316	254	1,015	249
Education	1,387	1,164	1,224	1,211	1,223	1,357	1,309	1,314	1,359	1,461	2,901	1,328
Environment	192	124	210	130	313	266	225	208	247	208	635	259
Foreign Affairs and International Assistance	131	131	131	131	131	131	131	131	131	131	131	131
General Services	680	905	930	705	810	633	645	710	610	602	4,436	702
Health	1,342	1,194	1,492	1,403	1,353	1,668	1,605	1,651	1,607	1,673	3,393	1,562
Housing	111	143	107	96	143	102	99	206	154	55	476	117
Labour	130	178	276	143	179	145	143	100	149	102	473	153
Other	173	196	172	198	187	217	114	137	200	139	1,159	191
Interest Payments	1,524	1,491	1,921	1,511	1,997	3,215	2,127	1,609	1,746	1,755	2,512	2,356
Protection of Persons and Property	708	947	1,683	1,726	707	976	919	543	782	750	1,827	885

Table 2.6: Total Government Spending Per Capita, 1990 (Dollars)

Function	Nfld	PEI	NS	NB	Que	Ont	Man	Sask	Alta	BC	Terr.	Cda
Regional Planning and Development	42	28	62	49	48	60	105	31	74	54	948	60
Resource Conservation and Industrial Development	442	810	423	401	332	280	582	1,601	1,279	372	2,797	481
Research Establishments	47	30	61	58	72	62	48	66	86	73	48	67
Social Services*	3,632	3,426	2,831	3,058	2,777	2,384	2,453	2,058	2,052	2,490	2,704	2,523
Transportation & Communi-cations	669	815	618	727	599	471	560	604	756	528	2,252	569
Total	**11,379**	**11,808**	**12,372**	**11,721**	**11,079**	**12,221**	**11,399**	**11,258**	**11,548**	**10,647**	**27,707**	**11,631**
Canada Pension Plan	360	428	575	471	6	547	523	503	383	541	138	383
Total + CPP	11,739	12,236	12,947	12,192	11,085	12,768	11,922	11,761	11,931	11,188	27,845	12,014

* excludes Canada Pension Plan revenues and expenditures.

We will provide more detail by level of government in the following chapters, which will, to some extent, relieve the difficulties associated with interpreting the aggregate national numbers by province.

Another difficulty with these data is the fact that they may reflect expenditures within particular provinces that were made to achieve national objectives. Nova Scotia and Prince Edward Island, for example, show very high expenditures on protection of persons and property. However, this is a reflection of national expenditure on defence and does not reflect a decision by the Nova Scotia and Prince Edward Island provincial governments to spend two or three times the national average on this particular service. As already noted, this ambiguity will be cleared up in subsequent chapters which consider the expenditure on each function by level of government.

Provincial spending versus national average

As a final comment on aggregate government expenditure per capita in each of the provinces, we compare the expenditures by province to the Canadian average expenditure taken from table 1.6 and reported as the last column in table 2.6. While bearing in mind the variety of reasons for provincial differences, it is nevertheless interesting to observe that this comparison does reveal wide variations from the average, especially for the major expense categories of health, education, and social security. These national distributions serve to whet the appetite for the consideration of individual provincial expenditure profiles undertaken in subsequent chapters.

While there are variations amongst the provinces in total spending per capita, that variation is not as pronounced as might be expected, given the wide variations amongst the provinces in total private income. Of course, at least part of the reason for this is the system of equalization payments that is part of the structure of Canadian Confederation. Although there is an unequal ability to pay for government services, there is less inequality in the actual distribution of government spending because the "have" provinces contribute towards the spending of the "have not" provinces.

Table 2.7: Total Government Spending as a Percentage of Provincial Gross Domestic Product

Province	1970	1975	1980	1985	1988	1990
Newfoundland	52.8%	78.5%	72.6%	85.2%	71.2%	73.9%
Prince Edward Island	72.7%	88.4%	78.7%	83.8%	76.1%	77.7%
Nova Scotia	59.7%	80.1%	94.1%	74.6%	66.3%	65.4%
New Brunswick	53.5%	70.0%	85.4%	65.6%	62.5%	64.4%
Quebec	35.6%	45.0%	48.7%	51.6%	45.5%	48.7%
Ontario	33.3%	38.0%	38.4%	42.7%	38.8%	43.8%
Manitoba	38.8%	45.2%	48.3%	53.0%	52.2%	52.5%
Saskatchewan	43.9%	44.4%	43.9%	56.5%	62.0%	54.9%
Alberta	37.6%	32.4%	30.6%	37.2%	43.2%	40.0%
British Columbia	31.6%	39.3%	36.2%	42.0%	38.1%	41.0%
Territories	63.4%	61.1%	57.1%	120.8%	71.2%	71.9%
Canada	35.9%	42.0%	42.5%	47.0%	43.7%	46.1%

The fact that there is relatively little variation in spending per capita amongst the provinces in the face of wide variations in total income implies wide variations in the relative presence of government spending in the provinces. Table 2.7 presents the total expenditures of government by province as a fraction of the gross domestic product in that province. As is clearly evident, there is, as expected, a wide range in the extent to which the various provinces are dependent on government sector expenditures. There have also been considerable changes over time in the extent of this dependency.

Reflecting the national movement towards government spending as a larger fraction of total income, all of the provinces have experienced an increase in the intensity of government during the period under study. By 1990, Prince Edward Island had moved from a government occupying a 73 percent share of GDP to one occupying a 78 percent share. Ontario moved from 33 percent to 44 percent. In Newfoundland, the current manifestation of the government sector at 74 percent of GDP reflects the fact that total government activity amounts to 2.8 times total private activity in that province. That and the high percentages enjoyed by Prince Edward Island, Nova Scotia, and New Brunswick can only be sustained by a significant inflow of resources from the federal government into those provinces. It is also interesting to speculate about the possibility for sustained private sector development when governments occupy such a significant percentage of total economic activity in a region.

As a final reflection on the data in table 2.7, reconsider the information in table 2.5. While the needs of what are called "slow growth regions" or the "have not" provinces in Canada are often offered up in explanation for the considerable amount of income redistribution and activity by the government, table 2.5 and figure 2.1 make clear that this is not, in aggregate terms, an accurate assessment of government expenditure requirements. For example, although it is true that the government sector makes up a significant fraction of the Newfoundland economy, the total amount of government expenditure in that province is only 2 percent of government activity in the country as a whole. Social security expenditures, which include the transfer payments to persons from all levels of government, and which serve to inflate the government presence in Newfoundland, represent only 3 percent of the total amount of social security spending in all provinces by all governments. Social security payments in total for all the Atlantic provinces amount to only 10.8 percent of total social security payments made in the country. By comparison, for example, social security payments in Quebec alone amounted to 28.0 percent of the nation's total.

Accordingly, while social security payments per capita in the Atlantic provinces are well above the national average and the presence of government in the Atlantic provinces' economies has reached a very high fraction of the total economies, the existence of the Atlantic provinces and the perceived greater need for social security payments in those regions are not good explanations for the configuration of social security payments that we observe in the country as a whole.

The archetype of the Atlantic fisherman drawing social welfare benefits at the expense of the rest of the country is accurate, but is not an explanation for the whole edifice of social welfare spending. To a much greater extent, the picture revealed in figure 2.1, which shows the distribution of social welfare spending by province, is one of the citizens of Ontario and Quebec (who collectively receive about 63 percent of all social welfare spending) receiving benefits at the expense of other citizens of those provinces.

This is a subject for further scrutiny when we consider the expenditure profiles of the federal government later in this book.

Figure 2.1: Percentage of Total Social Security Spending in Each Province, 1990

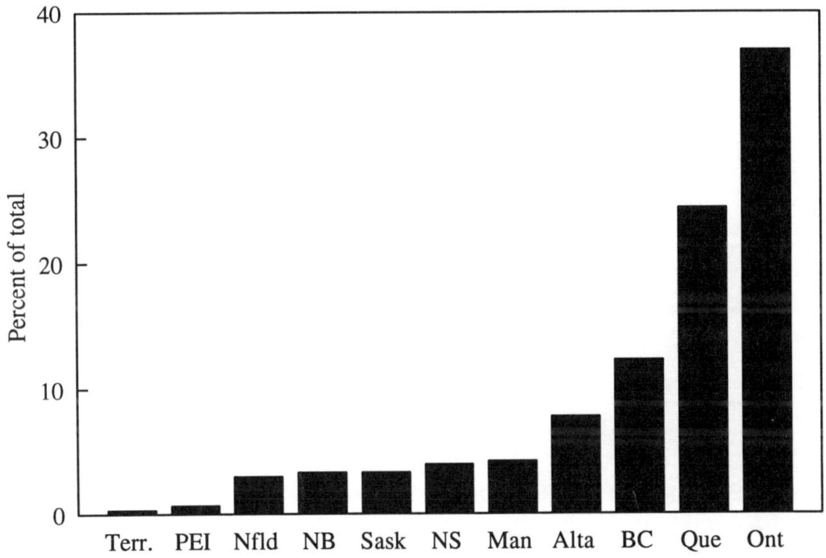

Chapter 3: Expenditures by the Federal Government

THIS CHAPTER PROVIDES A COMPILATION of the expenditures of the federal government by province as well as a comparison of total federal expenditure in each of the provinces with the revenue that is raised in the province.

First, let us consider the total level of expenditure. In doing so, we have to be clear about the distinction between who spends the money and who funds that spending. While it is ultimately true that taxpayers fund all the expenditures of government, it is nevertheless the case that different levels of government engage in the taxing activities which produce the revenue. In some instances, the government that raises the money is different than the one that spends it. This chapter attempts to specifically identify the amount of money which the federal government provides, either from tax revenue or from borrowing, to fund expenditures of different kinds in the provinces. Since all spending takes place in some province or territory, the total spending by the provinces and territories sums to total federal spending.

Spending distribution by province

Table 3.1 provides a province-by-province distribution of total federal funding of all government expenditures. From 1970 to 1990, total federal expenditure has gone from $15.6 billion to $151.8 billion, nearly a

Table 3.1: Gross Federal Government Funding of Total Government Spending, by Province (Millions of Dollars)

Year	Nfld	PEI	NS	NB	Que	Ont	Man	Sask	Alta	BC	Terr	Cda
1970	447	138	876	576	3,773	5,678	787	725	1,087	1,404	109	15,600
1975	1,084	288	2,273	1,518	9,097	12,924	1,704	1,684	2,484	3,397	277	36,728
1980	1,907	484	4,377	3,194	16,891	22,923	3,111	2,658	4,408	5,981	528	66,464
1985	3,896	832	6,292	4,008	26,657	40,942	5,048	4,887	9,433	11,083	2,253	115,330
1988	3,821	979	6,634	5,002	30,638	49,521	6,181	5,935	11,218	12,962	1,435	134,326
1990	4,096	1,053	7,197	5,469	35,062	60,750	6,244	5,390	11,002	14,743	747	151,753

Table 3.2: Composition of Federal Funding of Government Spending, 1970 to 1990 (Percent)

Function	1970	1975	1980	1985	1988	1990
Culture and Recreation	0.8%	1.1%	0.9%	0.8%	0.9%	0.9%
Education	7.0%	4.3%	4.9%	4.3%	4.2%	3.2%
Environment	0.1%	0.9%	0.6%	0.5%	0.5%	0.6%
Foreign Affairs & International Assistance	1.8%	2.0%	1.6%	1.8%	2.7%	2.3%
General Services	6.8%	7.2%	5.5%	4.8%	5.0%	5.3%
Health	10.1%	9.0%	7.8%	7.2%	7.0%	6.0%
Housing	0.3%	1.0%	1.6%	1.3%	1.2%	1.4%
Interest	11.9%	11.2%	17.0%	22.9%	25.6%	28.9%
Labour, Employment & Immigration	1.8%	2.0%	1.8%	1.6%	1.8%	1.8%
Other	1.9%	1.5%	2.3%	3.0%	1.7%	1.7%
Protection of Persons & Property	13.2%	9.5%	9.9%	10.5%	10.3%	10.1%
Regional Planning & Development	0.5%	0.6%	0.4%	0.3%	0.4%	0.4%
Resource Conservation & Industrial Development	7.2%	10.8%	11.3%	7.3%	6.0%	3.9%
Research Establishments	2.4%	1.4%	1.6%	0.9%	0.8%	0.9%
Social Services	29.1%	32.7%	28.4%	29.3%	28.7%	30.1%
Transportation & Communications	4.8%	4.9%	4.4%	3.4%	3.2%	2.7%
Total	100.0%	100.0%	100.0%	100.0%	100.0%	100.0%

tenfold increase. The composition of federal government expenditures by function is given in table 3.2. The same trends are found in federal spending by category as are found in the preceding two chapters. Education falls from 7.0 percent of total expenditure in 1970 to 3.2 percent in 1990; health drops from 10.1 percent to 6.0 percent; and interest rises from 11.9 percent to 28.9 percent.

While table 3.1 gives a sense of how the aggregate federal funding of expenditures has changed over time in each of the provinces, it is difficult to draw implications from these figures because the trends in particular provincial figures are obscured by movement in the overall totals. Accordingly, table 3.3 calculates the percentage distribution of gross federal funding of total expenditures across each of the provinces. The entries in table 3.3 provide the percentage of total federal funding that went to each province in each of the years. Thus, for example, the line for 1990 in the table shows that 2.7 percent of total federal funding went to the province of Newfoundland. In the same year, 40.0 percent went to Ontario and 9.7 percent went to British Columbia.

Common perceptions not validated

Quebec's share is not increasing

It is safe to say that the historical perspective on the distribution of federal funding provided by table 3.3 does not conform to the usual impressions people have about this spending. First, focusing on the province of Quebec, there is no evidence of any change over the 1970-1990 period in the extent to which federal funding has accrued to the benefit of the residents of that province. Federal expenditures in the province of Quebec comprised 24.2 percent of total federal spending in 1970; they comprised 23.1 percent in 1990. Given the changing population distribution, that may or may not mean that the average resident of the province of Quebec fared better or worse in 1990 than in 1970, but that is a subject to which we will turn below.

Table 3.3: Distribution of Federal Funding of Total Government Spending Across Canada (Percent)

Year	Nfld	PEI	NS	NB	Que	Ont	Man	Sask	Alta	BC	Terr	Cda
1970	2.9%	0.9%	5.6%	3.7%	24.2%	36.4%	5.0%	4.6%	7.0%	9.0%	0.7%	100.0%
1975	3.0%	0.8%	6.2%	4.1%	24.8%	35.2%	4.6%	4.6%	6.8%	9.2%	0.8%	100.0%
1980	2.9%	0.7%	6.6%	4.8%	25.4%	34.5%	4.7%	4.0%	6.6%	9.0%	0.8%	100.0%
1985	3.4%	0.7%	5.5%	3.5%	23.1%	35.5%	4.4%	4.2%	8.2%	9.6%	2.0%	100.0%
1988	2.8%	0.7%	4.9%	3.7%	22.8%	36.9%	4.6%	4.4%	8.4%	9.6%	1.1%	100.0%
1990	2.7%	0.7%	4.7%	3.6%	23.1%	40.0%	4.1%	3.6%	7.2%	9.7%	0.5%	100.0%

The Atlantic provinces' share has shrunk

Another of the widespread beliefs about government expenditure is not borne out by the distribution table, namely, what has been happening in the Atlantic region over the period 1970 to 1990.

In 1970, Newfoundland, Prince Edward Island, Nova Scotia, and New Brunswick together received 13.1 percent of the total federal funding made available. By 1990, those four provinces received in total only 11.7 percent, a decline of 1.4 percent of total federal expenditure over the twenty years. Over the period, the percentage going to the Atlantic provinces rose to 15.0 percent in 1980 and then fell to 11.7 percent by 1990. Equally surprisingly, both Alberta and British Columbia enjoyed an increase over the same period in the total fraction of federal expenditure received. From 9.0 percent in 1970, British Columbia's share of federal expenditure grew to 9.7 percent in 1990, while Alberta's share moved from 7.0 percent in 1970 to 7.2 percent in 1990.

Provincial distribution per capita

Part of the reason for the evolution of the distribution of expenditures seen in table 3.3, is the changing population structure of the country. It is therefore interesting to examine the distribution of total federal funding on a per capita basis over the period since 1970 (see table 3.4). The average expenditure per capita in 1990 was $5,703, and as table 3.4 demonstrates, there is considerable variation from this average among the different provinces.

The territories have consistently had the highest expenditure by the federal government per capita since 1970, with $9,346 per capita in 1990. Nova Scotians receive the second highest amount, or $8,320 in federal funding per capita. The province with the lowest level of funding is Alberta at $4,449 per capita. Those provinces enjoying an above-average per capita expenditure include Newfoundland, Prince Edward Island, Nova Scotia, New Brunswick, Ontario, and Manitoba. Lower than average expenditures were experienced by Alberta, British Columbia, Quebec, and Saskatchewan. Later in the chapter we will compare these

Table 3.4: Federal Funding of Total Government Spending Per Capita (Dollars)

Year	Nfld	PEI	NS	NB	Que	Ont	Man	Sask	Alta	BC	Terr	Cda
1970	865	1,250	1,120	919	628	752	801	771	682	660	2,179	733
1975	1,975	2,455	2,773	2,282	1,472	1,581	1,681	1,856	1,397	1,396	4,431	1,618
1980	3,371	3,944	5,179	4,594	2,645	2,675	3,036	2,770	2,059	2,244	7,886	2,764
1985	6,817	6,601	7,224	5,646	4,092	4,546	4,745	4,847	4,016	3,861	29,875	4,583
1988	6,718	7,619	7,522	7,003	4,614	5,251	5,702	5,856	4,696	4,350	18,534	5,184
1990	7,152	8,058	8,320	7,571	5,180	6,231	5,734	5,406	4,449	4,706	9,346	5,703

Table 3.5: Federal Funding of Government Spending by Function Per Capita, 1990 (Dollars)

Function	Nfld	PEI	NS	NB	Que	Ont	Man	Sask	Alta	BC	Terr	Cda
Culture and Recreation	63	95	108	66	42	49	61	44	37	41	202	49
Education	442	410	335	373	182	111	340	298	181	155	142	180
Environment	53	48	34	37	32	27	29	29	26	25	37	29
Foreign Affairs & International Assistance	131	131	136	131	131	131	131	131	131	131	131	131
General Services	385	599	753	431	255	318	346	244	212	243	859	303
Health	555	524	566	521	366	279	483	400	293	284	857	340
Housing	107	142	84	95	59	57	87	175	89	39	390	68
Labour	103	151	210	117	89	111	109	76	82	92	222	103
Other	130	176	157	164	103	69	65	62	70	57	271	83
Interest Payments	804	967	1,288	871	1,159	2,635	981	681	763	1,035	2,379	1,613
Protection of Persons and Property	486	777	1,491	1,493	422	574	635	268	435	418	654	548

Table 3.5: Federal Funding of Government Spending by Function Per Capita, 1990 (Dollars)

Function	Nfld	PEI	NS	NB	Que	Ont	Man	Sask	Alta	BC	Terr	Cda
Regional Planning & Development	20	19	25	21	19	25	24	9	12	13	17	20
Resource Conservation & Industrial Development	273	509	284	222	130	137	389	1,033	479	121	997	223
Research Establishments	47	30	56	50	52	55	47	51	52	54	30	53
Social Services*	3,245	3,072	2,451	2,664	2,016	1,517	1,828	1,736	1,446	1,890	1,590	1,807
Transportation & Communications	307	408	343	313	124	136	180	170	140	109	567	151
Total	**7,152**	**8,058**	**8,320**	**7,571**	**5,180**	**6,231**	**5,734**	**5,406**	**4,449**	**4,706**	**9,346**	**5,703**
Canada Pension Plan	206	56	497	340	42	5,335	570	502	946	1,694	11	10,199
Total + CPP	7,358	8,114	8,817	7,911	5,222	11,566	6,304	5,908	5,395	6,400	9,357	15,902

*excludes Canada Pension Plan revenues and expenditures.

per capita spending figures with per capita taxation numbers to acquire a better sense of the net level of federal activity in each province.

Spending by function per capita

Before turning to a consideration of the net flows into the provinces, we examine in table 3.5 the distribution of federal expenditure by function, by province. The per capita figures reveal a pattern of differences in the extent to which the federal government spends money in the different provinces.

Interest on public debt is the most variable

The category which varies the most among the provinces is the expenditure by the federal government on interest on the public debt. Interest payments on the debt, often the subject of concern and discussion when considered as an "unproductive" outlay of the federal government, are nevertheless received as income by Canadians and are thus properly considered a "benefit" even though there is no creation of a current program benefit. They are, moreover, an important aspect of federal government spending in the provinces. Because of the sheer size of these payments, the provincial distribution of interest payments on the public debt has a determining influence on the per capita distribution of overall federal spending. For example, the $2,635 per person spent by the federal government on interest payments in Ontario in 1990-91 served to boost the level of expenditure in that province above the per capita average for the country. The interest distribution is based on figures provided by Statistics Canada for the estimates of gross provincial product. Since a significant portion of the interest is paid into pension accounts (owned by Canadians across the country), and on holdings of debt by the Bank of Canada allocated to Ontario because of the location of the federal government, it may be more insightful to view total expenditure distribution by province *excluding* interest from the expenditure distribution profile. This distribution is provided in table 3.6.

Table 3.6: Distribution of Federal Funding of Total Government Spending, Net of Interest, Across Canada (Percent)

Year	Nfld	PEI	NS	NB	Que	Ont	Man	Sask	Alta	BC	Terr	Cda
1970	3.1%	0.9%	5.9%	3.9%	23.9%	34.5%	5.3%	5.0%	7.4%	9.3%	0.7%	100.0%
1975	3.2%	0.8%	6.5%	4.4%	25.2%	33.0%	4.8%	4.9%	7.0%	9.4%	0.8%	100.0%
1980	3.2%	0.8%	7.3%	5.5%	26.2%	30.5%	4.9%	4.4%	6.9%	9.4%	0.9%	100.0%
1985	4.0%	0.8%	6.1%	4.0%	23.8%	29.9%	4.7%	5.0%	9.1%	10.1%	2.4%	100.0%
1988	3.3%	0.9%	5.5%	4.4%	24.1%	30.3%	5.1%	5.3%	9.6%	10.2%	1.3%	100.0%
1990	3.3%	0.9%	5.6%	4.5%	24.9%	32.3%	4.8%	4.3%	8.4%	10.5%	0.5%	100.0%

Deleting the effect of interest expense

As tables 3.6 and 3.7 illustrate, subtracting interest payments from total federal expenditure by province does indeed produce a provincial profile that more closely matches our common sense expectations. That is to say, provinces such as Quebec, Ontario, British Columbia, and Alberta have expenditure levels below the national average. Newfoundland, Prince Edward Island, Nova Scotia, New Brunswick, and the territories, as well as Manitoba and Saskatchewan generally have federal expenditure levels above the national average.

Table 3.7: Federal Funding of Expenditure Per Capita, Net of Interest Charges, 1990 (Dollars)

Nfld	6,348
PEI	7,091
NS	7,032
NB	6,700
Que	4,021
Ont	3,596
Man	4,753
Sask	4,725
Alta	3,686
BC	3,671
Terr	6,967
Cda	4,090

It is important to bear in mind the structure of the compensation various provinces receive under the federal-provincial fiscal arrangements agreements. Broadly speaking, these are arrangements whereby the federal government has historically agreed to provide the provinces with funds for program spending in areas of provincial responsibility but where the federal government has sought to encourage national standards of service or national coverage for a particular program. Some of the funding for these programs is in the form of cost sharing, while other funding is provided on a fixed cash transfer basis. More recently, funds are provided by the federal government vacating, in favour of the provinces, a certain amount of "tax room" in the form of percentage points of the personal income tax.

Quebec, for example, elects to receive tax transfers from the federal government for the hospital portion of insured health services as well as for the Canada Assistance Plan and youth allowances. The total amount of such transfers for the fiscal year 1991 is estimated to be about \$2.2 billion or \$311 per capita.[1] These transfers must be added to the total per capita figure reported in the table to make the Quebec figure comparable with the other provinces. With this adjustment, the per capita figure for federal spending in Quebec is just above the national average. In all cases there has been a program of tax transfers to the provinces to finance insured health services and post secondary education. These transfers amounted to just over \$10 billion in 1991.

Social security expenditures per capita display a more or less expected pattern. The Atlantic provinces, with their above-average reliance on transfer income, have a much higher per capita participation in the social security programs than the national average. British Columbia also enjoys higher than average social security payments per capita, largely because of the higher fraction of people receiving Old Age Security in the province than elsewhere in Canada, but also because B.C. is a net recipient of Unemployment Insurance payments. Payments made to persons under Unemployment Insurance, Old Age Security, and Canada Pension Plan are detailed in tables 3.8, 3.9, and 3.10.

A scan of the resource conservation & industrial development distribution reveals an anomalous entry for Saskatchewan—it received a per capita expenditure of more than 4.5 times the national average in that category. Saskatchewan has historically enjoyed more support in this category than have other provinces, largely as a result of the payments that are made to it for agriculture. While recent per capita

---

1 The Canadian Tax Foundation, *The National Finances*, 1991, Table 16.2, Footnote (b).

Table 3.8: Unemployment Insurance Benefits (Millions of Dollars)

Province	1970	1975	1980	1985	1988	1990
Nfld	25	160	261	548	747	781
PEI	4	26	46	107	138	140
NS	26	129	208	454	524	593
NB	25	153	247	512	605	660
Que	212	1,077	1,586	3,138	3,372	4,274
Ont	230	978	1,220	2,524	2,354	3,453
Man	25	57	115	313	356	388
Sask	22	48	78	255	301	304
Alta	34	86	139	829	850	899
BC	92	432	421	1,401	1,492	1,577
Terr	0	8	10	35	40	47
Cda	695	3,155	4,332	10,118	10,781	13,119

Source: Statistics Canada, Provincial Economic Accounts, catalogue 13-213.

payments in Saskatchewan have been more than 4.5 times the Canadian average, in 1970 these payments were smaller, but still about 3.5 times the national average. The payments have increased steadily during the 1970s and '80s.

Federal expenditures on protection of persons and property reflects the allocation on defence installations across the country. Prince Edward Island, Nova Scotia, and New Brunswick are more significant beneficiaries in this category than are other provinces. Most significantly, Nova Scotia and New Brunswick receive expenditures of $1,491 and $1,493 per capita respectively, nearly three times the national average. While Nova Scotia and Prince Edward Island benefit significantly by federal spending on the protection of persons and property, it is

Table 3.9: Old Age Security Benefits (Millions of Dollars)

Province	1970	1975	1980	1985	1988	1990
Nfld	39	81	161	288	343	380
PEI	15	28	51	85	98	106
NS	81	163	303	520	611	670
NB	62	123	235	407	483	536
Que	454	952	1,820	3,185	3,877	4,410
Ont	664	1,308	2,417	4,151	5,096	5,768
Man	104	205	368	615	725	796
Sask	102	197	353	591	698	771
Alta	127	258	477	831	1,035	1,182
BC	212	434	828	1,465	1,819	2,068
Terr	2	4	7	12	16	18
Cda	1,862	3,753	7,020	12,150	14,801	16,705

Source: Statistics Canada, Provincial Economic Accounts, catalogue 13-213.

important to recognize that they obtain only 17.0 percent of total expenditures on this category.

The best way to discern the extent to which spending on particular categories varies amongst the provinces is to compare the share of spending under each heading to the share of total spending by the federal government in that province. So, for example, if a province receives a greater share of total spending than another province, it would be natural to find that the share of some particular category of spending was larger for that province. The interesting analytical question is whether the share of a particular program exceeds the share that a province receives overall. The reason why this is interesting, particularly in a time of retrenchment of programs, is that those provinces that are disproportionate recipients under a particular program are likely to be more affected by cutbacks in that area than are other provinces.

Table 3.10: Canada Pension Plan Payments to Persons (Millions of Dollars)

Province	1970	1975	1980	1985	1988	1990
Nfld	1	10	37	98	162	206
PEI	0	3	11	28	44	56
NS	4	30	101	238	402	497
NB	3	19	69	164	278	340
Que	0	2	8	19	34	42
Ont	42	281	1,005	2,440	4,221	5,335
Man	5	35	117	276	459	570
Sask	5	26	100	243	405	502
Alta	7	44	159	412	741	946
BC	11	76	294	753	1,341	1,694
Terr	0	1	2	5	8	11
Cda	78	527	1,903	4,676	8,095	10,199

Source: Statistics Canada, Provincial Economic Accounts, catalogue 13-213.

Federal taxes compared to federal spending by province

Tables 3.5 and 3.7 convey an impression about the total benefit or expenditure per capita in each of the provinces generated by the activities of the federal government. Of course, the federal government does not create these benefits. It transfers them from the taxpayers to the beneficiaries. An obvious question arises: to what extent are the taxes raised by the federal government in one province spent in another province? In this section we examine this issue on a province-by-province basis.

Table 3.11 presents a distribution of total federal tax levied on the provinces. This distribution, it should be noted, ignores that portion of federal tax which is raised by taxing non-residents of Canada, and therefore looks only at the domestic distribution of the federal tax burden. It is evident by comparing the distribution line in table 3.11 with the distribution line in table 3.3 for 1990 that there is an imbalance in the sharing of the total federal tax burden and the total distribution of expenditures across Canada.

The winners and the losers

The province of Newfoundland receives 2.7 percent of total federal expenditure and pays just over 1 percent of the total federal tax burden. In fact, all the Atlantic provinces are winners in the sense that they bear a smaller fraction of the total tax burden than they receive in total federal expenditures. The only provinces for which that is not true are Ontario, Alberta, and British Columbia.

Net "benefits" per capita

This different distribution of expenditures and tax revenues is also reflected in table 3.12, which provides a per capita statement of the spending and taxation activities of the federal government by province. The first line in the table simply repeats the per capita federal expenditure by province from table 3.4. The second line reports CPP payments to persons. The third lists the estimates of total federal taxes (CPP contributions are considered to be taxes) paid, on average, by residents of each of the provinces according to the calculations provided in The Fraser Institute's biennial study of taxation, *Tax Facts*. The fourth line records the apparent benefit or current benefit that is enjoyed by individuals in each of the provinces—the difference between total spending by the federal government and the total taxes raised by the federal government in the particular province.

For example, on average, a resident of Newfoundland receives $4,876 more in benefits than he or she pays in total taxes to the federal government. The average citizen of Alberta receives $269 more in current benefits from the federal government than the amount paid in taxes.

Table 3.11: Distribution of Deficit Taxes

Function	Nfld	PEI	NS	NB	Que	Ont	Man	Sask	Alta	BC
1970										
Distribution of Total Federal Tax (millions of dollars)	181	37	376	267	3,066	6,694	617	401	1,142	1,694
Distribution (%)	1.3%	0.3%	2.6%	1.8%	21.2%	46.2%	4.3%	2.8%	7.9%	11.7%
Deficit Taxes (millions of dollars)	12	3	26	18	210	459	42	27	78	116
Deficit Taxes per Capita (dollars)	24	23	33	29	35	61	43	29	49	55
1990										
Distribution of Total Federal Tax (millions of dollars)	1,509	380	3,207	2,334	24,473	53,328	4,094	3,475	11,282	15,324
Distribution (%)	1.3%	0.3%	2.7%	1.9%	20.4%	44.5%	3.4%	2.9%	9.4%	12.8%
Deficit Taxes (millions of dollars)	365	92	775	564	5,918	12,895	990	840	2,728	3,705
Deficit Taxes per Capita (dollars)	637	702	896	781	874	1,323	909	843	1,103	1,183

Accounting for the deficit

The fifth line in the table reports the amount of tax per capita deferred by the deficits incurred by the federal government. Every dollar of deficit is a dollar of taxes that must be collected in the future to pay the interest on the debt which is incurred in the form of the deficit. Since the taxes incurred today that are deferred to the future also generate an interest expense at the current government bond rate, it is appropriate to regard the current deficit as the liability associated with the future tax burdens.[2]

Subtracting taxes deferred by the deficit from current benefits produces the net current benefit for residents and is the barometer of net activities of the federal government in taxing and spending across the various provinces.

The last line of table 3.12 reveals that, within the financial structure of Confederation as it presently operates, seven provinces are net fiscal beneficiaries and three provinces are net fiscal losers. Newfoundland, Prince Edward Island, Nova Scotia, New Brunswick, Quebec, Manitoba, and Saskatchewan all receive more in current expenditures than they pay in terms of current or deferred tax liabilities. The net current benefit per capita ranges from $696 in Quebec to as high as $4,879 in Prince Edward Island.

Deferred taxes can also be regionally distributed by two other methods that lead to similar conclusions, as table 3.13 shows. In the first case, we assume that money not already earmarked for a particular transfer program to the provinces will be available to pay interest on the public debt. This is approximated by the regional distribution of federal tax collected net of transfer payments to provincial and municipal

---

2 This is because of a concept economists refer to as "present value." If deferred taxes bear interest at the government bond rate, and if we discount the future interest on those taxes at the same government bond rate, then in effect, the force of interest cancels out over the period. So the current deficit is a good estimate of the present value of the tax liability associated with the extra spending. The deferred taxes are distributed amongst the provinces according to the share of actual federal tax revenues collected in that province.

Table 3.12: Federal Net Spending Benefits Per Capita, by Province (Dollars)

Function	Nfld	PEI	NS	NB	Que	Ont	Man	Sask	Alta	BC
1970										
Federal Government Services*	865	1,250	1,120	919	628	752	801	771	682	660
plus CPP payments to persons	2	0	5	5	0	6	5	5	4	5
less Taxes Paid	350	340	481	425	510	886	627	426	716	796
equals Gross Current Benefit	517	910	644	499	118	-129	178	350	-31	-131
less Taxes Deferred	24	23	33	29	35	61	43	29	49	55
equals Net Current Benefit	493	887	611	469	83	-190	135	321	-80	-186

* Excludes Canada Pension Plan Expenditures

Table 3.12: Federal Net Spending Benefits Per Capita, by Province (Dollars)

Function	Nfld	PEI	NS	NB	Que	Ont	Man	Sask	Alta	BC
1990										
Federal Government Services*	7,152	8,058	8,320	7,571	5,180	6,231	5,734	5,406	4,449	4,706
plus CPP Payments to Persons	360	428	575	471	6	547	523	503	383	541
less Taxes Paid	2,635	2,905	3,707	3,232	3,616	5,470	3,760	3,485	4,562	4,892
equals Gross Current Benefit	4,876	5,582	5,187	4,810	1,571	1,308	2,497	2,424	269	355
less Taxes Deferred	637	702	896	781	874	1,323	909	843	1,103	1,183
equals Net Current Benefit	4,239	4,879	4,291	4,029	696	-14	1,588	1,581	-834	-828

* Excludes Canada Pension Plan Expenditures

Table 3.13: Federal Net Spending Benefits Per Capita, by Province, 1990 (Dollars)

Nfld	PEI	NS	NB	Que	Ont	Man	Sask	Alta	BC
Method 1: Taxes Deferred Regionally Allocated by Share of Federal Tax Revenue Collected in Each Province									
4,239	4,879	4,291	4,029	696	-14	1,588	1,581	-834	-828
Method 2: Taxes Deferred Regionally Allocated by Share of Federal Tax Revenue Collected Less Transfer Payments to Provincial and Municipal Governments in Each Province									
3,436	4,021	3,905	3,447	534	380	1,284	1,131	-975	-904
Method 3: Taxes Deferred Regionally Allocated by Share of Federal Tax Revenue Less CPP Payments Less Transfer Payments to Provincial and Municipal Governments in Each Province									
4,393	5,040	4,378	4,148	653	-54	1,663	1,671	-781	-797

governments. In the second case, we further exclude payments to the Canada Pension Plan from the tax total as M. A. Raynauld does in his fiscal flow study.[3]

The provinces of British Columbia, Alberta, and Ontario are all net fiscal losers in the sense that the net current benefit is actually negative, implying that the total of current and deferred taxes exceeds the fiscal flow into those provinces from the federal government, either in the form of direct transfers or expenditures. The loss ranges from a low of $14 per capita in Ontario to $834 in Alberta.

The movement from line four to line six in table 3.12 (deducting deferred taxes) swings the same three provinces from net beneficiaries to net losers. This swing and the importance of deficit financing suggests the need for another calculation, the province-by-province distribution of the inflows and outflows associated with the interest on the federal public debt. This calculation is provided in table 3.14.

Who pays the interest on the debt?

The first row in table 3.14 provides the total tax cost of the federal interest payments. In other words, it represents the distribution, according to the average distribution of total federal revenue by province, of the total amount of interest paid during 1990. Each province is assumed to bear the cost of interest payments in proportion to the percentage of total federal revenue that it provides. The second line provides the per capita distribution of these figures. Line three in the table presents the total amount of interest paid out in each province, and line four provides the per capita amount of interest. The fifth line shows the calculation of the net flow of money into or out of the province, a figure that is determined by the payment of interest on the public debt and the taxes that must be raised to pay for it.

The figure for Newfoundland, for instance, is negative $80 million, which indicates that Newfoundlanders receive fewer dollars in interest payments than the total taxes they are assessed in order to pay for

---

3 M. André Raynauld, *Les Enjeux Economiques de la Souveraineté*, Conseil de Patronat du Québec, Octobre 1990.

Table 3.14: Distribution of the Tax and Expenditure Flows Associated with Interest on the Federal Public Debt, 1990

	Nfld	PEI	NS	NB	Que	Ont	Man	Sask	Alta	BC
Tax Cost of Interest (Federal Government Funding of Interest distributed according to distribution of Federal tax collection):										
(millions of dollars)	540	136	1,148	836	8,761	19,091	1,466	1,244	4,039	5,486
(dollars per capita)	943	1,040	1,327	1,157	1,294	1,958	1,346	1,248	1,633	1,751
Interest Payments:										
(millions of dollars)	460	126	1,114	629	7,846	25,687	1,068	679	1,887	3,242
(dollars per capita)	804	967	1,288	871	1,159	2,635	981	681	763	1,035
Net Flow:										
(millions of dollars)	-80	-10	-34	-206	-916	6,596	-397	-565	-2,152	-2,244
(dollars per capita)	-139	-73	-39	-286	-135	677	-365	-567	-870	-716

interest on the public debt. The latter figure is calculated by observing the percentage of total federal tax collected in Newfoundland, and assuming that any taxes raised to pay the interest on the debt would be raised in the same way that current revenues are raised. An examination of the provinces reveals that most provinces are losers when it comes to the financial flows associated with interest on the public debt. The exception is Ontario. Ontario is a very significant net beneficiary when it comes to interest on the public debt. It receives $6.6 billion more in interest payments than would be attributed to it by the overall distribution of the tax costs associated with financing those interest payments. It must be said that these figures are distorted to the extent that financial institutions, such as pension funds, hold government of Canada debt in Ontario on behalf of residents in other provinces. The figures are also distorted by the location of the Bank of Canada, which holds significant amounts of government of Canada debt. It is not possible at present to estimate how much distortion these factors induce.

Some insights onto old issues

The data in table 3.14 cast some light on two statements that are part of everyday conversation, and which deserve somewhat closer scrutiny. One of these is that we don't have to worry about the national debt because we owe it to ourselves. As the net flows associated with the public debt outstanding make quite clear, for the most part, the public debt is something which the rest of the country owes to Ontario. Ontario is a net beneficiary in that total interest payments from the federal government received by residents of Ontario exceeds by $6.6 billion the total expenses incurred by residents of Ontario associated with interest on the debt in the form of higher taxes. To put it somewhat differently, Ontario receives 60 percent of all of the interest paid on the outstanding public debt, but it bears only 45 percent of the total taxes paid to the federal government.

A second issue is the notion that, by quitting the Canadian confederation, Quebec has an opportunity to rid itself of a very significant liability in the form of the interest payments on the public debt. The story goes that with $456 billion in total federal net public debt outstanding in 1990, Quebeckers have a $93 billion incentive (their share of the total if their share is the portion of the interest borne by the province of Quebec, or $115 billion if their share is determined by population) to quit the Canadian confederation and hence rid themselves of this encumbrance. Such an analysis implicitly assumes that all of the residents of Quebec regard the public debt as a burden and a future tax liability. It fails to recognize that Quebec is a beneficiary of the public debt in the sense that $7.8 billion in 1990 was paid to residents of Quebec as holders of that same government debt in the form of government bonds.

It is, however, true for Quebec (as for all the other provinces save Ontario) that the public debt is a net burden amounting to an annual flow of $1 billion out of the province, or $128 per capita.

There are several issues associated with these calculations that bear further discussion. First and most importantly, it is inappropriate to regard the payment of interest on the public debt as creating a net benefit in any overall sense. Obviously, all provinces and the country as a whole would be better off if there were no public debt at all. The public debt is an expense incurred because of past spending by the federal government. There are no current program benefits conferred by the necessity of paying the interest on the debt. Interest payments on the public debt are a transfer from current taxpayers to past recipients of government program expenses. For example, payments that were made to program beneficiaries in 1984 when the federal deficit amounted to $38 billion are now being paid for by current taxpayers in the form of the interest on the bonds that the government issued in 1984 to enable it to make those payments. That said, given that there is a national debt and interest payments on it, the holders of the debt are the recipients of the interest and current taxpayers are the payers of the interest. To the extent that on average those who receive and those who pay are resident in different provinces, there is a regional redistribution involved in the interest payments on the public debt.

Second, it is clear that the "net benefits" that are enjoyed by provinces holding above average amounts of government debt are directly determined by the choice of the citizens of that province to hold Government of Canada bonds. So, for example, the province of Quebec, which is a net loser, could change its standing by the simple expedient of buying more Government of Canada bonds. Apart from anything else, this fact does place in sharp relief the tendentious nature of the calculation and its sensitivity to variables which have nothing to do with the federal government's proclivity to spend money in one province or another.

Chapter 3 Appendix: The Fiscal Outlook for ROC

ONE OF THE MOST PRESSING QUESTIONS that may face Canadians late in 1994 is what to do if the people of Quebec have voted for the separatist option in their provincial election campaign. This option, presented by the Parti Québécois at the provincial level, would sooner or later require the separation of Quebec's finances from those of the rest of Canada (or ROC as it is sometimes referred to in abbreviation). While the authors of this book are not in favour of such an outcome and certainly do not wish to see it happen, it may nevertheless be useful to construct a pro-forma net balance position for ROC and its constituent provinces.

In order to construct such a fiscal position, it is necessary to make certain assumptions about continuing obligations. In particular, what would be done about the national debt? While some assume a distribution by population—roughly 25 per cent—would be appropriate, others argue for a smaller fraction based on some analysis of the amount of federal spending done in the province of Quebec. For the purpose of this analysis, we assume that there would be no change from the present in the amount of the federal debt effectively assumed by Quebec. While there have been many assertions about what would actually happen, it would undoubtedly be a "fair" sharing of the debt burden because the province of Quebec would want to have cordial trade relations with

ROC, since 54 percent of its trade is with ROC, and a considerable fraction of that is related to the automobile industry as a by-product of the auto-pact provisions of NAFTA. Quebec would want to continue to have the benefits of NAFTA but would not be able to be a signatory unless Canada agreed, according to the provisions of NAFTA. Canada, not Quebec, is the signatory to NAFTA. Accordingly, the assumption that there would be a continuation of Quebec's current debt interest payments is not a "heroic" assumption.

From the point of view of the fiscal balance of ROC, the assumption by Quebec of a share of the debt would be equivalent to Quebec continuing to provide a certain amount of revenue equal to their current share of debt interest. All other tax revenue from Quebec would cease. On the other hand, all spending going to the province of Quebec would also cease. There would be a net balance in the flows to and from Quebec made up by the interest payments and the reduction in the net contribution which the federal government currently makes to the province of Quebec. In 1990, this net turn-around in the federal government's fiscal position would be $10.6 billion.

The implications for the rest of the fiscal position of the government would of course depend on what the government decided to do with its improved position. It could reduce the federal deficit by an equivalent amount. Under those circumstances, the deficit would fall from $32.1 billion to $21.5 billion according to the 1990 figures, implying a reduction of $10.6 billion in the forthcoming fiscal year with a corresponding deficit to GDP ratio of 4.2 percent.

Of course, the bonds of the government of Canada corresponding to the portion of the national debt owed by the province of Quebec would still be outstanding and there would therefore be no reduction in the debt to GDP ratio for the government of Canada. However, since there would be no interest on the part of the new government of Quebec to carry this burden of Canada bonds indefinitely, there probably would be a debt repayment scheme agreed to so that Quebec could amortise its share of the national debt in the same way that families amortise their mortgages. As families discover, there is very little difference between the regular mortgage payment and an interest only mortgage payment if the period of amortization is long enough. Accordingly, it would actually be possible for the government of the new Quebec to pay off its debt to Canada over a reasonable period of time.

Our calculation is that Quebec's prorated share of the national debt is $93.0 billion, based on the current share of interest borne by the province of Quebec.[4] If the agreement between Canada and Quebec were to provide for an amortization over, say, 30 years, the total annual payment would be $9.6 billion as opposed to the interest cost of $8.8 billion currently being incurred. Under this arrangement, the eventual debt to GDP ratio for ROC would fall from the present level of 88.8 per cent to 70.7 percent.

Evidently, ROC would have a far preferred fiscal balance position if it did not have the added burden of the province of Quebec. Quebec, on the other hand would have no change in its interest coverage position since it is already servicing its share of the debt, but it would have a serious short-term deterioration in its apparent balance sheet position since the $93.0 billion national debt position attributable to Quebec would be added to its previously existing debt outstanding. This is only an apparent deterioration, of course, since Quebec does indeed currently bear the burden associated with its share of the national debt.

---

4 If population is used to determine Quebec's share of the federal debt, then Quebec's share is $115.1 billion in 1990. This figure compares with the estimated share of $150.6 billion in 1994 in Robin Richardson's study, "The Public Debt of an Independent Quebec," *Fraser Forum Critical Issues Bulletin*, The Fraser Institute, August 1994. If the population share is used, then annual interest payments are $11.9 billion as of 1990.

Chapter 4: An Analysis of Provincial/Territorial and Municipal Government Spending Priorities

Funding and spending

THE PURPOSE OF THIS CHAPTER is to examine the distribution of provincial (here "province" means both provinces and territories) and municipal funding of expenditures to determine the spending priorities for the different provinces and how these priorities have changed over the past twenty years. We are concerned about the provincial funding of expenditures because there is a difference between the total expenditure on an item and the amount of that expenditure which is funded by the province itself. So, for example, in 1990 total expenditure per capita on education in Newfoundland amounted to $1,387 per capita. Of that amount, $442 was funded by the federal government, $899 was funded by the provincial government, and $46 was funded by municipal governments.

The source of all revenue for every level of government is, of course, the taxpayer. In some sense, therefore, it is meaningless to distinguish

Table 4.1: Provincial Funding of Government Spending by Function, 1970 (Millions of Dollars)

Function	Nfld	PEI	NS	NB	Que	Ont	Man	Sask	Alta	BC	Terr	Cda
Culture and Recreation	2	1	2	5	37	61	10	6	11	14	1	150
Education	47	2	87	92	719	1,308	117	95	416	273	13	3,168
Environment	2	1	1	3	21	25	1	0	4	6	1	66
Foreign Affairs and International Assistance	0	0	0	0	0	0	0	0	0	0	0	0
General Services	14	3	20	22	203	282	24	15	53	70	20	727
Health	22	4	51	39	736	938	95	71	196	219	3	2,375
Housing	2	1	1	0	13	9	0	8	0	4	2	39
Labour	5	1	3	8	43	53	0	1	5	1	0	120
Other	0	0	2	6	0	1	0	0	1	0	0	11
Interest Payments	23	4	43	23	182	506	42	37	69	29	2	960

Table 4.1: Provincial Funding of Government Spending by Function, 1970 (Millions of Dollars)

Function	Nfld	PEI	NS	NB	Que	Ont	Man	Sask	Alta	BC	Terr	Cda
Protection of Persons and Property	6	1	10	9	130	212	16	16	50	43	3	495
Regional Planning and Development	8	0	6	3	36	38	3	2	7	1	3	107
Resource Conservation and Industrial Development	0	0	8	0	105	147	28	22	56	75	0	441
Research Establishments	0	0	1	1	0	4	0	2	4	0	0	11
Social Services	16	3	17	17	491	399	32	27	84	164	2	1,252
Transportation and Communications	27	7	49	56	353	505	46	73	97	138	5	1,355
Total	174	28	302	283	3,069	4,486	416	374	1,052	1,038	54	11,277

Note: Figures may not add up due to rounding.

Table 4.2: Provincial Funding of Government Spending by Function, 1990 (Millions of Dollars)

Function	Nfld	PEI	NS	NB	Que	Ont	Man	Sask	Alta	BC	Terr	Cda
Culture and Recreation	30	10	47	47	419	578	99	104	240	214	49	1,836
Education	515	99	643	605	7,046	7,216	872	728	2,351	3,353	220	23,646
Environment	48	9	31	43	455	646	33	51	267	228	20	1,829
Foreign Affairs and International Assistance	0	0	0	0	0	0	0	0	0	0	0	0
General Services	129	37	128	179	2,775	1,942	212	377	702	919	264	7,664
Health	451	88	846	635	6,671	13,475	1,196	1,204	3,249	4,243	202	32,260
Housing	1	0	19	0	563	339	11	30	139	33	1	1,137
Labour	15	3	66	19	612	330	37	24	165	31	20	1,323
Other	21	2	10	22	205	948	26	58	197	212	70	1,770
Interest Payments	365	62	556	440	4,363	5,097	1,126	865	1,782	1,707	7	16,369

Table 4.2: Provincial Funding of Government Spending by Function, 1990 (Millions of Dollars)

Function	Nfld	PEI	NS	NB	Que	Ont	Man	Sask	Alta	BC	Terr	Cda
Protection of Persons and Property	108	17	124	113	927	2,100	151	154	484	520	87	4,786
Regional Planning and Development	12	1	34	20	110	259	78	14	52	88	74	743
Resource Conservation and Industrial Development	97	39	133	125	1,292	1,356	198	566	1,979	746	144	6,676
Research Establishments	0	0	6	6	137	69	1	15	83	59	1	378
Social Services	221	46	288	284	5,153	8,027	671	304	1,501	1,881	89	18,465
Transportation and Communications	154	48	194	249	1,517	2,405	220	229	903	877	112	6,908
Total	2,166	461	3,126	2,787	32,245	44,787	4,932	4,722	14,092	15,111	1,361	125,791

Note: Figures may not add up due to rounding.

which level of government is actually responsible for funding expenditures. However, the objective of this chapter is to reveal how the provincial and municipal governments allocate the money they receive directly from taxpayers. It is appropriate to focus on those expenditures that emerge from both funding sources since they are the only unambiguous indicators of provincial preference and priority. Expenditures made by a province that are funded and controlled by a federal government program cannot be regarded as a provincial government spending priority. So too, expenditures made by municipal governments in areas funded and controlled by federal and provincial government programs cannot be regarded as municipal government spending priorities. The first part of the chapter analyzes how the provincial government allocates the money it receives from its own sources. The second section looks at how municipal governments allocate their own source funds.

How spending flows have changed

A comparison of tables 4.1 and 4.2 reveals the very significant growth that has occurred in the gross flow of provincial government expenditure since 1970. However, it is difficult to draw any inferences from these comparative data since growth in provincial population and inflation obscure the underlying developments. Consequently, tables 4.3 and 4.4 provide per capita provincial funding for various provinces, while tables 4.5 and 4.6 provide these per capita figures on an inflation-adjusted basis. Finally, tables 4.7 and 4.8 provide the percentage distribution by function of total provincial expenditure in each of the two years examined.

The leading provincial expenses

Tables 4.3 and 4.4 provide an impression of the extent to which there is variation among the provinces in the support provided for the different expenditure functions from provincial revenue. In 1970, the biggest per capita expenditure in all provinces except for Prince Edward Island was for education. The next most significant expenditures were on health care, and on transportation and communication—an expenditure dominated by road construction and maintenance.

The territories and Alberta—the leading spenders

On average, the territorial governments spent $1,089 per capita in 1970—more than twice the national average. The second highest spender was Alberta, at $660 per capita.

While the priorities assigned by the provinces were basically similar, the ability of the provinces to dispense funds to the prioritized functions obviously varied according to their general affluence. As well, the quantity of funds dispensed varied according to the extent to which the provincial governments were inclined to tax their citizens and spend the resulting revenues on the various programs. So, for example, total expenditure per capita from own sources in 1970 ranged from $254 in Prince Edward Island to $660 in Alberta. The finding that Alberta spends more per capita than other provinces is something of a surprise in view of the fact that it has the reputation of being the least taxing province, and the most fiscally conservative one. The paradox is explained by the fact that while Alberta does not levy a sales tax, and therefore seems to tax less than other provinces, it does obtain extensive revenues from resource taxation, which are not regarded as taxes by the ordinary observer.[1] Similarly, Alberta has and does spend considerable amounts per capita on the petroleum and natural resource industries in its jurisdiction.

Calculating total expenditure net of interest payments per capita in the provinces as a fraction of the national Canadian average yields an impression of the variability. In 1970, Alberta was able to sustain expenditures from its own sources 27 percent above the national average, whereas Prince Edward Island managed only 45 percent of the national average (see table 4.3). Alberta and Ontario were above average spenders while the rest were below the national average. While by 1990 all of

---

1 Further information about the taxation levied in the various provinces and how taxes affect the average resident can be found in the companion volume to this study, *Tax Facts 8* by Isabella Horry, Filip Palda, and Michael A. Walker, Vancouver: The Fraser Institute, 1992.

Table 4.3: Provincial Funding of Government Spending by Function Per Capita, 1970 (dollars)

Function	Nfld	PEI	NS	NB	Que	Ont	Man	Sask	Alta	BC	Terr	Cda
Culture and Recreation	3	7	3	8	6	8	10	6	7	7	22	7
Education	90	15	111	147	120	173	119	101	261	128	264	149
Environment	3	5	1	5	4	3	2	0	2	3	12	3
Foreign Affairs & International Assistance	0	0	0	0	0	0	0	0	0	0	0	0
General Services	28	29	26	35	34	37	25	16	33	33	402	34
Health	43	39	66	63	122	124	97	76	123	103	51	111
Housing	4	7	1	0	2	1	0	8	0	2	35	2
Labour	9	11	4	12	7	7	0	1	3	1	8	6
Other	1	3	3	9	0	0	0	0	1	0	0	1
Interest Payments	45	37	56	37	30	67	43	39	43	14	32	45
Protection of Persons and Property	11	8	12	15	22	28	17	17	31	20	53	23

Table 4.3: Provincial Funding of Government Spending by Function Per Capita, 1970 (dollars)

Function	Nfld	PEI	NS	NB	Que	Ont	Man	Sask	Alta	BC	Terr	Cda
Regional Planning and Development	15	3	8	4	6	5	3	2	4	1	63	5
Resource Conservation and Industrial Development	0	0	11	0	17	19	29	23	35	35	0	21
Research Establishments	0	0	1	1	0	1	0	2	2	0	0	1
Social Services	31	25	22	27	82	53	32	29	53	77	42	59
Transportation & Communications	52	64	63	89	59	67	47	78	61	65	105	64
Total	336	254	387	452	510	594	424	397	660	488	1,087	530
Total Net of Interest Payments	290	217	331	415	480	527	381	358	616	474	1,055	484
Total Net of Interest Payments as a Percentage of the Canadian Average	59.9%	44.9%	68.4%	85.7%	99.1%	108.8%	78.6%	73.9%	127.2%	97.9%	217.9%	100.0%

Note: Figures may not add up due to rounding.

Table 4.4: Provincial Funding of Government Spending by Function Per Capita, 1990 (Dollars)

Function	Nfld	PEI	NS	NB	Que	Ont	Man	Sask	Alta	BC	Terr	Cda
Culture and Recreation	53	76	55	65	62	59	91	104	97	68	617	69
Education	899	754	743	838	1,041	740	801	730	951	1,070	2,759	889
Environment	83	65	35	60	67	66	31	51	108	73	246	69
Foreign Affairs & International Assistance	0	0	0	0	0	0	0	0	0	0	0	0
General Services	225	280	148	247	410	199	195	379	284	293	3,305	288
Health	787	670	978	879	986	1,382	1,099	1,208	1,314	1,355	2,528	1,212
Housing	2	0	22	0	83	35	10	30	56	11	19	43
Labour	27	27	76	26	90	34	34	24	67	10	250	50
Other	36	19	12	30	30	97	23	58	80	68	873	67
Interest Payments	637	474	643	609	645	523	1,034	867	720	545	87	615
Protection of Persons and Property	188	132	143	156	137	215	139	154	196	166	1,085	180

Table 4.4: Provincial Funding of Government Spending by Function Per Capita, 1990 (Dollars)

Function	Nfld	PEI	NS	NB	Que	Ont	Man	Sask	Alta	BC	Terr	Cda
Regional Planning and Development	21	9	39	28	16	27	72	14	21	28	932	28
Resource Conservation and Industrial Development	169	301	154	173	191	139	182	568	800	238	1,801	251
Research Establishments	0	0	7	9	20	7	1	15	33	19	17	14
Social Services	387	354	333	393	761	823	616	305	607	601	1,114	694
Transportation & Communications	268	365	225	345	224	247	202	230	365	280	1,407	260
Total	3,782	3,526	3,613	3,858	4,764	4,594	4,529	4,736	5,698	4,824	17,039	4,727
Total Net of Interest Payments	3,145	3,053	2,971	3,249	4,120	4,071	3,495	3,869	4,978	4,279	16,952	4,112
Total Net of Interest Payments as a Percentage of the Canadian Average	76.5%	74.2%	72.2%	79.0%	100.2%	99.0%	85.0%	94.1%	121.1%	104.1%	412.3%	100.0%

Note: Figures may not add up due to rounding.

the provinces were, of course, expending considerably more per capita on all of the functions, there was still a very wide range in the extent of total spending and expenditures on particular items among the provinces. In 1990, Alberta's provincial expenditures were 21 percent above the national average, whereas Prince Edward Island managed only 74 percent of the average.

Interest expense crowds out other spending

By 1990, all the provinces had reordered their spending priorities. Health care has emerged as the area where the most dollars per capita are now spent by all governments. Education falls in second place—in some provinces a distant second place. One reason for the apparent shift in priorities is the emergence of interest as a prominent expense. On average, interest costs are the fourth largest demand on the resources that provinces raise from their own sources.

Manitoba and Saskatchewan spend most on debt interest

The territories and Alberta have retained their dominance as the two top spenders. Significantly, the territories are the top per capita spenders in all categories but interest, where they are the lowest spenders. Of the ten provinces, Alberta spent the most per capita in 1990 on resource conservation and industrial development, on the environment, and on transportation and communication. Ontario spent the most on health care, on protection of persons and property, and on social services. Saskatchewan and Manitoba paid the most provincial debt interest charges in 1990. Saskatchewan, with annual interest payments of $947 per capita, spent $243 per capita less than Manitoba, which is the top interest spender. Since both provinces are recipients of transfers from the federal government which paid at least part of these interest payments, the provincially-sourced spending on interest was $867 and $1,034 for Saskatchewan and Manitoba, respectively.

Changing priorities

The impressions from table 4.3 and 4.4 are not in any way altered by adjusting them for inflation, although that adjustment does give us an opportunity to compare the change in the real per capita allocations by the provincial governments over the period since 1970. By examining the increases in these real per capita figures we can ascertain a sense of the changing priorities within the provincial budgets of the various provinces. These percentage increases are presented in table 4.7. Other than for a few unusual expenditures like those on labour, housing, environment, or research establishments, which are relatively small in the provinces' overall expenditures, the spending priorities that received the most attention over the period were interest on provincial debt and social services. On average, the provinces experienced a 254 percent increase in interest costs in real terms over the period since 1970, nearly double the increase in per capita expenditures on health care and five times the increase allocated to education. Social services increased by 206 percent over the same period.

Of the major expenditure categories, those with an average or below average increase over the period included general services, education, the protection of persons and property, and transportation and communications. Those receiving above average—in many cases significantly above average—growth included health care, social services, resource conservation and industrial development expenditures, and, of course, interest payments. Figure 4.1 provides a graphic illustration of the development with regard to the major expenditure categories over the period since 1970.

While a comparison of the Canada-wide totals over the period gives an impression of the general direction of change in the provincial expenditure priorities, it is difficult to make comparisons among the provinces because the total expenditure by each from its own revenue sources has grown at different rates. For instance, Ontario's real per capita expenditures have increased by only 97 percent, whereas the Canadian average was 132 percent. On the other hand, Nova Scotia's real per capita expenditures grew by a very large 282 percent. Accordingly, the developments in the real per capita expenditures over the period need in some way to be adjusted for growth in the overall

Figure 4.1: Percentage Increase in Real Per Capita Provincial Funding of Government Spending

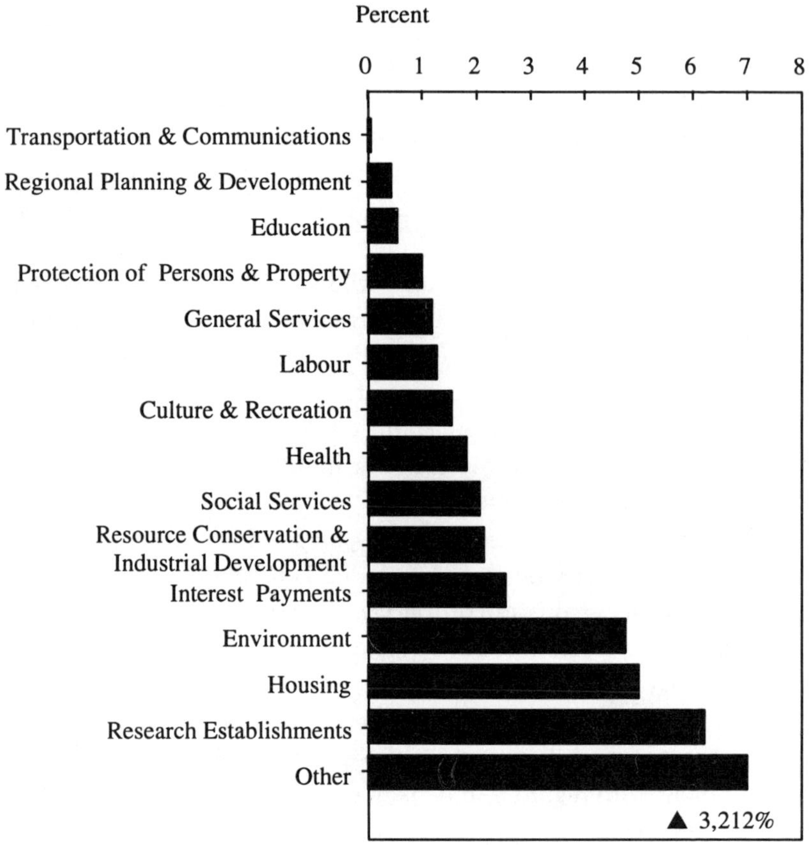

expenditure pattern within the individual provinces. Tables 4.8 and 4.9 accomplish this by expressing expenditures on individual items as a fraction of total expenditure.

Before examining that data, however, it is interesting to consider the correlation between the increase in overall expenditures that originated from provincial sources and the increase in interest payments per capita in the individual provinces (see table 4.6). For example, while Saskatchewan chose to increase its total spending by 224 percent during the period, it also experienced a 499 percent increase in interest payments because the source of much of the spending increase came from provincial deficits. Access to deficit financing also explains, to some extent, the narrowing between 1970 and 1990 in own-source financing of expenditures noted above.

Tables 4.8 and 4.9 present the provincial budget allocation decisions in the form of proportions of total funding by function in each province. For example, in 1970 the national average expenditure on education was 28 cents out of each budgetary dollar raised from provincial sources. However, there was considerable variation among the provinces: Alberta spent 40 cents out of each dollar on education whereas Quebec spent only 23 cents and Prince Edward Island just 6 cents of each dollar. Expenditures on the protection of persons and property absorbed an average of 4 cents of provincial-source revenues during the period. Fluctuations among the provinces, however, ranged from 5 cents in Alberta and the Territories to 3 cents in the Atlantic provinces.

To some extent, the variations among the provinces in the fraction of their total funding allocated to different functions is a reflection of the way in which each province is organized *vis-à-vis* the federal government on the one hand, and the municipal governments on the other. For example, in 1970 in Quebec, 24 cents out of every dollar of provincial funding was allocated to health care when the Canadian average was only 21 cents. That variation is explained by the fact that Quebec relies on own-source revenue in the form of tax points transferred from the federal government to finance some aspects of health care and some aspects of its social security net. It is therefore not surprising to discover that in the social security expenditure area Quebec also spent well above the national average, at 16 cents out of the total spending dollar during 1970 compared with a national average of 11 cents per dollar.

Table 4.9 provides the proportion of funding by function in each province for 1990. Comparing this table with the contents of table 4.8 provides a sense of the shift in spending priorities over time. The most dramatic change in the allocation of provincial budgets, as we have seen in other forms in previous tables, is the allocation for interest expense. In 1970 the provincial average was only 9 cents per dollar of provincial funding; by 1990 this had risen to 13 cents per dollar. An almost equally

Table 4.5: Provincial Funding of Government Spending Per Capita in Real Dollars, 1970 (in 1986 Dollars)

Function	Nfld	PEI	NS	NB	Que	Ont	Man	Sask	Alta	BC	Terr	Cda
Culture and Recreation	10	23	10	26	20	26	31	19	21	21	78	23
Education	310	48	350	478	387	556	379	310	817	408	919	480
Environment	12	17	4	18	12	11	5	1	8	10	42	10
Foreign Affairs and International Assistance	0	0	0	0	0	0	0	0	0	0	0	0
General Services	95	91	81	113	109	120	79	49	104	105	1,401	110
Health	148	120	206	204	396	399	308	234	385	327	177	360
Housing	13	21	3	0	7	4	1	25	0	6	123	6
Labour	31	33	14	39	23	23	1	4	9	2	27	18
Other	2	10	10	29	0	0	1	0	2	0	0	2
Interest Payments	157	115	175	120	98	215	136	121	136	43	110	145

Table 4.5: Provincial Funding of Government Spending Per Capita in Real Dollars, 1970 (in 1986 Dollars)

Function	Nfld	PEI	NS	NB	Que	Ont	Man	Sask	Alta	BC	Terr	Cda
Protection of Persons and Property	40	25	39	48	70	90	53	52	98	64	184	75
Regional Planning and Development	53	11	24	14	20	16	11	5	13	2	218	16
Resource Conservation and Industrial Development	0	0	33	0	56	63	91	70	110	113	0	67
Research Establishments	0	0	3	4	0	2	0	5	7	0	0	2
Social Services	107	78	68	87	264	170	103	89	165	246	147	190
Transportation and Communications	179	198	197	289	190	215	148	239	190	206	365	205
Total	1,157	789	1,217	1,469	1,652	1,908	1,346	1,223	2,065	1,553	3,791	1,708

Note: Figures may not add up due to rounding.

Table 4.6: Provincial Funding of Government Spending Per Capita in Real Dollars, 1990 (in 1986 Dollars)

Function	Nfld	PEI	NS	NB	Que	Ont	Man	Sask	Alta	BC	Terr	Cda
Culture and Recreation	47	65	46	56	53	49	76	87	82	58	537	58
Education	790	644	632	718	884	607	673	611	808	910	2,401	744
Environment	73	56	30	51	57	54	26	43	92	62	214	58
Foreign Affairs and International Assistance	0	0	0	0	0	0	0	0	0	0	0	0
General Services	197	239	126	212	348	163	164	317	241	249	2,876	241
Health	691	572	833	754	837	1,133	924	1,011	1,116	1,152	2,200	1,014
Housing	2	0	19	0	71	29	9	25	48	9	16	36
Labour	24	23	65	23	77	28	28	20	57	8	218	42
Other	32	16	10	26	26	80	20	48	68	58	759	56
Interest Payments	560	404	547	522	548	428	869	726	612	463	75	515

Table 4.6: Provincial Funding of Government Spending Per Capita in Real Dollars, 1990 (in 1986 Dollars)

Function	Nfld	PEI	NS	NB	Que	Ont	Man	Sask	Alta	BC	Terr	Cda
Protection of Persons and Property	166	113	122	134	116	177	117	129	166	141	945	150
Regional Planning and Development	18	7	34	24	14	22	61	12	18	24	811	23
Resource Conservation and Industrial Development	149	257	131	148	162	114	153	475	680	203	1,567	210
Research Establishments	0	0	6	7	17	6	1	13	28	16	15	12
Social Services	340	303	283	337	647	675	518	255	515	511	970	581
Transportation and Communications	236	312	191	296	190	202	170	192	310	238	1,224	217
Total	3,323	3,011	3,075	3,309	4,048	3,765	3,809	3,963	4,841	4,102	14,829	3,956

Note: Figures may not add up due to rounding.

Table 4.7: Percentage Increase in Real Per Capita Provincial Funding of Government Spending Between 1970 and 1990 (Percent)

Function	Nfld	PEI	NS	NB	Que	Ont	Man	Sask	Alta	BC	Terr	Cda
Culture and Recreation	360%	181%	366%	111%	163%	87%	146%	357%	291%	176%	592%	155%
Education	154%	1,254%	81%	50%	129%	9%	78%	97%	-1%	123%	161%	55%
Environment	535%	227%	583%	190%	395%	408%	438%	7,206%	1,114%	541%	415%	476%
Foreign Affairs & International Assistance	*	*	*	*	*	*	*	*	*	*	*	*
General Services	108%	163%	56%	89%	219%	36%	107%	545%	131%	138%	105%	119%
Health	368%	378%	303%	269%	111%	184%	200%	332%	190%	252%	1,141%	182%
Housing	-86%	-100%	606%	**	890%	666%	1,281%	0%	199,430 %	41%	-87%	500%
Labour	-23%	-32%	378%	-42%	235%	23%	1,867%	424%	529%	363%	699%	128%
Other	1,650%	58%	1%	-12%	121,985 %	23,518%	2,409%	**	2,946%	24,290%	1,571,839 %	3,212%
Interest Payments	257%	253%	213%	336%	460%	99%	541%	499%	351%	969%	-31%	254%

Table 4.7: Percentage Increase in Real Per Capita Provincial Funding of Government Spending Between 1970 and 1990 (Percent)

Function	Nfld	PEI	NS	NB	Que	Ont	Man	Sask	Alta	BC	Terr	Cda
Protection of Persons and Property	318%	356%	214%	181%	67%	96%	120%	149%	69%	121%	414%	101%
Regional Planning and Development	-66%	-32%	41%	68%	-30%	37%	457%	129%	36%	1,174%	271%	44%
Resource Conservation & Industrial Development	**	**	294%	**	188%	82%	69%	575%	518%	80%	6,298,368 %	214%
Research Establishments	*	*	98%	107%	**	220%	**	154%	297%	**	**	622%
Social Services	216%	290%	314%	286%	145%	298%	405%	187%	212%	108%	560%	206%
Transportation & Communications	31%	57%	-3%	2%	0%	-6%	15%	-20%	63%	15%	235%	6%
Total	187%	282%	153%	125%	145%	97%	183%	224%	134%	164%	291%	132%

*There is no expenditure in either 1970 or in 1990.
**Denotes an increase over 1970, but since the value was zero in 1970, the percentage increase is undefined.

dramatic change occurred in educational expenditure which declined from 28 percent of the average provincial budget in 1970 to 19 percent of the average budget in 1990. As noted above, this reflects demographic changes, but also, like the other aspects of provincial expenditure, reflects crowding out by the expansion in interest payments.

Health care, which has received considerable attention in recent years as an absorber of funding, has indeed increased in provincial priorities over the period; it absorbed 21 cents per dollar of the budget in 1970, but by 1990 it had risen to absorb 26 cents of the budget. Transportation and communication, a traditional sector of heavy government expenditure, declined significantly as a provincial priority, from 12 percent of total funding in 1970 to only 5 percent by 1990. Protection of persons and property dropped from 4.4 percent of the provincial budget to 3.8 percent in 1990. Social security expenditures increased from 11 to 15 cents of the average funding dollar. Also increasing over the period was expenditures on resource conservation and industrial development, which took 4 cents of the average provincial budget in 1970, and 5 cents in 1990.

Overall assessment of provincial priorities

In summary, while priorities vary, the average provincial priority during the last twenty years has moved away from educational funding, protection of persons and property, and the building of provincial infrastructure towards social security expenditures, subsidization of industry, and payment of interest on debt accumulated.

A cursory analysis of municipal expenditure

What follows is a cursory analysis of municipal government funding of expenditures—cursory because the analysis of municipal spending provides special problems caused by variation among the provinces in the allocation of expenditure responsibility.

In 1970, municipal governments funded $5,088 million, or 16 percent of total government spending, and in 1990, they funded $31,956 million, or 10 percent of the total. When we refer to municipal government spending, we in fact mean only that portion of spending which the municipalities fund from their own taxes.

Tables 4.10 and 4.11 show the increase in municipal government expenditure over the period since 1970. However, as noted in the provincial analysis, it is difficult to draw conclusions from these data since growth in provincial population and inflation obscure the underlying developments.

The figures are given on a per capita basis in tables 4.12 and 4.13. Tables 4.14 and 4.15 provide these per capita figures on an inflation-adjusted basis. Tables 4.17 and 4.18 provide the percentage distribution by function of total municipal expenditure.

As tables 4.12 and 4.13 show, spending by municipalities from their own sources on various functions is highly variable across the provinces. In 1970, the largest per capita expenditure in all provinces except Newfoundland and New Brunswick was on education. Spending on education ranged from zero in New Brunswick to $105 per capita in Ontario. The next most significant expenditures were on transportation and communication, protection of persons and property, environment, and interest on debt.

Alberta cities top spenders

In 1970, total expenditures per capita from municipalities' own sources ranged from $29 in Newfoundland to $293 in Ontario. The more affluent the province, the greater the ability is of municipalities in the province to tax and consequently to spend the revenue on various programs. Ontario, Saskatchewan, Alberta, and British Columbia were able to sustain expenditure from their own sources at or above the national average, while the other provinces were below it. Ontario managed to sustain expenditure 23 percent above the national average, while Newfoundland managed only 12 percent of the national average. By 1990, Alberta's municipal governments, considered as a whole, had surpassed those of Ontario as the highest spenders per capita. Ontario and Alberta maintained per capita expenditure above the national average. The Territories achieved higher than average per capita expenditure in 1990. The other provinces, including British Columbia, were below the

Table 4.8: Distribution of Provincial Funding of Government Spending by Province, 1970 (Percent)

Function	Nfld	PEI	NS	NB	Que	Ont	Man	Sask	Alta	BC	Terr	Cda
Culture and Recreation	0.9%	2.9%	0.8%	1.8%	1.2%	1.4%	2.3%	1.6%	1.0%	1.4%	2.0%	1.3%
Education	26.8%	6.0%	28.8%	32.5%	23.4%	29.2%	28.2%	25.4%	39.6%	26.3%	24.2%	28.1%
Environment	1.0%	2.2%	0.4%	1.2%	0.7%	0.6%	0.4%	0.0%	0.4%	0.6%	1.1%	0.6%
Foreign Affairs and International Assistance	0.0%	0.0%	0.0%	0.0%	0.0%	0.0%	0.0%	0.0%	0.0%	0.0%	0.0%	0.0%
General Services	8.2%	11.5%	6.6%	7.7%	6.6%	6.3%	5.9%	4.0%	5.1%	6.7%	37.0%	6.4%
Health	12.8%	15.2%	17.0%	13.9%	24.0%	20.9%	22.9%	19.1%	18.6%	21.1%	4.7%	21.1%
Housing	1.2%	2.7%	0.2%	0.0%	0.4%	0.2%	0.0%	2.0%	0.0%	0.4%	3.3%	0.3%
Labour	2.7%	4.2%	1.1%	2.6%	1.4%	1.2%	0.1%	0.3%	0.4%	0.1%	0.7%	1.1%
Other	0.2%	1.3%	0.8%	2.0%	0.0%	0.0%	0.1%	0.0%	0.1%	0.0%	0.0%	0.1%
Interest Payments	13.5%	14.5%	14.4%	8.1%	5.9%	11.3%	10.1%	9.9%	6.6%	2.8%	2.9%	8.5%

Table 4.8: Distribution of Provincial Funding of Government Spending by Province, 1970 (Percent)

Function	Nfld	PEI	NS	NB	Que	Ont	Man	Sask	Alta	BC	Terr	Cda
Protection of Persons and Property	3.4%	3.1%	3.2%	3.2%	4.2%	4.7%	3.9%	4.2%	4.8%	4.1%	4.8%	4.4%
Regional Planning and Development	4.6%	1.4%	2.0%	1.0%	1.2%	0.8%	0.8%	0.4%	0.6%	0.1%	5.8%	0.9%
Resource Conservation and Industrial Development	0.0%	0.0%	2.7%	0.0%	3.4%	3.3%	6.7%	5.8%	5.3%	7.3%	0.0%	3.9%
Research Establishments	0.0%	0.0%	0.3%	0.2%	0.0%	0.1%	0.0%	0.4%	0.3%	0.0%	0.0%	0.1%
Social Services	9.3%	9.8%	5.6%	5.9%	16.0%	8.9%	7.6%	7.3%	8.0%	15.8%	3.9%	11.1%
Transportation and Communications	15.5%	25.1%	16.2%	19.7%	11.5%	11.2%	11.0%	19.5%	9.2%	13.3%	9.6%	12.0%
Total	100.0%	100.0%	100.0%	100.0%	100.0%	100.0%	100.0%	100.0%	100.0%	100.0%	100.0%	100.0%

Note: Figures may not add up due to rounding.

Table 4.9: Distribution of Provincial Funding of Government Spending by Province, 1990 (Percent)

Function	Nfld	PEI	NS	NB	Que	Ont	Man	Sask	Alta	BC	Terr	Cda
Culture and Recreation	1.4%	2.1%	1.5%	1.7%	1.3%	1.3%	2.0%	2.2%	1.7%	1.4%	3.6%	1.5%
Education	23.8%	21.4%	20.6%	21.7%	21.9%	16.1%	17.7%	15.4%	16.7%	22.2%	16.2%	18.8%
Environment	2.2%	1.8%	1.0%	1.6%	1.4%	1.4%	0.7%	1.1%	1.9%	1.5%	1.4%	1.5%
Foreign Affairs and International Assistance	0.0%	0.0%	0.0%	0.0%	0.0%	0.0%	0.0%	0.0%	0.0%	0.0%	0.0%	0.0%
General Services	5.9%	7.9%	4.1%	6.4%	8.6%	4.3%	4.3%	8.0%	5.0%	6.1%	19.4%	6.1%
Health	20.8%	19.0%	27.1%	22.8%	20.7%	30.1%	24.3%	25.5%	23.1%	28.1%	14.8%	25.6%
Housing	0.1%	0.0%	0.6%	0.0%	1.7%	0.8%	0.2%	0.6%	1.0%	0.2%	0.1%	0.9%
Labour	0.7%	0.8%	2.1%	0.7%	1.9%	0.7%	0.7%	0.5%	1.2%	0.2%	1.5%	1.1%
Other	1.0%	0.5%	0.3%	0.8%	0.6%	2.1%	0.5%	1.2%	1.4%	1.4%	5.1%	1.4%
Interest Payments	16.8%	13.4%	17.8%	15.8%	13.5%	11.4%	22.8%	18.3%	12.6%	11.3%	0.5%	13.0%

Table 4.9: Distribution of Provincial Funding of Government Spending by Province, 1990 (Percent)

Function	Nfld	PEI	NS	NB	Que	Ont	Man	Sask	Alta	BC	Terr	Cda
Protection of Persons and Property	5.0%	3.7%	4.0%	4.1%	2.9%	4.7%	3.1%	3.3%	3.4%	3.4%	6.4%	3.8%
Regional Planning and Development	0.5%	0.2%	1.1%	0.7%	0.3%	0.6%	1.6%	0.3%	0.4%	0.6%	5.5%	0.6%
Resource Conservation and Industrial Development	4.5%	8.5%	4.3%	4.5%	4.0%	3.0%	4.0%	12.0%	14.0%	4.9%	10.6%	5.3%
Research Establishments	0.0%	0.0%	0.2%	0.2%	0.4%	0.2%	0.0%	0.3%	0.6%	0.4%	0.1%	0.3%
Social Services	10.2%	10.1%	9.2%	10.2%	16.0%	17.9%	13.6%	6.4%	10.6%	12.4%	6.5%	14.7%
Transportation and Communications	7.1%	10.4%	6.2%	8.9%	4.7%	5.4%	4.5%	4.8%	6.4%	5.8%	8.3%	5.5%
Total	100.0%	100.0%	100.0%	100.0%	100.0%	100.0%	100.0%	100.0%	100.0%	100.0%	100.0%	100.0%

Note: Figures may not add up due to rounding.

national average. Prince Edward Island had the lowest per capita expenditure, $223.

Overall program priorities did not change much between 1970 and 1990. Education, transportation and communication, protection of persons and property, the environment, and interest charges are still the major expenditures. Other categories such as health care, culture and recreation, general services and other took on greater importance.

Municipal governments in provinces other than Alberta are dominant per capita spenders only in specific categories. Ontario is the largest per capita spender on education and protection of persons and property. Nova Scotia spends the largest amount on social security, $145 per capita, which is 562 percent above the national average.

Adjusting for inflation does not alter the observations made in tables 4.12 and 4.13. But the adjustment does allow us to compare the change in real per capita allocations by municipal governments between 1970 and 1988 and to observe changes in the spending priorities of various provinces. These percentage increases are found in table 4.16.

Of the major expenditure categories, three of them—environment, other, and protection of persons and property—enjoyed above average increases over the period. Those growing at below average rates were transportation and communication, and education.

Tables 4.17 and 4.18 present municipal budget allocation decisions according to the proportion of total funding by function in each province. For example, in 1970 (see table 4.17), the national average expenditure on education was 32 cents out of each budgetary dollar raised by municipal governments. Spending among the provinces varied greatly: Newfoundland spent 5 cents on education, Ontario and British Columbia spent 36 cents each, and Prince Edward Island spent 55 cents out of each dollar funded in 1970.

The proportion of funding by function in each province in 1990 is provided in table 4.18. Comparing tables 4.17 and 4.18 gives a sense of the shift in municipal spending priorities over the period. For example, the national average expenditure on health care was greatly reduced between 1970 and 1990. In 1970, 8 cents out of each budgetary dollar raised by municipal governments went to health; in 1990 just one cent went to health care. The reduction was greatest in Alberta where spending on health care fell from 22 cents to zero cents out of each dollar. Protection of persons and property rose from 10 percent of total funding in 1970 to 13 percent in 1990. Transportation and communication dropped from 14 percent in 1970 to 13 percent in 1990. The environment rose from 9 percent to 13 percent. Education fell from 32 percent to 22 percent. These changes reflect not only demographic changes but also changes in spending responsibility among the three levels of government.

In Prince Edward Island education fell from 55 percent of municipal spending in 1970 to zero percent in 1990. At the same time, the provincial government's spending on education rose dramatically. In 1970, provincial government spending on education from own sources comprised 6 percent of provincial spending; in 1990, spending on education had reached 21 percent. Appendix D, which details the funding composition of a dollar spent by government by category of spending, better illustrates the above point. In 1970, each dollar spent on education by government in Prince Edward Island was composed of 72 cents of federal funding, 7 cents of provincial funding, and 21 cents of municipal funding. In 1990, by comparison, 35 cents came from federal funding and the remaining 65 cents from the provincial funding. The share of municipal own-source revenue allocated to education fell in all provinces except Newfoundland where it rose from 5 percent to 10 percent.

Over the period from 1970 to 1990, although municipal government spending priorities varied among provinces, on average the major expenditure categories—environment, interest, other, protection of persons and property, and transportation and communication—remained fairly constant. Municipal priorities, however, did move away from educational and health care funding toward expenditure on culture and recreation, general services, and other.

Much of the variation in expenditure across provinces, at both the provincial and municipal government levels, reflects local taste in how to split the responsibility between provincial and municipal governments. As noted above, in the case of spending on education in Prince Edward Island, the responsibility can also shift between levels of government over time. Between 1970 and 1990, the responsibility of funding

Table 4.10: Municipal Funding of Government Spending by Function, 1970 (Millions of Dollars)

Function	Nfld	PEI	NS	NB	Que	Ont	Man	Sask	Alta	BC	Terr	Cda
Culture and Recreation	1	1	3	3	60	147	12	11	31	36	0	304
Education	1	5	46	0	311	793	80	75	128	184	0	1,622
Environment	2	0	16	7	119	186	21	20	50	59	1	481
Foreign Affairs and International Assistance	0	0	0	0	0	0	0	0	0	0	0	0
General Services	4	0	10	3	130	109	19	15	24	31	1	345
Health	0	0	30	0	9	163	23	47	117	5	0	394
Housing	0	0	0	0	1	0	0	0	0	0	0	1
Labour	0	0	0	0	0	0	0	0	0	0	0	0
Other	1	0	2	0	0	28	5	1	4	2	0	42
Interest Payments	4	1	11	3	187	199	21	17	45	45	0	533

Table 4.10: Municipal Funding of Government Spending by Function, 1970 (Millions of Dollars)

Function	Nfld	PEI	NS	NB	Que	Ont	Man	Sask	Alta	BC	Terr	Cda
Protection of Persons and Property	1	1	10	6	143	226	19	15	39	56	0	516
Regional Planning and Development	0	0	0	0	0	4	0	1	11	2	0	19
Resource Conservation and Industrial Development	0	0	2	0	0	14	0	1	0	1	0	17
Research Establishments	0	0	0	0	0	0	0	0	0	0	0	0
Social Services	0	0	7	0	5	80	0	3	3	23	0	121
Transportation and Communications	3	1	10	9	200	267	27	33	79	63	1	692
Total	15	10	146	32	1,166	2,216	226	237	529	506	3	5,088

Note: Figures may not add up due to rounding.

Table 4.11: Municipal Funding of Government Spending by Function, 1990 (Millions of Dollars)

Function	Nfld	PEI	NS	NB	Que	Ont	Man	Sask	Alta	BC	Terr	Cda
Culture and Recreation	30	7	66	31	697	1,390	198	141	450	453	16	3,478
Education	26	0	164	0	0	4,930	183	286	563	736	0	6,888
Environment	32	1	128	24	1,448	1,686	180	128	279	345	28	4,279
Foreign Affairs and International Assistance	0	0	0	0	0	0	0	0	0	0	0	0
General Services	40	3	53	19	983	1,129	114	87	282	208	22	2,939
Health	0	0	0	2	10	62	25	44	0	109	1	253
Housing	1	0	4	0	0	107	2	1	22	17	5	160
Labour	0	0	0	0	0	0	0	0	0	0	0	0
Other	4	0	8	2	367	501	28	18	125	45	1	1,100
Interest Payments	48	7	49	22	1,309	565	122	61	649	547	4	3,383

Table 4.11: Municipal Funding of Government Spending by Function, 1990 (Millions of Dollars)

Function	Nfld	PEI	NS	NB	Que	Ont	Man	Sask	Alta	BC	Terr	Cda
Protection of Persons and Property	19	5	93	55	1,005	1,819	158	120	374	522	7	4,178
Regional Planning and Development	1	0	0	0	83	88	10	7	100	38	0	327
Resource Conservation and Industrial Development	0	0	0	5	72	40	12	0	0	42	0	172
Research Establishments	0	0	0	0	0	0	0	0	0	0	0	0
Social Services	0	0	125	0	0	431	10	17	0	0	0	583
Transportation and Communications	54	6	62	50	1,703	864	194	204	621	435	22	4,214
Total	255	29	751	211	7,678	13,613	1,237	1,113	3,466	3,498	106	31,956

Note: Figures may not add up due to rounding.

Table 4.12: Municipal Funding of Government Spending by Function Per Capita, 1970 (Dollars)

Function	Nfld	PEI	NS	NB	Que	Ont	Man	Sask	Alta	BC	Terr	Cda
Culture and Recreation	1	5	4	5	10	20	12	11	19	17	6	14
Education	1	49	59	0	52	105	81	79	80	86	0	76
Environment	3	2	21	11	20	25	21	21	31	28	26	23
Foreign Affairs and International Assistance	0	0	0	0	0	0	0	0	0	0	0	0
General Services	8	4	13	5	22	14	19	16	15	14	12	16
Health	0	0	38	0	2	22	23	50	73	2	1	19
Housing	0	0	0	0	0	0	0	0	0	0	0	0
Labour	0	0	0	0	0	0	0	0	0	0	0	0
Other	1	0	2	0	0	4	5	1	2	1	0	2
Interest Payments	8	13	14	5	31	26	21	18	28	21	2	25

Table 4.12: Municipal Funding of Government Spending by Function Per Capita, 1970 (Dollars)

Function	Nfld	PEI	NS	NB	Que	Ont	Man	Sask	Alta	BC	Terr	Cda
Protection of Persons and Property	1	6	13	10	24	30	20	16	24	26	6	24
Regional Planning and Development	0	0	0	1	0	1	0	1	7	1	0	1
Resource Conservation and Industrial Development	0	0	2	0	0	2	0	1	0	0	0	1
Research Establishments	0	0	0	0	0	0	0	0	0	0	0	0
Social Services	0	0	8	0	1	11	0	3	2	11	0	6
Transportation and Communications	6	9	13	14	33	35	27	35	50	30	13	32
Total	29	89	187	51	194	293	230	252	332	238	67	239

Note: Figures may not add up due to rounding.

Table 4.13: Municipal Funding of Government Spending by Function Per Capita, 1990 (Dollars)

Function	Nfld	PEI	NS	NB	Que	Ont	Man	Sask	Alta	BC	Terr	Cda
Culture and Recreation	52	53	76	43	103	143	182	141	182	145	196	131
Education	46	0	189	0	0	506	168	286	228	235	0	259
Environment	56	10	148	33	214	173	166	128	113	110	352	161
Foreign Affairs and International Assistance	0	0	0	0	0	0	0	0	0	0	0	0
General Services	70	26	61	26	145	116	105	87	114	66	272	110
Health	0	0	0	3	2	6	23	44	0	35	7	10
Housing	2	0	4	0	0	11	2	1	9	5	67	6
Labour	0	0	0	0	0	0	0	0	0	0	0	0
Other	6	1	9	3	54	51	26	18	51	14	16	41
Interest Payments	84	51	57	31	193	58	112	61	262	175	46	127

Table 4.13: Municipal Funding of Government Spending by Function Per Capita, 1990 (Dollars)

Function	Nfld	PEI	NS	NB	Que	Ont	Man	Sask	Alta	BC	Terr	Cda
Protection of Persons and Property	34	38	107	77	149	187	145	121	151	167	88	157
Regional Planning and Development	2	0	0	0	12	9	9	7	41	12	0	12
Resource Conservation and Industrial Development	0	0	0	6	11	4	11	0	0	14	0	6
Research Establishments	0	0	0	0	0	0	0	0	0	0	0	0
Social Services	0	0	145	0	0	44	9	17	0	0	0	22
Transportation and Communications	93	42	71	69	252	89	178	205	251	139	278	158
Total	446	223	868	292	1,134	1,396	1,136	1,116	1,401	1,117	1,322	1,201

Note: Figures may not add up due to rounding.

Table 4.14: Municipal Funding of Government Spending by Function Per Capita in Real Dollars, 1970 (in 1986 Dollars)

Function	Nfld	PEI	NS	NB	Que	Ont	Man	Sask	Alta	BC	Terr	Cda
Culture and Recreation	5	16	14	16	32	63	39	34	60	53	19	46
Education	5	153	185	0	168	337	258	244	251	275	0	246
Environment	10	6	65	37	64	79	66	66	97	89	91	73
Foreign Affairs and International Assistance	0	0	0	0	0	0	0	0	0	0	0	0
General Services	26	12	41	16	70	46	60	48	46	46	43	52
Health	0	0	119	1	5	69	74	155	229	7	3	60
Housing	0	0	0	0	0	0	0	0	0	0	1	0
Labour	0	0	0	0	0	0	0	0	0	0	0	0
Other	3	0	6	1	0	12	17	4	8	3	1	6
Interest Payments	27	41	45	15	101	85	67	55	88	68	8	81

Table 4.14: Municipal Funding of Government Spending by Function Per Capita in Real Dollars, 1970 (in 1986 Dollars)

Function	Nfld	PEI	NS	NB	Que	Ont	Man	Sask	Alta	BC	Terr	Cda
Protection of Persons and Property	5	20	41	33	77	96	62	49	76	83	20	78
Regional Planning and Development	0	1	0	2	0	2	0	4	22	3	0	3
Resource Conservation and Industrial Development	0	0	7	0	0	6	0	2	0	1	0	3
Research Establishments	0	0	0	0	0	0	0	0	0	0	0	0
Social Services	0	1	27	0	3	34	0	9	5	35	0	18
Transportation and Communications	19	28	41	45	108	113	87	107	156	94	46	105
Total	100	277	589	166	628	942	731	777	1,039	757	232	771

Note: Figures may not add up due to rounding.

Table 4.15: Municipal Funding of Government Spending by Function Per Capita in Real Dollars, 1990 (in 1986 Dollars)

Function	Nfld	PEI	NS	NB	Que	Ont	Man	Sask	Alta	BC	Terr	Cda
Culture and Recreation	46	46	65	37	88	117	153	118	155	123	171	109
Education	40	0	161	0	0	414	142	240	193	200	0	217
Environment	49	9	126	29	182	142	139	107	96	94	307	135
Foreign Affairs and International Assistance	0	0	0	0	0	0	0	0	0	0	0	0
General Services	62	22	52	22	123	95	88	73	97	56	237	92
Health	0	0	0	3	1	5	20	37	0	30	6	8
Housing	2	0	4	0	0	9	2	0	8	5	58	5
Labour	0	0	0	0	0	0	0	0	0	0	0	0
Other	5	1	8	3	46	42	22	15	43	12	14	35
Interest Payments	74	43	49	27	164	48	95	51	223	148	40	106

Table 4.15: Municipal Funding of Government Spending by Function Per Capita in Real Dollars, 1990 (in 1986 Dollars)

Function	Nfld	PEI	NS	NB	Que	Ont	Man	Sask	Alta	BC	Terr	Cda
Protection of Persons and Property	30	33	91	66	126	153	122	101	128	142	77	131
Regional Planning and Development	1	0	0	0	10	7	8	6	34	10	0	10
Resource Conservation and Industrial Development	0	0	0	6	9	3	10	0	0	12	0	5
Research Establishments	0	0	0	0	0	0	0	0	0	0	0	0
Social Services	0	0	123	0	0	36	8	14	0	0	0	18
Transportation and Communications	82	36	61	59	214	73	150	171	213	118	242	133
Total	392	191	739	250	964	1,144	956	934	1,191	950	1,151	1,005

Note: Figures may not add up due to rounding.

Table 4.16: Percentage Increase in Real Per Capita Municipal Funding of Government Spending Between 1970 and 1990 (Percent)

Function	Nfld	PEI	NS	NB	Que	Ont	Man	Sask	Alta	BC	Terr	Cda
Culture and Recreation	905%	194%	377%	128%	172%	87%	296%	243%	156%	130%	781%	138%
Education	721%	-100%	-13%	**	-100%	23%	-45%	-2%	-23%	-27%	*	-12%
Environment	374%	36%	93%	-23%	183%	79%	110%	63%	-1%	6%	237%	85%
Foreign Affairs & International Assistance	*	*	*	*	*	*	*	*	*	*	*	*
General Services	138%	92%	28%	37%	76%	105%	46%	52%	109%	22%	450%	77%
Health	-10%	32%	-100%	249%	-74%	-93%	-74%	-76%	-100%	330%	92%	-87%
Housing	41,782 %	**	**	**	-100%	**	**	**	2,321%	**	5,092%	3,558%
Labour	*	*	*	*	*	*	*	*	*	*	*	*
Other	64%	1,611%	29%	349%	29,202 %	256%	28%	278%	453%	381%	2,482%	438%
Interest Payments	176%	7%	9%	72%	63%	-44%	41%	-6%	152%	119%	387%	32%

Table 4.16: Percentage Increase in Real Per Capita Municipal Funding of Government Spending Between 1970 and 1990 (Percent)

Function	Nfld	PEI	NS	NB	Que	Ont	Man	Sask	Alta	BC	Terr	Cda
Protection of Persons and Property	536%	64%	122%	100%	64%	59%	95%	108%	69%	71%	286%	68%
Regional Planning and Development	**	-100%	**	-100%	**	344%	**	57%	58%	236%	*	263%
Resource Conservation and Industrial Development	*	*	-100%	**	**	-44%	**	-100%	*	1,028%	-101%	108%
Research Establishments	*	*	*	*	*	*	*	*	*	*	*	*
Social Services	*	-100%	363%	*	-100%	6%	**	52%	-100%	-100%	*	0%
Transportation & Communications	326%	30%	49%	32%	98%	-36%	73%	61%	37%	26%	431%	26%
Total	292%	-31%	25%	51%	54%	21%	31%	20%	15%	25%	395%	30%

* There is no expenditure in either 1970 or in 1990.
** Denotes an increase over 1970, but since the value was zero in 1970, the percentage increase is undefined.

Table 4.17: Distribution of Municipal Funding of Government Spending by Province, 1970 (Percent)

Function	Nfld	PEI	NS	NB	Que	Ont	Man	Sask	Alta	BC	Terr	Cda
Culture and Recreation	4.6%	5.6%	2.3%	9.7%	5.1%	6.6%	5.3%	4.4%	5.8%	7.0%	8.3%	6.0%
Education	4.9%	55.2%	31.4%	0.0%	26.7%	35.8%	35.3%	31.4%	24.1%	36.4%	0.0%	31.9%
Environment	10.4%	2.3%	11.1%	22.4%	10.2%	8.4%	9.1%	8.5%	9.4%	11.7%	39.2%	9.5%
Foreign Affairs and International Assistance	0.0%	0.0%	0.0%	0.0%	0.0%	0.0%	0.0%	0.0%	0.0%	0.0%	0.0%	0.0%
General Services	26.0%	4.2%	6.9%	9.8%	11.2%	4.9%	8.2%	6.2%	4.5%	6.1%	18.5%	6.8%
Health	0.0%	0.0%	20.2%	0.5%	0.8%	7.4%	10.2%	20.0%	22.0%	0.9%	1.4%	7.7%
Housing	0.0%	0.0%	0.0%	0.0%	0.1%	0.0%	0.0%	0.0%	0.0%	0.0%	0.5%	0.0%
Labour	0.0%	0.0%	0.0%	0.0%	0.0%	0.0%	0.0%	0.0%	0.0%	0.0%	0.0%	0.0%
Other	3.4%	0.0%	1.0%	0.4%	0.0%	1.3%	2.3%	0.5%	0.7%	0.3%	0.2%	0.8%
Interest Payments	26.7%	14.6%	7.6%	9.3%	16.0%	9.0%	9.2%	7.1%	8.5%	9.0%	3.5%	10.5%

Table 4.17: Distribution of Municipal Funding of Government Spending by Province, 1970 (Percent)

Function	Nfld	PEI	NS	NB	Que	Ont	Man	Sask	Alta	BC	Terr	Cda
Protection of Persons and Property	4.6%	7.2%	7.0%	19.8%	12.2%	10.2%	8.5%	6.3%	7.3%	11.0%	8.6%	10.1%
Regional Planning and Development	0.0%	0.3%	0.0%	1.2%	0.0%	0.2%	0.0%	0.5%	2.1%	0.4%	0.0%	0.4%
Resource Conservation and Industrial Development	0.0%	0.0%	1.1%	0.0%	0.0%	0.6%	0.0%	0.3%	0.0%	0.1%	0.1%	0.3%
Research Establishments	0.0%	0.0%	0.0%	0.0%	0.0%	0.0%	0.0%	0.0%	0.0%	0.0%	0.0%	0.0%
Social Services	0.0%	0.4%	4.5%	0.0%	0.5%	3.6%	0.0%	1.2%	0.5%	4.6%	0.0%	2.4%
Transportation and Communications	19.3%	10.0%	6.9%	27.0%	17.2%	12.0%	11.9%	13.7%	15.0%	12.4%	19.6%	13.6%
Total	100.0%	100.0%	100.0%	100.0%	100.0%	100.0%	100.0%	100.0%	100.0%	100.0%	100.0%	100.0%

Note: Figures may not add up due to rounding.

Table 4.18: Distribution of Municipal Funding of Government Spending by Province, 1990 (Percent)

Function	Nfld	PEI	NS	NB	Que	Ont	Man	Sask	Alta	BC	Terr	Cda
Culture and Recreation	11.8%	23.9%	8.8%	14.6%	9.1%	10.2%	16.0%	12.6%	13.0%	12.9%	14.8%	10.9%
Education	10.3%	0.0%	21.8%	0.0%	0.0%	36.2%	14.8%	25.7%	16.2%	21.0%	0.0%	21.6%
Environment	12.6%	4.6%	17.0%	11.4%	18.9%	12.4%	14.6%	11.5%	8.1%	9.9%	26.7%	13.4%
Foreign Affairs and International Assistance	0.0%	0.0%	0.0%	0.0%	0.0%	0.0%	0.0%	0.0%	0.0%	0.0%	0.0%	0.0%
General Services	15.8%	11.8%	7.0%	8.9%	12.8%	8.3%	9.2%	7.8%	8.1%	5.9%	20.6%	9.2%
Health	0.0%	0.0%	0.0%	1.1%	0.1%	0.5%	2.1%	3.9%	0.0%	3.1%	0.6%	0.8%
Housing	0.4%	0.2%	0.5%	0.1%	0.0%	0.8%	0.2%	0.0%	0.6%	0.5%	5.0%	0.5%
Labour	0.0%	0.0%	0.0%	0.0%	0.0%	0.0%	0.0%	0.0%	0.0%	0.0%	0.0%	0.0%
Other	1.4%	0.7%	1.1%	1.2%	4.8%	3.7%	2.3%	1.6%	3.6%	1.3%	1.2%	3.4%
Interest Payments	18.8%	22.6%	6.6%	10.6%	17.0%	4.2%	9.9%	5.5%	18.7%	15.6%	3.5%	10.6%

Table 4.18: Distribution of Municipal Funding of Government Spending by Province, 1990 (Percent)

Function	Nfld	PEI	NS	NB	Que	Ont	Man	Sask	Alta	BC	Terr	Cda
Protection of Persons and Property	7.5%	17.2%	12.4%	26.3%	13.1%	13.4%	12.7%	10.8%	10.8%	14.9%	6.7%	13.1%
Regional Planning and Development	0.4%	0.0%	0.0%	0.0%	1.1%	0.6%	0.8%	0.7%	2.9%	1.1%	0.0%	1.0%
Resource Conservation and Industrial Development	0.0%	0.0%	0.0%	2.2%	0.9%	0.3%	1.0%	0.0%	0.0%	1.2%	0.0%	0.5%
Research Establishments	0.0%	0.0%	0.0%	0.0%	0.0%	0.0%	0.0%	0.0%	0.0%	0.0%	0.0%	0.0%
Social Services	0.0%	0.0%	16.7%	0.0%	0.0%	3.2%	0.8%	1.5%	0.0%	0.0%	0.0%	1.8%
Transportation and Communications	21.0%	18.9%	8.2%	23.7%	22.2%	6.3%	15.7%	18.3%	17.9%	12.4%	21.0%	13.2%
Total	100.0%	100.0%	100.0%	100.0%	100.0%	100.0%	100.0%	100.0%	100.0%	100.0%	100.0%	100.0%

Note: Figures may not add up due to rounding.

education moved away from Prince Edward Island's municipal governments to its provincial government.

Tables 4.19 to 4.25 combine provincial and municipal government spending. Tables 4.19 and 4.20 detail per capita spending; tables 4.21 and 4.22 give per capita spending in 1986 dollars; table 4.23 gives the percentage increase in real provincial and municipal funding of spending between 1970 and 1990; tables 4.24 and 4.25 detail the distribution of each dollar of budgetary revenue of provincial and municipal governments combined.

In 1970, the three major spending categories were education, health, and transportation and communication (see table 4.19). By 1990, the three major categories were health, education, and interest payments(see table 4.20). Transportation and communication had fallen to fifth position in 1990. These observations are consistent with those made earlier in the chapter.

In 1970, the national average spending on education was 29 cents of each budgetary dollar raised by provincial and municipal governments combined. Prince Edward Island spent the least on education, 19 cents of every budgetary dollar, while Alberta spent the most, 34 cents. At the municipal level, spending ranged from zero cents in New Brunswick to 55 cents in Prince Edward Island. At the provincial level, spending ranged from 6 cents in Prince Edward Island to 33 cents in New Brunswick. The range of spending on health by the provincial and municipal governments combined is also smaller than the individual provincial or municipal governments' ranges. In 1990, on average, 21 cents of each budgetary dollar raised by provincial and municipal governments combined were spent on health. The provincial and municipal governments combined allocated between 14 cents (the Territories) and 23 cents (British Columbia) of each budgetary dollar to that category. The provincial governments spent between 15 cents (the Territories) and 30 cents (Ontario) of each budgetary dollar on health, while the municipal governments spent from 0 cents, in Alberta, Newfoundland, Prince Edward Island, and Nova Scotia, to 4 cents, in Saskatchewan.

Much of the variability among the provinces regarding either provincial or municipal government spending is due to differences in responsibilities between provincial and municipal levels across the provinces. When provincial and municipal governments are combined, the responsibility differences are factored out, and the variability in spending from province to provinces is noticeably reduced.

Table 4.19: Provincial and Municipal Funding of Spending Per Capita by Function, 1970 (Dollars)

Function	Nfld	PEI	NS	NB	Que	Ont	Man	Sask	Alta	BC	Terr	Cda
Culture and Recreation	4	12	8	13	16	28	22	17	26	23	28	21
Education	91	65	170	147	171	278	201	180	341	215	264	225
Environment	6	8	22	17	23	28	22	22	34	31	38	26
Foreign Affairs and International Assistance	0	0	0	0	0	0	0	0	0	0	0	0
General Services	35	33	39	40	55	52	44	32	48	47	414	50
Health	43	39	104	63	124	146	120	126	196	105	52	130
Housing	4	7	1	0	2	1	0	8	0	2	36	2
Labour	9	11	4	12	7	7	0	1	3	1	8	6
Other	2	3	5	9	0	4	6	1	3	1	0	3
Interest Payments	53	50	70	42	61	93	64	57	72	35	34	70

Table 4.19: Provincial and Municipal Funding of Spending Per Capita by Function, 1970 (Dollars)

Function	Nfld	PEI	NS	NB	Que	Ont	Man	Sask	Alta	BC	Terr	Cda
Protection of Persons and Property	13	14	25	25	45	58	36	33	56	46	58	47
Regional Planning and Development	15	4	8	5	6	5	3	3	11	2	63	6
Resource conservation and Industrial Development	0	0	13	0	17	21	29	24	35	36	0	22
Research Establishments	0	0	1	1	0	1	0	2	2	0	0	1
Social Services	31	25	30	27	83	63	32	32	54	88	42	64
Transportation and Communications	58	73	75	103	92	102	74	112	110	94	118	96
Total	365	344	574	503	704	888	654	650	992	725	1,154	768

Note: Figures may not add up due to rounding.

Table 4.20: Provincial and Municipal Funding of Spending Per Capita by Function, 1990 (Dollars)

Function	Nfld	PEI	NS	NB	Que	Ont	Man	Sask	Alta	BC	Terr	Cda
Culture and Recreation	106	129	131	107	165	202	272	245	279	213	813	200
Education	944	754	932	838	1,041	1,246	969	1,016	1,178	1,306	2,759	1,147
Environment	140	76	183	93	281	239	196	179	221	183	598	230
Foreign Affairs and International Assistance	0	0	0	0	0	0	0	0	0	0	0	0
General Services	295	306	209	273	555	315	299	466	398	360	3,576	398
Health	787	670	978	882	987	1,388	1,122	1,252	1,314	1,389	2,536	1,222
Housing	4	1	27	1	83	46	13	30	65	16	85	49
Labour	27	27	76	26	90	34	34	24	67	10	250	50
Other	43	20	21	34	85	149	49	76	130	82	888	108
Interest Payments	721	524	700	640	838	581	1,146	928	983	720	133	742

Table 4.20: Provincial and Municipal Funding of Spending Per Capita by Function, 1990 (Dollars)

Function	Nfld	PEI	NS	NB	Que	Ont	Man	Sask	Alta	BC	Terr	Cda
Protection of Persons and Property	222	171	251	233	286	402	284	275	347	333	1,174	337
Regional Planning and Development	22	9	39	28	28	36	81	22	61	40	932	40
Resource conservation and Industrial Development	169	301	154	179	202	143	194	568	800	252	1,801	257
Research Establishments	0	0	7	9	20	7	1	15	33	19	17	14
Social Services	387	354	478	393	761	867	625	322	607	601	1,114	716
Transportation and Communications	362	407	296	414	476	335	380	434	616	419	1,685	418
Total	4,227	3,750	4,482	4,150	5,899	5,990	5,665	5,852	7,099	5,941	18,361	5,928

Note: Figures may not add up due to rounding.

Table 4.21: Provincial and Municipal Funding of Spending Per Capita by Function in Real Dollars, 1970 (in 1986 Dollars)

Function	Nfld	PEI	NS	NB	Que	Ont	Man	Sask	Alta	BC	Terr	Cda
Culture and Recreation	15	38	24	42	52	89	70	53	82	74	97	69
Education	315	201	535	478	555	893	638	554	1,068	683	919	726
Environment	22	24	70	55	76	90	71	66	105	98	133	83
Foreign Affairs and International Assistance	0	0	0	0	0	0	0	0	0	0	0	0
General Services	121	103	122	129	179	166	139	97	151	151	1,444	162
Health	148	120	326	205	401	468	383	389	614	334	181	419
Housing	13	21	3	0	8	4	1	25	0	6	124	6
Labour	31	33	14	39	23	23	1	4	9	2	27	18
Other	5	10	16	30	0	12	18	4	10	3	1	8
Interest Payments	183	155	220	135	198	300	203	176	224	111	118	226

Table 4.21: Provincial and Municipal Funding of Spending Per Capita by Function in Real Dollars, 1970 (in 1986 Dollars)

Function	Nfld	PEI	NS	NB	Que	Ont	Man	Sask	Alta	BC	Terr	Cda
Protection of Persons and Property	44	45	80	81	147	186	115	101	174	147	204	153
Regional Planning and Development	53	12	24	16	20	18	11	9	35	5	218	19
Resource conservation and Industrial Development	0	0	40	0	56	69	91	73	110	114	0	69
Research Establishments	0	0	3	4	0	2	0	5	7	0	0	2
Social Services	107	79	95	87	267	204	103	98	170	281	147	208
Transportation and Communications	199	226	237	334	298	328	235	346	346	300	411	310
Total	1,257	1,066	1,806	1,635	2,280	2,850	2,077	2,000	3,104	2,309	4,024	2,479

Note: Figures may not add up due to rounding.

Table 4.22: Provincial and Municipal Funding of Spending Per Capita by Function in Real Dollars, 1990 (in 1986 Dollars)

Function	Nfld	PEI	NS	NB	Que	Ont	Man	Sask	Alta	BC	Terr	Cda
Culture and Recreation	93	110	111	92	140	165	229	205	237	181	708	167
Education	830	644	793	718	884	1,021	815	850	1,001	1,110	2,401	960
Environment	123	65	156	80	239	196	165	150	188	155	521	192
Foreign Affairs and International Assistance	0	0	0	0	0	0	0	0	0	0	0	0
General Services	259	262	178	234	472	258	252	390	338	306	3,113	333
Health	691	572	833	757	839	1,138	944	1,047	1,116	1,181	2,207	1,022
Housing	4	0	23	1	71	38	11	25	55	14	74	41
Labour	24	23	65	23	77	28	28	20	57	8	218	42
Other	37	17	18	29	72	122	42	63	111	70	773	90
Interest Payments	633	448	596	549	712	476	964	777	835	612	116	621

Table 4.22: Provincial and Municipal Funding of Spending Per Capita by Function in Real Dollars, 1990 (in 1986 Dollars)

Function	Nfld	PEI	NS	NB	Que	Ont	Man	Sask	Alta	BC	Terr	Cda
Protection of Persons and Property	195	146	213	200	243	330	238	230	295	283	1,021	282
Regional Planning and Development	20	7	34	24	24	29	68	18	52	34	811	34
Resource conservation and Industrial Development	149	257	131	153	171	117	163	475	680	214	1,567	215
Research Establishments	0	0	6	7	17	6	1	13	28	16	15	12
Social Services	340	303	407	337	647	711	526	270	515	511	970	599
Transportation and Communications	318	348	252	355	404	275	319	363	523	356	1,466	350
Total	3,715	3,202	3,814	3,559	5,012	4,910	4,765	4,897	6,032	5,052	15,980	4,961

Note: Figures may not add up due to rounding.

Table 4.23: Percentage Increase in Real Provincial and Municipal Funding of Spending by Function Between 1990 and 1970 (Percent)

Function	Nfld	PEI	NS	NB	Que	Ont	Man	Sask	Alta	BC	Terr	Cda
Culture and Recreation	630%	286%	472%	217%	268%	187%	329%	383%	291%	243%	729%	243%
Education	263%	321%	148%	150%	159%	114%	128%	153%	94%	163%	261%	132%
Environment	558%	274%	224%	146%	315%	218%	232%	226%	179%	158%	393%	232%
Foreign Affairs and International Assistance	*	*	*	*	*	*	*	*	*	*	*	*
General Services	214%	255%	146%	182%	263%	155%	181%	401%	224%	203%	216%	205%
Health	467%	478%	256%	369%	209%	243%	247%	269%	182%	354%	1,222%	244%
Housing	27%	2%	841%	**	938%	1,007%	1,678%	102%	16,263%	214%	60%	669%
Labour	77%	68%	478%	58%	335%	123%	1,967%	524%	629%	463%	799%	228%
Other	723%	170%	112%	96%	40,280%	1,000%	232%	1,596%	1,109%	2,529%	**	1,113%
Interest Payments	345%	289%	271%	406%	359%	159%	476%	441%	373%	550%	98%	275%

Table 4.23: Percentage Increase in Real Provincial and Municipal Funding of Spending by Function Between 1990 and 1970 (Percent)

Function	Nfld	PEI	NS	NB	Que	Ont	Man	Sask	Alta	BC	Terr	Cda
Protection of Persons and Property	441%	326%	267%	248%	165%	177%	207%	229%	169%	192%	502%	184%
Regional Planning and Development	37%	63%	141%	147%	123%	166%	627%	198%	149%	690%	371%	177%
Resource conservation and Industrial Development	**	**	328%	**	304%	171%	179%	655%	618%	188%	527,656 %	310%
Research Establishments	*	*	198%	207%	**	320%	**	254%	397%	**	**	722%
Social Services	316%	385%	427%	386%	242%	349%	512%	274%	303%	182%	660%	288%
Transportation & Communications	160%	154%	106%	106%	136%	84%	136%	105%	151%	119%	357%	113%
Total	296%	300%	211%	218%	220%	172%	229%	245%	194%	219%	397%	200%

* There is no expenditure in either 1970 or 1990.
** Denotes an increase over 1970, but since the value was zero in 1970, the percentage increase is undefined.

Table 4.24: Distribution of Provincial and Municipal Funding of Spending Across Functions, 1970 (Percent)

Function	Nfld	PEI	NS	NB	Que	Ont	Man	Sask	Alta	BC	Terr	Cda
Culture and Recreation	1.2%	3.6%	1.3%	2.6%	2.3%	3.1%	3.4%	2.7%	2.6%	3.2%	2.4%	2.8%
Education	25.1%	18.8%	29.6%	29.2%	24.3%	31.3%	30.7%	27.7%	34.4%	29.6%	22.8%	29.3%
Environment	1.7%	2.2%	3.9%	3.4%	3.3%	3.2%	3.4%	3.3%	3.4%	4.3%	3.3%	3.3%
Foreign Affairs and International Assistance	0.0%	0.0%	0.0%	0.0%	0.0%	0.0%	0.0%	0.0%	0.0%	0.0%	0.0%	0.0%
General Services	9.6%	9.6%	6.7%	7.9%	7.9%	5.8%	6.7%	4.9%	4.9%	6.5%	35.9%	6.6%
Health	11.8%	11.2%	18.0%	12.6%	17.6%	16.4%	18.4%	19.5%	19.8%	14.5%	4.5%	16.9%
Housing	1.1%	2.0%	0.1%	0.0%	0.3%	0.1%	0.0%	1.2%	0.0%	0.3%	3.1%	0.2%
Labour	2.5%	3.1%	0.8%	2.4%	1.0%	0.8%	0.1%	0.2%	0.3%	0.1%	0.7%	0.7%
Other	0.4%	0.9%	0.9%	1.8%	0.0%	0.4%	0.9%	0.2%	0.3%	0.1%	0.0%	0.3%
Interest Payments	14.6%	14.5%	12.2%	8.3%	8.7%	10.5%	9.8%	8.8%	7.2%	4.8%	2.9%	9.1%

Table 4.24: Distribution of Provincial and Municipal Funding of Spending Across Functions, 1970 (Percent)

Function	Nfld	PEI	NS	NB	Que	Ont	Man	Sask	Alta	BC	Terr	Cda
Protection of Persons and Property	3.5%	4.2%	4.4%	4.9%	6.4%	6.5%	5.6%	5.0%	5.6%	6.4%	5.1%	6.2%
Regional Planning and Development	4.2%	1.1%	1.3%	1.0%	0.9%	0.6%	0.5%	0.5%	1.1%	0.2%	5.4%	0.8%
Resource conservation and Industrial Development	0.0%	0.0%	2.2%	0.0%	2.5%	2.4%	4.4%	3.6%	3.5%	4.9%	0.0%	2.8%
Research Establishments	0.0%	0.0%	0.2%	0.2%	0.0%	0.1%	0.0%	0.3%	0.2%	0.0%	0.0%	0.1%
Social Services	8.5%	7.4%	5.3%	5.3%	11.7%	7.2%	4.9%	4.9%	5.5%	12.2%	3.6%	8.4%
Transportation and Communications	15.8%	21.2%	13.1%	20.4%	13.1%	11.5%	11.3%	17.3%	11.1%	13.0%	10.2%	12.5%
Total	100.0%	100.0%	100.0%	100.0%	100.0%	100.0%	100.0%	100.0%	100.0%	100.0%	100.0%	100.0%

Note: Figures may not add up due to rounding.

Table 4.25: Distribution of Provincial and Municipal Funding of Spending Across Functions, 1990 (Percent)

Function	Nfld	PEI	NS	NB	Que	Ont	Man	Sask	Alta	BC	Terr	Cda
Culture and Recreation	2.5%	3.4%	2.9%	2.6%	2.8%	3.4%	4.8%	4.2%	3.9%	3.6%	4.4%	3.4%
Education	22.3%	20.1%	20.8%	20.2%	17.6%	20.8%	17.1%	17.4%	16.6%	22.0%	15.0%	19.4%
Environment	3.3%	2.0%	4.1%	2.2%	4.8%	4.0%	3.5%	3.1%	3.1%	3.1%	3.3%	3.9%
Foreign Affairs and International Assistance	0.0%	0.0%	0.0%	0.0%	0.0%	0.0%	0.0%	0.0%	0.0%	0.0%	0.0%	0.0%
General Services	7.0%	8.2%	4.7%	6.6%	9.4%	5.3%	5.3%	8.0%	5.6%	6.1%	19.5%	6.7%
Health	18.6%	17.9%	21.8%	21.3%	16.7%	23.2%	19.8%	21.4%	18.5%	23.4%	13.8%	20.6%
Housing	0.1%	0.0%	0.6%	0.0%	1.4%	0.8%	0.2%	0.5%	0.9%	0.3%	0.5%	0.8%
Labour	0.6%	0.7%	1.7%	0.6%	1.5%	0.6%	0.6%	0.4%	0.9%	0.2%	1.4%	0.8%
Other	1.0%	0.5%	0.5%	0.8%	1.4%	2.5%	0.9%	1.3%	1.8%	1.4%	4.8%	1.8%
Interest Payments	17.0%	14.0%	15.6%	15.4%	14.2%	9.7%	20.2%	15.9%	13.8%	12.1%	0.7%	12.5%

Table 4.25: Distribution of Provincial and Municipal Funding of Spending Across Functions, 1990 (Percent)

Function	Nfld	PEI	NS	NB	Que	Ont	Man	Sask	Alta	BC	Terr	Cda
Protection of Persons and Property	5.3%	4.6%	5.6%	5.6%	4.8%	6.7%	5.0%	4.7%	4.9%	5.6%	6.4%	5.7%
Regional Planning and Development	0.5%	0.2%	0.9%	0.7%	0.5%	0.6%	1.4%	0.4%	0.9%	0.7%	5.1%	0.7%
Resource conservation and Industrial Development	4.0%	8.0%	3.4%	4.3%	3.4%	2.4%	3.4%	9.7%	11.3%	4.2%	9.8%	4.3%
Research Establishments	0.0%	0.0%	0.2%	0.2%	0.3%	0.1%	0.0%	0.3%	0.5%	0.3%	0.1%	0.2%
Social Services	9.1%	9.5%	10.7%	9.5%	12.9%	14.5%	11.0%	5.5%	8.5%	10.1%	6.1%	12.1%
Transportation and Communications	8.6%	10.9%	6.6%	10.0%	8.1%	5.6%	6.7%	7.4%	8.7%	7.1%	9.2%	7.1%
Total	100.0%	100.0%	100.0%	100.0%	100.0%	100.0%	100.0%	100.0%	100.0%	100.0%	100.0%	100.0%

Note: Numbers may not add up due to rounding.

Chapter 5: An Analysis of Government Spending on Interest Charges

Deficits are deferred taxes

IN THE FRASER INSTITUTE'S WORK ON TAXATION published every other year in *Tax Facts*, the deficits that are incurred by governments are treated as deferred taxation. There is an explicit acknowledgement of the fact that expenditures undertaken during a current period for which tax revenues are not secured imply a future tax burden equal to the excess expenditures made during the current period. Another way of making the same statement is to say that for every current expenditure not matched by a current tax there will be a future tax not matched by a future program expenditure.

The practical way in which this deferred taxation enters the budgetary process is through interest payments on past borrowing. As we have observed in previous chapters, these interest payments for all levels of government have been escalating dramatically during the past two decades. It is the purpose of this chapter to provide a catalogue of the debt charges that have to be borne by citizens in the individual provinces, and to show how the debt charges vary from province to province.

Table 5.1: Municipal Government Spending on Interest Payments (Millions of Dollars)

Year	Nfld	PEI	NS	NB	Que	Ont	Man	Sask	Alta	BC	Cda
1970	5	2	12	5	219	212	22	17	50	51	595
1975	9	3	21	10	328	296	43	19	99	116	945
1980	42	5	45	26	846	425	89	34	234	255	2,002
1985	47	6	53	41	1,150	582	126	61	699	511	3,279
1988	56	8	52	41	1,281	539	116	70	696	539	3,401
1990	59	8	55	39	1,406	622	137	70	707	586	3,696

Table 5.2: Provincial Government Spending on Interest Payments (Millions of Dollars)

Year	Nfld	PEI	NS	NB	Que	Ont	Man	Sask	Alta	BC	Cda
1970	38	8	58	29	202	518	48	42	68	25	1,039
1975	106	13	94	53	469	1,134	96	63	128	58	2,226
1980	262	29	194	145	1,386	2,092	279	237	264	205	5,097
1985	451	56	563	407	3,634	4,286	785	851	601	975	12,608
1988	513	73	626	471	4,281	5,093	1,134	1,151	1,021	1,492	15,921
1990	491	85	705	555	4,811	5,181	1,295	944	1,794	1,721	17,589

The basic facts about government interest charges

Tables 5.1, 5.2, and 5.3 provide the actual dollar amounts of interest charges in each of the provinces. The meaning of the data in the tables is quite straightforward and the totals in each year for each province report the amount of interest actually incurred by the province or by the municipality in each case. An ambiguity arises, however, with regard to how the interest charges of the federal government should be allocated since they are incurred, in some sense, on behalf of all Canadians. In the case of provincial expenditure on interest, the amount incurred by a particular province should clearly be allocated within that province. Similarly, there is no lack of clarity about the allocation of municipal government debt charges. The appropriate allocation of federal government interest charges, however, must reflect the manner in which the burden of interest charges is actually shared amongst the provinces, i.e., according to the provinces' contribution to total federal government tax revenues. The federal government's interest charges reported in table 5.3 are allocated according to the total contribution to federal government revenues by residents of the particular province in that particular year.

Interest costs per capita

Tables 5.4, 5.5, and 5.6 present the debt charges in a more meaningful way, namely, as a cost per capita. Canadians in different parts of the country bear very different interest cost burdens depending on the province in which they live. In 1990, for example, municipal government debt charges per capita ranged from a low of $54 per capita in New Brunswick to a high of $286 per capita in Alberta.

Manitoba the top borrower

As Table 5.5 reveals, the debt charges associated with provincial government borrowing cover an even wider range. While the national average per capita is $661, the range is from a low of $531 per capita in Ontario to a high of $1,190 per capita in Manitoba.

Table 5.3: Federal Spending on Interest Payments (Distributed by Federal Tax Collection) (Millions Of Dollars)

Year	Nfld	PEI	NS	NB	Que	Ont	Man	Sask	Alta	BC	Cda
1970	22	5	46	33	375	819	75	49	140	207	1,778
1975	54	11	102	79	791	1,675	164	151	437	487	3,968
1980	139	30	269	206	2,207	4,269	388	366	1,427	1,441	10,784
1985	379	85	741	549	6,078	10,183	973	799	2,619	2,851	25,417
1988	411	104	899	649	7,067	14,556	1,190	1,051	3,128	3,988	33,167
1990	530	135	1,132	823	8,811	19,117	1,483	1,262	3,973	5,188	42,630

Table 5.4: Municipal Government Spending on Interest Charges Per Capita (Dollars)

Year	Nfld	PEI	NS	NB	Que	Ont	Man	Sask	Alta	BC	Cda
1970	10	14	15	7	36	28	23	18	31	24	28
1975	16	22	25	16	53	36	43	21	56	48	42
1980	74	38	53	38	132	50	87	35	109	96	83
1985	82	48	60	58	177	65	119	60	297	178	130
1988	99	59	59	58	193	57	107	69	291	181	131
1990	104	62	62	54	208	64	126	71	286	187	139

Table 5.5: Provincial Government Spending on Interest Charges Per Capita (Dollars)

Year	Nfld	PEI	NS	NB	Que	Ont	Man	Sask	Alta	BC	Cda
1970	73	69	75	47	34	69	48	45	43	12	49
1975	193	108	115	80	76	139	95	69	72	24	98
1980	463	239	229	209	217	244	273	247	123	77	212
1985	788	448	646	574	558	476	738	844	256	340	501
1988	901	568	709	660	645	540	1,046	1,136	427	501	614
1990	858	650	787	768	711	531	1,190	947	726	549	661

Table 5.6: Federal Government Spending on Interest Charges (According to Tax Burdens) Per Capita (Dollars)

Year	Nfld	PEI	NS	NB	Que	Ont	Man	Sask	Alta	BC	Cda
1970	43	42	59	52	62	109	77	52	88	97	83
1975	98	96	125	119	128	205	162	167	246	200	175
1980	246	241	318	296	346	498	378	381	667	540	449
1985	664	673	850	773	933	1,131	914	792	1,115	993	1,010
1988	722	807	1,019	909	1,064	1,543	1,098	1,037	1,309	1,338	1,280
1990	925	1,030	1,265	1,140	1,302	1,961	1,362	1,265	1,606	1,656	1,602

Ontario residents bear largest share of federal interest charges

Table 5.6 presents the per capita cost of the federal debt. The pattern of the incidence of that cost reflects the contribution that the individual provinces make to the total federal government revenue. As the table indicates, the have-not provinces, such as the Atlantic provinces and some of the Prairies, make less of a contribution toward the cost of carrying the public debt, and thus have a relatively low cost per capita. Ontario, Alberta, and British Columbia, major contributors to federal government revenue, correspondingly bear a higher burden of the interest cost associated with past deficits.

Tables 5.7 and 5.8 present the total interest burden imposed on residents of each province by the interest charges incurred by all three levels of government. Table 5.8 presents the data in a per capita form. For 1990, for example, where the total interest burden per capita was $1,886 in Newfoundland, $2,556 in Ontario, and $2,393 in British Columbia, it is evident that the variation in the range of debt servicing cost per capita for all three levels of government is narrower than that observed in comparing interest charges incurred by the individual provinces and municipalities. This is because Ontario and British Columbia, which have relatively low provincial debt servicing costs, are saddled with a much higher than average share of the burden of federal interest charges—$1,961 per capita for Ontario, and $1,656 for British Columbia. The reverse is true for Newfoundland and Saskatchewan, provinces with relatively high provincial debt servicing charges, $858 and $947 per capita respectively, but which are allocated relatively smaller portions of the total federal interest charges at $925 and $1265 per capita respectively.

From the point of view of the residents of these "have" provinces, it is almost as though provincial parsimony and the corresponding tight control of provincial debt accumulation has been rewarded by a more than counter-balancing burden associated with federal expenditures. However, the reality is that the data are explained by the fact that those provinces in the "have" category—Ontario, Alberta, and British Columbia—with greater access to resources, have had less need to borrow, and have been better able to contribute to the bearing of the federal tax

Table 5.7: Total Government Spending on Interest Charges (Millions of Dollars)

Year	Nfld	PEI	NS	NB	Que	Ont	Man	Sask	Alta	BC	Cda
1970	65	14	116	67	796	1,549	145	109	258	284	3,412
1975	168	26	217	142	1,588	3,105	303	233	665	661	7,140
1980	443	64	507	377	4,438	6,786	756	636	1,925	1,901	17,883
1985	876	147	1,356	997	10,862	15,050	1,884	1,710	3,919	4,337	41,304
1988	979	184	1,576	1,162	12,630	20,188	2,440	2,273	4,844	6,019	52,489
1990	1,080	228	1,893	1,417	15,028	24,921	2,916	2,276	6,474	7,495	63,915

Table 5.8: Total Government Spending on Interest Charges Per Capita (Dollars)

Year	Nfld	PEI	NS	NB	Que	Ont	Man	Sask	Alta	BC	Cda
1970	125	125	149	106	132	205	148	115	162	133	160
1975	307	226	265	214	257	380	299	257	374	272	315
1980	783	519	600	542	695	792	738	663	899	713	744
1985	1,534	1,168	1,557	1,405	1,667	1,671	1,771	1,696	1,669	1,511	1,641
1988	1,722	1,434	1,788	1,627	1,902	2,141	2,251	2,242	2,028	2,020	2,026
1990	1,886	1,742	2,114	1,962	2,220	2,556	2,678	2,283	2,618	2,393	2,402

Table 5.9: Gross Domestic Product Per Capita (Dollars)

Year	Nfld	PEI	NS	NB	Que	Ont	Man	Sask	Alta	BC	Cda
1970	2,329	2,191	2,839	2,657	3,739	4,917	3,752	3,234	4,450	4,378	4,184
1975	4,058	3,937	4,752	4,678	6,626	8,341	6,822	7,612	10,458	8,008	7,558
1980	7,240	6,889	7,445	7,217	11,309	13,419	10,916	12,925	20,157	14,343	12,889
1985	11,171	10,508	13,699	12,709	16,502	20,400	16,639	17,326	27,858	19,014	18,994
1988	14,132	13,829	17,103	16,597	21,436	26,820	19,953	17,952	26,133	23,509	23,432
1990	15,390	15,203	18,912	18,210	22,732	27,927	21,717	20,487	28,874	25,988	25,214

Table 5.10: Total Interest Per Capita as a Percentage of Income Per Capita (Percent)

Year	Nfld	PEI	NS	NB	Que	Ont	Man	Sask	Alta	BC	Cda
1970	5.39%	5.71%	5.24%	3.99%	3.54%	4.17%	3.95%	3.57%	3.64%	3.05%	3.83%
1975	7.56%	5.74%	5.57%	4.58%	3.88%	4.56%	4.39%	3.37%	3.58%	3.39%	4.16%
1980	10.81%	7.54%	8.06%	7.51%	6.15%	5.90%	6.76%	5.13%	4.46%	4.97%	5.77%
1985	13.73%	11.12%	11.37%	11.05%	10.10%	8.19%	10.64%	9.79%	5.99%	7.95%	8.64%
1988	12.18%	10.37%	10.45%	9.80%	8.87%	7.98%	11.28%	12.49%	7.76%	8.59%	8.65%
1990	12.26%	11.46%	11.18%	10.77%	9.77%	9.15%	12.33%	11.14%	9.07%	9.21%	9.53%

burden. This is made more readily evident by comparing the per capita government debt servicing cost with the per capita income in the various provinces.

Interest burden grows faster than ability to pay

As table 5.9 illustrates, there is a wide variation among the provinces in per capita income. From a high of $28,874 in Alberta, total income per capita ranges to as low as $15,203 in Prince Edward Island. As a consequence, even though provinces like Alberta and Ontario bear relatively high per capita interest cost burdens, the fraction of their incomes devoted to these interest costs is actually below the average. That is not the central message suggested by the data, however. Rather, the data suggest that attention should be focused on the extent to which *all* of the provinces have increased the fraction of the total per capita income which is being devoted to servicing debt interest.

Because that income per capita, or ability to bear the interest burden, grew less rapidly than the interest expense, by 1990 Canadians were devoting, on average, one dollar in 10 of their income to the payment of interest charges on debt acquired by the various levels of government. This was a significant increase from 1970 when less than one dollar in 26 was required to service debt charges. Both the wealthy and the poor provinces have experienced a significant increase in their interest burdens. The range in 1990 was from one dollar in 8 in Manitoba to one in 11 in Alberta.

Some moderation in the relative interest burden is evident in the comparison of the 1985 data with those for 1990. The growth in per capita interest payments slowed dramatically from the pace established up to 1985, and over the five years to 1990 was actually exceeded by per capita income growth.

Chapter 6: Who Benefits from Government Spending?

After years of research on taxation, the economics profession in general and The Fraser Institute in particular have a fairly precise notion about who pays the national tax bill. We know much less about who benefits from government spending. This chapter will discuss several approaches to answer the question, "Who benefits from government?" In the previous edition of this book published in 1992, we conducted a preliminary analysis of the distribution of government spending using distribution methods based on averages. In this revised chapter, we use the income and expenditure activities of a sample of 44,500 Canadians to revisit this question.

Knowing who benefits from government spending may be an important step leading to an understanding of why governments spend in the way they do and with such little restraint. Our analysis suggests there are three reasons why government is large and has trouble shrinking:

1) At any given time, a majority of Canadians get more spent on them by government than they pay in taxes.

2) Many Canadians who benefit now from government spending do not realize that over the course of their lives the benefits will not be as great as they believe.

3) Some groups benefit disproportionately from certain government programs and have the incentive to invest considerable effort to defend the programs against cuts.

The Canadians who fall into these three categories form a strong constituency against change. In such a climate, politicians will see no urgent need to control the flow of money from public coffers.

This chapter describes in detail who, *at any given moment,* benefits from public spending. In some cases, we found surprising results that do not accord with the popular perception of government as a sort of Robin Hood, taking from the well-to-do and giving to those with low incomes. For example: high income families get the most out of government-funded university education, and high income farmers get the most out of farm support programs. It is even true that more than half of the benefits from programs like unemployment insurance go to families whose incomes are above the average. In other words, the facts suggest that governments are helping many people who are actually well-equipped to take care of themselves.

We also find that the "good deal" many people think they are getting out of government may be an illusion. What any given Canadian gets *now* and what he or she will get *over his or her life* are different things. Many of the people who benefit from government spending today do not see that they will pay more fully for this privilege later in their lives. In this chapter we attempt to calculate, for the first time, how Canadians relate to their government over their lifetime.

Following the public dollar

To figure out what benefits people receive from public spending, we must "follow" the public dollar as it makes its way from government treasuries to the people. As noted above, to follow this dollar we used a survey of 44,500 Canadian families. The survey shows how much straight government transfer each family gets (such as UI and CPP) and gives clues to the amount of government services (education, infrastructure, et cetera) these families use. In Appendix B we have explained in detail how we followed these clues and put together the picture of who benefits from government spending.

Expenditures are not benefits

Following where government dollars go is not the only wrinkle in figuring out who benefits from government spending. We must also have some idea of whether people value a dollar that government spends on their behalf as much as they value a dollar of their own money. Just because government spends a dollar on you does not mean that you get the same benefit as if government put that dollar in your hand.

Table 6.1 gives an idea of the difference that might exist between how much government spends on families and the benefits they get from that spending. The table focuses on two families of different income levels drawn from the Statistics Canada survey. In the left column of table 6.1, we have calculated how much each family gets *spent* on it by all levels of government, the taxes it pays, and the difference between taxes and spending (the "net amount spent" on the average

Table 6.1: Two Views of What Two Families Get Out of Government, 1990

	Assumption 1: $1 govt. spending=$1 benefit	Assumption 2: $1 govt. spending=$.44 benefit
A Family with an Income of $35,000		
Taxes	14,245	14,245
Government Spending	19,792	19,792
Benefits	19,792	13,282
Net Benefits*	5,547	-963
A Family with an Income of $60,000		
Taxes	28,440	28,440
Government Spending	22,789	22,789
Benefits	22,789	13,981
Net Benefits*	-5,651	-14,459

* Net Benefits=Benefits-Taxes

person in the income group). Canadian families with an average income of $35,000 get $5,547 in net benefits from government. Families making $65,000 on average lose $5,651 to government.

The story looks different, though, when we try to calculate the net *benefit* to the family of government spending instead of simply calculating the amount *spent* on it. There are two assumptions to make in order to calculate benefit:

1) We assume that the family counts a dollar of straight transfer money, such as welfare or unemployment insurance, as being worth a dollar.

2) We speculate that the family puts a smaller value on other types of spending, such as spending on culture, education, the military, and so on. Such expenditures are not made in a voluntary, individual market purchase arrangement where the individual making the purchase could reasonably have selected alternative services. The supplier, for the most part, receives the funding for the expenditure directly from the treasury and is not, therefore, required to win the support of "customers" in the normal way. Therefore, it would not be appropriate to assert, for example, that all of the money spent on education created a benefit for those upon whose behalf the money is spent. A study by Katsaikis (1987) suggests that a dollar of such spending is worth about 44 cents to Canadians.

Combining these two assumptions gives the right column in table 6.1, which shows that now both families get less net benefit from government spending than they did under the assumption that a dollar of government spending on a family is worth a dollar to that family. This exercise is highly speculative, because we really do not know with precision how much people value the government dollar. Throughout the rest of the chapter we adhere to the notion that a dollar of government spending leads to a dollar of benefit (the left column of table 6.1). But we present the results in the right column of table 1 to caution readers that the benefits from government we present throughout this chapter are probably overstated.

The great fairness debate: do the rich pay enough?

We often hear that the "rich" do not pay their "fair" share of taxes. This is a highly charged statement that is often made without a proper grasp of the facts. Facts which can help form an informed opinion on what is fair are set out in table 6.2. This table shows how much government spent on average on families in different income groups, and how much tax those groups paid. As noted earlier, the assumptions we used to get these results are from Appendix B.

The first two columns of table 6.2 show that as people's incomes rise, so do their taxes and the amount that government spends on them. The question for those interested in fairness is how fast do taxes and spending rise as income rises. Two quantities are relevant here. First, we would like to know at which income level Canadians make the switch from being net recipients of government spending to being net contributors to government. We would also like to know how much Canadians from different income groups "pay" for each dollar of government service they receive. These two quantities appear in the last two columns of table 6.2.

The middle column of table 6.2 shows that, on average, a Canadian family stops being a net recipient of government aid when it has an income of $50,000 to $60,000. Fifty-one percent of all families are net recipients. This translates into 49 percent of the voting age population.[1] Table 6.3 offers a slightly different perspective on how the benefits of spending are distributed. This table is identical to table 6.2 except in the way the families are grouped. Table 6.3 provides a distribution of government expenditures by *income deciles*. That is, if we imagine the families lined up according to income from lowest to highest, and then divided them into ten equally sized groups, we can then calculate how families in each of these ten groups benefit from government spending.

---

1 The percentage of families receiving a positive net benefit from government does not translate directly into the percentage of voting age citizens these families represent. To get this correspondence we have to account for how many people of voting age there are in each family.

Table 6.2: What Families in Different Income Groups Get Out of Government

Income Group ($'000s)	Average Tax in Group	Average Benefit in Group	Average Net Benefit in Group	Ratio: Tax/Benefit	Percentage of all Taxes Paid by Group	Percentage of all Benefits Received by Group	Percentage of the Population
<20	$2,483	$19,601	$17,118	0.13	3%	19%	15%
20-30	9,021	23,471	14,449	0.38	5%	13%	11%
30-40	15,106	23,641	8,535	0.64	8%	12%	11%
40-50	20,502	24,528	4,026	0.84	10%	11%	12%
50-60	26,254	26,080	-175	1.01	11%	10%	11%
60-70	31,247	28,050	-3,197	1.11	11%	9%	10%
70-80	37,307	28,408	-8,899	1.31	9%	7%	7%
80-90	41,602	27,828	-13,774	1.49	8%	5%	6%
90-100	48,252	29,302	-18,950	1.65	7%	4%	4%
>100	77,160	31,925	-45,235	2.42	28%	11%	11%

Table 6.3: What Families in Different Income Deciles Get Out of Government, 1990

Decile	Average Tax in Group	Average Benefit in Group	Average Net Benefit in Group	Ratio: Tax/Benefit	Percentage of all Taxes Paid by Group	Percentage of all Benefits Received by Group	Percentage of Population in Group*
1	$899	$16,405	$15,506	0.05	0%	6%	7%
2	2,473	21,786	19,313	0.11	1%	8%	5%
3	6,059	22,466	16,407	0.27	2%	8%	6%
4	9,632	23,546	13,913	0.41	4%	9%	7%
5	13,892	23,422	9,530	0.59	6%	9%	8%
6	18,341	23,937	5,596	0.77	8%	10%	10%
7	23,047	25,380	2,334	0.91	10%	10%	11%
8	28,862	26,868	-1,995	1.07	13%	11%	12%
9	36,851	28,390	-8,461	1.30	18%	13%	14%
10	65,470	30,761	-34,709	2.13	38%	17%	18%

*Note that 10% of all families is found in each decile, but since family size differs by income decile, the percentage of the population found in each decile also differs across income deciles.

The second decile received the most benefit from government expenditure, with an average expenditure per family of $19,313. The group that benefitted the least was the tenth decile, with an average benefit of -$34,707.

Knowing how much an income group benefits is not the only relevant statistic for those interested in fairness. It is also important to know how fast benefits change relative to the tax a family pays. The fourth column of table 6.2 shows how much Canadian families in different income groups pay in taxes for their government services. *A family earning on average less than $20,000 will pay 13 cents for each dollar of government services it receives.* A family earning on average between $20,000 and $30,000 will pay 38 cents for the same dollar of government services. In other words, as a family's income doubles it pays three times as much for government services. This progressivity is evident for all the higher income levels. Families earning six times as much as the poorest category pay nearly ten times as much for each dollar of government services. The middle column of table 6.3 shows the same kind of information for families grouped according to deciles. This table shows that the top 30 percent of income earners paid 69 percent of all taxes and received 41 percent of all benefits.

Tables 6.2 and 6.3 do not prove that our governments tax and spend fairly or unfairly. No one can prove fairness. These numbers simply give some basis on which to form opinions. The last columns of these tables suggest that high income Canadians pay more per dollar of government services than do lower income Canadians. However, the reader will note that on average, high income families receive more government services than do the poor. We look at the reason for this in the following section.

Who gets what?

Looking at who benefits from total government spending gives only a rough idea of where the money goes. Table 6.4(a) fine tunes the analysis by showing how the average family in each income group benefits from different types of government spending.[2]

The major expenditure items—health and education—generate increasing benefits for families as their incomes increase. The reason for this relationship is that higher income families include the majority of Canada's children (70 percent in the top 50 percent of income earners) and most of the university attenders (65 percent in the top 50 percent).

Social security expenditures (which comprise the overall leading expenditure type) generate the single biggest benefit flow for low income Canadian families; the largest transfer payments are made to the lowest and second lowest income groups. Those receiving maximum benefits are families earning between $20,000 and $30,000 per year. They enjoyed average benefits of $8,176.

Agriculture, education, and health care benefit the wealthy

When families are grouped into income deciles we can more precisely compare the benefits proffered to the wealthy and the poor. Table 6.5(a) suggests that agricultural expenditures predominantly benefit the top three income deciles. On the assumption that agricultural subsidies benefit people in proportion to the extent to which they receive farm

---

2 Total spending and spending per family do not include interest spending by government, since we are here concerned only with total program spending, or the distribution of current benefits to citizens during the current year. Interest payments on the public debt reflect payment for past expenditures in the sense that if during a particular period the government spends more than it takes in in tax revenue, it finances the difference by borrowing, the interest costs of which are reflected in current government spending. It is obvious, however, that no current program benefit is being delivered for that interest cost except to the extent that capital structures such as highways or public buildings have been financed with the deficit spending. It might also be said that education is a form of investment and that it, like highways and buildings, will produce a flow of services over time which ought appropriately to be paid for over time and reflected in interest charges. To that extent, there is a benefit flow from past spending that is not picked up in total spending if that total is reduced by the amount of interest expense.

Table 6.4a: What Families in Different Income Groups on Average Get Out of Specific Government Expenditures, 1990, Canada (Excluding the Territories) (Dollars)

Income Group ('000s):	<20	20-30	30-40	40-50	50-60	60-70	70-80	80-90	90-100	>100
User Benefit Goods:										
Culture & Recreation	193	333	483	615	742	865	974	1,072	1,207	1,501
Health	3,256	3,815	3,710	3,900	4,107	4,406	4,523	4,488	4,628	4,974
Housing	380	333	305	276	252	235	220	219	215	218
Labour	56	179	289	402	497	581	663	759	813	905
Regional Planning & Development	48	90	119	134	158	179	203	200	245	420
Education	2,354	2,064	2,763	3,406	3,977	4,549	4,679	4,893	4,767	4,994
Resource Conservation & Industrial Development	658	988	1,197	1,230	1,349	1,475	1,488	1,494	1,745	2,073
of which: Trade & Industry	108	204	268	297	341	385	436	422	507	854
of which: Agriculture	222	380	454	414	435	463	434	432	560	557
of which: Other Resource Conservation & Industrial Development	327	403	475	518	572	627	619	641	678	662
Transportation & Communication	694	1,032	1,291	1,462	1,633	1,813	1,935	1,958	2,151	2,841

Table 6.4a: What Families in Different Income Groups on Average Get Out of Specific Government Expenditures, 1990, Canada (Excluding the Territories) (Dollars)

Income Group ('000s):	<20	20-30	30-40	40-50	50-60	60-70	70-80	80-90	90-100	>100
Social Services(excl. CPP)	7,223	8,176	6,728	5,876	5,695	5,695	5,346	4,484	5,037	5,026
CPP/QPP	1,065	1,895	1,491	1,258	1,154	1,224	1,171	772	997	1,214
sub total	15,926	18,904	18,376	18,558	19,563	21,022	21,204	20,339	21,804	24,167
Public Goods:										
Environment	426	526	607	692	753	821	843	886	868	911
General Services	1,164	1,449	1,662	1,876	2,022	2,180	2,229	2,293	2,254	2,332
Other(excl. interest charges)	307	379	440	501	552	601	619	657	657	687
Protection of Persons & Property	1,449	1,806	2,084	2,369	2,609	2,794	2,867	2,983	3,050	3,134
Research Establishments	112	137	159	180	196	214	218	226	225	233
Foreign Affairs & International Assistance	218	269	312	352	385	418	428	444	444	461
sub total	3,675	4,566	5,265	5,970	6,516	7,028	7,204	7,489	7,498	7,757
Average Total	19,601	23,471	23,641	24,528	26,080	28,050	28,408	27,828	29,302	31,925
Average Tax	2,483	9,021	15,106	20,502	26,254	31,247	37,307	41,602	48,252	77,160
Average Net Benefits	17,118	14,449	8,535	4,026	-175	-3,197	-8,899	-13,774	-18,950	-45,235

Table 6.4b: Total Government Spending and Tax Collection by Income Group, 1990, Canada (Excluding the Territories) (Millions of Dollars)

Income Group ('000s)	<20	20-30	30-40	40-50	50-60	60-70	70-80	80-90	90-100	>100	Total
User Benefit Goods:											
Culture & Recreation	477	472	619	738	770	697	579	497	399	1,288	6,536
Health	8,065	5,408	4,762	4,686	4,267	3,551	2,686	2,079	1,529	4,267	41,299
Housing	940	472	392	331	262	189	131	101	71	187	3,077
Labour	138	253	372	483	516	468	394	352	268	776	4,022
Regional Planning & Development	120	128	153	161	164	144	121	92	81	361	1,525
Education	5,830	2,925	3,547	4,093	4,131	3,666	2,778	2,267	1,575	4,284	35,097
Resource Conservation & Industrial Development	1,629	1,400	1,536	1,478	1,401	1,189	884	692	576	1,779	12,563
of which: Trade & Industry	269	290	344	357	355	310	259	195	167	733	3,280
of which: Agriculture	551	538	582	498	452	373	257	200	185	478	4,115
of which: Other Resource Conservation & Industrial Development	810	572	609	623	594	505	367	297	224	568	5,169
Transportation & Communication	1,719	1,463	1,656	1,757	1,697	1,461	1,149	907	710	2,437	14,956

Table 6.4b: Total Government Spending and Tax Collection by Income Group, 1990, Canada (Excluding the Territories) (Millions of Dollars)

Income Group ('000s)	<20	20-30	30-40	40-50	50-60	60-70	70-80	80-90	90-100	>100	Total
Social Services(excl. CPP)	17,891	11,590	8,636	7,061	5,916	4,590	3,175	2,078	1,664	4,312	66,912
CPP/QPP	2,637	2,686	1,914	1,512	1,199	986	696	358	329	1,042	13,358
sub total	39,447	26,798	23,586	22,300	20,323	16,942	12,591	9,424	7,203	20,732	199,345
Public Goods:											
Environment	1,055	745	780	831	782	661	501	410	287	781	6,833
General Services	2,883	2,053	2,134	2,254	2,101	1,757	1,324	1,063	745	2,000	18,314
Other(excl. interest charges)	759	538	565	602	573	485	367	304	217	589	4,999
Protection of Persons & Property	3,589	2,560	2,674	2,846	2,710	2,252	1,702	1,382	1,007	2,688	23,411
Research Establishments	276	195	204	216	204	172	130	105	74	200	1,776
Foreign Affairs & International Assistance	539	382	401	424	400	337	254	206	147	395	3,484
sub total	9,102	6,473	6,758	7,173	6,770	5,664	4,278	3,470	2,477	6,655	58,818
Total Spending	48,549	33,270	30,344	29,473	27,093	22,606	16,869	12,894	9,679	27,386	258,163
Total Tax	6,149	12,788	19,389	24,636	27,274	25,182	22,153	19,276	15,939	66,191	238,978
Total Net Benefit	42,400	20,482	10,955	4,837	-182	-2,577	-5,284	-6,382	-6,260	-38,805	19,185

Table 6.5a: What Families in Different Income Deciles on Average Get Out of Specific Government Expenditures, 1990, Canada (Excluding the Territories) (Dollars)

Decile:	1	2	3	4	5	6	7	8	9	10
User Benefit Goods:										
Culture & Recreation	184	171	250	357	458	563	673	799	979	1,371
Health	2,670	3,738	3,692	3,759	3,717	3,749	4,012	4,304	4,490	4,812
Housing	402	367	350	333	308	288	263	244	223	218
Labour	30	54	115	197	271	353	452	536	669	864
Regional Planning & Development	37	48	75	92	114	129	142	170	196	349
Education	3,457	1,490	1,783	2,179	2,673	3,071	3,817	4,134	4,723	4,959
Resource Conservation & Industrial Development	637	608	791	1,056	1,147	1,237	1,320	1,361	1,494	1,926
of which: Trade & Industry	83	108	168	209	259	288	312	365	420	714
of which: Agriculture	209	205	259	439	420	453	454	404	451	546
of which: Other Resource Conservation & Industrial Development	345	294	364	408	468	496	554	592	623	666
Transportation & Communication	663	649	872	1,064	1,252	1,386	1,546	1,719	1,915	2,559

Table 6.5a: What Families in Different Income Deciles on Average Get Out of Specific Government Expenditures, 1990, Canada (Excluding the Territories) (Dollars)

Decile:	1	2	3	4	5	6	7	8	9	10
Social Services(excl. CPP)	4,125	9,876	8,640	7,945	6,787	6,241	5,660	5,608	5,346	4,964
CPP/QPP	261	1,466	1,904	1,875	1,550	1,313	1,152	1,264	1,087	1,089
sub total	12,467	18,467	18,473	18,859	18,277	18,330	19,039	20,141	21,122	23,109
Public Goods:										
Environment	460	385	457	539	592	651	733	781	853	896
General Services	1,251	1,049	1,260	1,491	1,627	1,763	1,985	2,083	2,248	2,305
Other(excl. interest charges)	329	278	331	388	428	472	533	573	626	675
Protection of Persons & Property	1,542	1,311	1,589	1,852	2,038	2,218	2,524	2,688	2,889	3,092
Research Establishments	120	100	121	141	156	170	191	203	220	230
Foreign Affairs & International Assistance	234	197	235	276	305	332	374	399	432	454
sub total	3,938	3,319	3,993	4,687	5,145	5,607	6,341	6,727	7,268	7,652
Average Total	16,405	21,786	22,466	23,546	23,422	23,937	25,380	26,868	28,390	30,761
Average Tax	899	2,473	6,059	9,632	13,892	18,341	23,047	28,862	36,851	65,470
Average Net Benefits	15,506	19,313	16,407	13,913	9,530	5,596	2,334	-1,995	-8,461	-34,709

Table 6.5b: Government Spending by Decile, 1990, Canada (Excluding the Territories) (Millions of Dollars)

Decile	1	2	3	4	5	6	7	8	9	10	Total
User Benefit Goods:											
Culture & Recreation	184	160	239	333	434	578	706	868	1,133	1,902	6,536
Health	2,660	3,483	3,524	3,507	3,521	3,849	4,206	4,673	5,196	6,678	41,299
Housing	401	342	335	310	292	296	276	265	258	302	3,077
Labour	30	50	110	184	256	362	474	582	774	1,198	4,022
Regional Planning & Development	37	45	72	86	108	133	149	185	227	484	1,525
Education	3,446	1,389	1,702	2,033	2,533	3,153	4,003	4,490	5,466	6,883	35,097
Resource Conservation & Industrial Development	635	567	755	986	1,087	1,270	1,385	1,478	1,729	2,672	12,563
of which: Trade & Industry	82	101	161	195	245	296	328	396	486	990	3,280
of which: Agriculture	208	191	247	410	398	465	476	439	522	758	4,115
of which: Other Resource Conservation & Industrial Development	344	274	348	381	444	510	581	643	721	924	5,169
Transportation & Communication	661	605	832	993	1,186	1,423	1,621	1,867	2,216	3,551	14,956

Table 6.5b: Government Spending by Decile, 1990, Canada (Excluding the Territories) (Millions of Dollars)

Decile	1	2	3	4	5	6	7	8	9	10	Total
Social Services(excl. CPP)	4,111	9,202	8,247	7,412	6,431	6,408	5,935	6,090	6,186	6,890	66,912
CPP/QPP	260	1,366	1,817	1,749	1,468	1,348	1,208	1,373	1,258	1,511	13,358
sub total	12,425	17,208	17,634	17,593	17,316	18,820	19,963	21,871	24,443	32,072	199,345
Public Goods:											
Environment	459	358	436	503	561	669	768	848	987	1,243	6,833
General Services	1,247	977	1,203	1,391	1,542	1,810	2,082	2,262	2,601	3,198	18,314
Other(excl. interest charges)	328	259	316	362	405	485	559	622	725	937	4,999
Protection of Persons & Property	1,537	1,221	1,516	1,727	1,930	2,278	2,647	2,919	3,343	4,291	23,411
Research Establishments	120	94	115	131	147	174	200	220	254	319	1,776
Foreign Affairs & International Assistance	233	183	225	258	289	341	393	433	500	630	3,484
sub total	3,924	3,093	3,812	4,372	4,875	5,757	6,649	7,305	8,410	10,620	58,818
Total Spending	16,349	20,301	21,445	21,965	22,191	24,578	26,612	29,176	32,853	42,692	258,163
Total Tax	896	2,304	5,783	8,986	13,162	18,832	24,165	31,342	42,644	90,863	238,978
Total Net Benefit	15,454	17,996	15,662	12,979	9,029	5,746	2,447	-2,166	-9,791	-48,171	19,185

income—a reasonable assumption since subsidies are generally proportional—this top 30 percent of Canadian income earners received 41.7 percent of all of the benefits distributed to agriculture. The bottom 30 percent of income earners received 15.6 percent of all payments to agriculture. These results may surprise those who believe that agricultural aid is in place to benefit poor farmers.

The pattern of educational spending also progresses strongly with income. More than 48 percent of educational benefits accrue to the top thirty percent of income earners, and fully 68.4 percent accrues to those in the top five deciles. As noted, this pattern occurs partly because the number of children of school age in a family rises as the income of the family rises. Furthermore, high income Canadians are most likely to send their children to university. University students pay only about a fifth of what the university spends on them. This comes to roughly an $8,000 subsidy per year, per student. A family with two children at university will be getting $16,000 of government subsidy each year for the four years of their children's education.

A similar pattern emerges for health care. Governments spend 68.4 percent of their health care budget on those in the top 50 percent of the income distribution. The top thirty percent receive 40.1 percent of the benefits. This seems to be paradoxical in a single-payer health care system designed to provide equal and untrammelled access to health care. The result is likely a reflection of the number of children in higher income families, and the greater proclivity of those with higher incomes to live in urban centres where the use of health care services is much greater per capita.

Of the major expenditure functions, only social security expenditures are distributed primarily to the lower income deciles: 59.1 percent of all social security benefits were distributed to the lowest five income deciles.

Tables 6.4(b) and 6.5(b) show similar information not on a per family basis, but on how much total government spending went to each income group. Chapter 6 Appendix contains the same information for the provinces.

Two illusions of large government benefits

Canadians may face two illusions that make it hard to determine whether government spending is a good deal for them or not. The first illusion is that people may judge the benefits they will get over their lifetimes by the benefits they get today. The second illusion is that people may not realize that future taxes will be higher if debt is used to finance government spending. The next two sections look at these illusions more closely.

The snapshot view versus the lifetime view

Peoples' views about government spending and taxes change over their lives. Often we find the young and the elderly to be the biggest supporters of government programs, while the middle-aged grumble the loudest about taxes. Table 6.6 suggests why these different ages hold different views. Families headed by people 35 and younger tend to be net-recipients of government spending. Families headed by people between 36 and 65 pay more than they get. Families with heads above 65 are net recipients. Families headed by individuals over 65 receive the most on health care, social services, and the Canada and Quebec Pension Plans. Families headed by people under 56 receive the most on education. The greatest educational benefits go to families headed by people between the ages of 36 and 55, which pay more to government than they receive.

Table 6.6 only gives a snapshot of Canadians of different ages. Unfortunately, this is the snapshot that many people may use in forming their impressions about government. The young Canadian of 20 who lives in a well-to-do family sees all the benefits of government spending but may not realize that years of high taxes will follow. Rational, calculating people should not just look at how they are doing today. They should also ask themselves how much net government benefit they will get over their lifetimes.

Table 6.7 gives the perspective of families that start out their lives in different income deciles. The table follows these families throughout their lifetimes. For example, a family that started out in the seventh

Table 6.6: What Families on Average Get From Government, Broken Down by Age of the Family Head, 1990

Age Group:	<25	26-35	36-45	46-55	56-65	66-75	>75
Average Age of Head of the family	23	31	40	50	60	70	79
Average size of family	1.59	2.59	3.18	2.91	2.25	1.78	1.48
Average number of children	0.24	0.95	1.27	0.51	0.11	0.03	0.01
Average Benefit per family($)	14,202	21,694	25,567	24,099	22,494	35,412	33,228
Average Tax Bill per family($)	9,762	19,262	26,008	30,826	27,865	20,436	16,004
Average Net Benefit per family($)	4,441	2,432	-440	-6,727	-5,371	14,976	17,224
Average Net Benefit per family member($)	2,794	940	-139	-2,314	-2,387	8,419	11,602
Average Family Income($)	23,768	43,988	56,649	65,377	51,696	40,350	33,392
Average Government Spending per Family by Age Group of Head (Dollars)							
Culture & Recreation	461	667	761	809	575	391	276
Health	2,088	3,530	3,650	3,992	3,773	4,947	7,414
Housing	414	308	259	250	278	305	328
Labour	240	431	542	588	333	66	29
Regional Planning & Development	65	90	116	146	218	251	216

Table 6.6: What Families on Average Get From Government, Broken Down by Age of the Family Head, 1990

Age Group:	<25	26-35	36-45	46-55	56-65	66-75	>75
Average Government Spending per Family by Age Group of Head (Dollars)							
Education	3,037	4,167	5,799	4,187	1,299	224	126
Resource Conservation & Industrial Development	586	1,068	1,307	1,404	1,452	1,281	935
Transportation & Communication	817	1,241	1,524	1,596	1,678	1,602	1,335
Social Service (excl. CPP/QPP)	2,753	4,196	4,170	4,029	5,502	16,760	15,960
CPP/QPP	101	117	214	481	2,202	5,523	3,231
Environment	415	681	838	766	595	467	386
General Services	1,118	1,822	2,244	2,050	1,586	1,260	1,050
Other (excl. Interest Payments)	303	499	612	560	435	341	282
Protection of Persons & Property	1,427	2,329	2,859	2,625	2,032	1,613	1,359
Research Establishments	110	178	218	199	153	121	100
Foreign Affairs & International Assistance	214	347	426	390	302	239	200

Table 6.7: Average Annual Net Benefit of Government Spending to a Family at Different Stages of its Life (1990 Dollars)

Family begins life in decile	Age group of the head of the family												
Decile	20-25	26-30	31-35	36-40	41-45	46-50	51-55	56-60	61-65	66-70	71-75	>75	Total*
1	15,597	15,718	21,074	18,527	17,662	14,976	8,240	10,182	11,296	21,289	19,593	19,388	330,083
2	11,478	8,765	17,167	19,554	13,261	10,682	11,554	7,292	13,798	21,875	19,641	18,484	266,045
3	9,805	8,999	11,466	14,353	7,247	7,971	12,456	9,754	14,174	23,791	22,713	19,586	224,385
4	8,877	8,965	12,495	10,123	3,883	4,927	6,176	7,551	11,458	23,005	22,768	19,745	193,900
5	7,514	4,837	9,590	9,092	7,868	366	-3,239	545	2,133	22,206	23,068	18,291	141,737
6	4,447	758	6,091	6,654	2,909	-918	1,553	-6,375	-3,714	17,347	22,311	19,404	81,179
7	134	-880	1,417	275	-2,610	-6,613	-14,512	-15,225	-5,739	13,303	14,054	16,962	-19,997
8	-841	-1,104	-4,259	-6,611	-8,290	-16,906	-8,798	-14,947	-8,086	6,907	14,357	9,786	-80,062
9	-3,320	-10,639	-16,616	-12,262	-17,395	-20,423	-27,895	-24,367	-15,383	-3,865	-2,058	-3,414	-238,949
10	-13,525	-20,308	-25,094	-25,020	-37,474	-47,037	-34,491	-43,014	-38,515	-22,644	-11,044	-12,338	-494,652

* Total discounted (5% rate) net benefit over lifetime. (Assume a lifespan of 85 years for the family head.)

decile will receive on average positive net government benefits when the head of that family is between 20 and 40 years old, but will in fact receive negative total net benefits over its lifetime. The lifetime benefits of this family are shown in the last column.[3] This table shows that even though government benefits may look good to a certain income group for a few years, over a lifetime the net benefits may actually be negative.

Don't forget the debt!

The tax figures presented so far underestimate the total tax burden people will pay for government spending. The federal government finances roughly 25 percent of its spending by issuing debt. Government expenditures that are financed by deficits become future tax burdens and this deferred tax burden ought to be included in our analysis. To the extent that governments incur deficits, they are able to produce an aggregate program expenditure and an expenditure per family that are greater than the apparent tax liability they are imposing on the family during the current period. In order to figure out the actual position of families, table 6.8 calculates the deferred tax burden per family by income level.

---

3 The families we are talking about here are really "pseudo" families made up from survey data on actual families alive today. The exercise in table 6.7 is to take a family today and follow its progress throughout its life. We cannot do this precisely because we cannot predict the future. Nor do we have surveys that have followed a group of families throughout their lives and looked at their spending and what they get from government. So we have improvised by turning the snapshot *Survey of Consumer Expenditures* into a lifetime profile. Our technique was to sample 500 families from each age group. We then lined families in each age group into income deciles. We created 500 pseudo-families by taking a family from a given decile in the first age group and assuming that once it reached the next age group it would have moved up or down in its income ranking according to some random force. We linked this first family to the family corresponding to this new ranking in the second age group. We continued the process for all age groups. This gave a lifetime view of a synthetic family made up of snapshots of many different families in different age groups. We did this for all 500 families. The procedure is similar, though less sophisticated, than the one used by Davies, St.-Hillaire, and Whalley (1984).

Table 6.8: Government Spending and Tax Paid per Family by Income Group, Canada, 1990 (Dollars)

Income Groups ('000s)	Average Income	Average Tax Paid per Family	Average Benefit per Family	Average Net Benefit per Family	Average Deferred Tax per Family	Net Benefit Less Deferred Tax per Family
<20	10,323	2,483	19,601	17,118	420	16,698
20-30	24,828	9,021	23,471	14,449	1,528	12,921
30-40	35,016	15,106	23,641	8,535	2,545	5,990
40-50	44,900	20,502	24,528	4,026	3,444	581
50-60	54,884	26,254	26,080	-175	4,398	-4,572
60-70	64,671	31,247	28,050	-3,197	5,236	-8,433
70-80	74,924	37,307	28,408	-8,899	6,221	-15,120
80-90	84,502	41,602	27,828	-13,774	6,921	-20,695
90-100	94,792	48,252	29,302	-18,950	8,019	-26,969
>100	142,895	77,160	31,925	-45,235	12,696	-57,931

Although we talk about the burden of the deficit as burdening all Canadians equally, taxes vary with family income, so that the actual burden that a family will one day bear depends on how high its income is. For example, the deferred tax per family for a family earning less than $20,000 a year is only $420 per year, whereas the deferred tax associated with deficits for a family with an income of $50,000-$60,000 is $4,398.

There are a number of fascinating aspects to the distribution of taxes and expenditures provided in table 6.8. The first is that for a very large number of Canadians there is a net benefit flow in the sense that total program expenditures for many families are greater than the tax burden which must be borne by each such family. Excluding deferred taxes, this is true for all families up to an income level of $54,884 per year. Beyond $50,000 per year, the total tax cost to the family exceeds by a fairly wide margin the expenditures on behalf of the family.

These data provide some very interesting reflections on a current and indeed perennial question concerning the control of government expenditure and deficit cutting, subjects that were broached in chapter one, namely, if there were a desire to cut the size of the deficit or cut government expenditure, where should those cuts be made and why aren't they being made?

Why we don't do something about the deficit

It is evident why the issue of deficit finance is not a pressing concern for the vast majority of tax payers. That is because is they are net beneficiaries of the ongoing process. As is clear from figure 6.1, even including the cost of the future deferred tax cost implied by the deficit, families who earn less than $44,900 are beneficiaries of the governmental tax and expenditure process. Assuming they perceive themselves to be net gainers, they will be in favour of further expansions in expenditures even if that is accomplished by deferred tax or deficit financing. Since the total number of families earning less than $44,900 is 5.784 million and the number earning more than $44,900 is 4.686 million, the majority of citizens may actually benefit from a continuation of the current deficit financed government spending process. (More to the point, from an electoral point of view, 45 percent of Canadian adults are in the less than

$44,900 income group and 57 percent of adults are in the group whose incomes are below $54,884, which is the net beneficiary group if deferred taxes are ignored.)

In a system of majority rule, it cannot be expected that there will be a turnaround in political sentiment until an effective majority of the population is or perceives itself to be adversely affected by spending and tax developments. As has been illustrated in both the 1990 election in Ontario and the federal election of 1993, an effective plurality of the population can be much less than 50 percent and in the case of Ontario it was less than 39 percent. These facts suggest some observations about the benefits distribution and its interaction with the political process.

First, looking at the situation from a practical perspective, there seems to be very little hope that in the short term there will be much political support for doing something constructive about deficit reduction and/or spending control despite the vast amount of rhetoric in that direction. This is true in spite of the fact that the average Canadian family will lose $644 per year as a result of the current activities of government. The reason, as is now clear, is the distribution of the losses and gains. Even though on average we lose as a nation, the majority of families continues to gain. The rhetoric evidently serves to assuage the feelings of those who are on the contributing side of the ledger, while failure to act continues to deliver goodies to those who are the net beneficiaries—the majority of the electorate. While it might be possible to convince those who are marginal net beneficiaries, that is to say, those who earn around $44,900 per year (using the tax line including deferred taxation), or those who earn around $54,884 (using the tax line excluding deferred taxation), the unfortunate reality is that a majority of families gains from government and the average net benefit of this majority is $15,571 per family.

Second, even if it were possible to mobilize the top income group, which bears a very large net burden, there would not be political solidarity within this group because some members of the group would be or would regard themselves as significant net beneficiaries of programs such as the health care system and post secondary education spending. (These expenditures, remember, are distributed disproportionately to the benefit of the higher income groups.) Accordingly, there may not be unanimity amongst the top income group about cutting back on the very programs that constitute some of the largest source of spending pressure and lead the top income groups to be net supporters of the system.

Third, the situation is getting worse, not better with the passage of time. Figure 6.2 presents the tax and spending profiles from a study of this kind that was done for the year 1969 by Irwin Gillespie. That study showed, as the figure illustrates, that there was a balance between expenditure and taxation (excluding deferred taxation which was negligible in 1969) at an income level (in 1990 dollars) of about $30,500. The study showed that 48 percent of families had incomes below that level. There was, therefore, a smaller group of net beneficiaries in 1969, and a majority of electors was in the net burden-bearing group. There was, therefore, less inherent political interest in spending growth, and more inherent intolerance of assuming more fiscal burdens.

Fourth, from the point of view of marshalling the political will to "do something" about the level of government spending, the benefits distribution indicates that even if there are great inefficiencies in the conduct of government programs, a majority will still be net beneficiaries. Those voters receiving a positive net benefit from government get $82.3 billion of positive net benefit. This sum represents the room government has to be inefficient. This is an important finding since it suggests that not withstanding the great public outcry against it, and even allowing for great inefficiency in the supply of government services, it is in the personal interest of a majority of Canadians to support expansion in both the level of government spending and the deficit as long as there is no change in the way in which the cost of spending is distributed.

Implications for public policy

The foregoing analysis suggests a number of conclusions for public policy. First, when politicians ask, "Where should we begin to cut government spending," they are asking a safe question, since a large majority of the electorate would perceive themselves to be net beneficiaries and therefore not rational supporters of cut-backs. Moreover, even those who are net payers into the system will have little interest in

Figure 6.1: Government Spending and Tax Paid per Family by Income Level, 1990 (Thousands of Dollars)

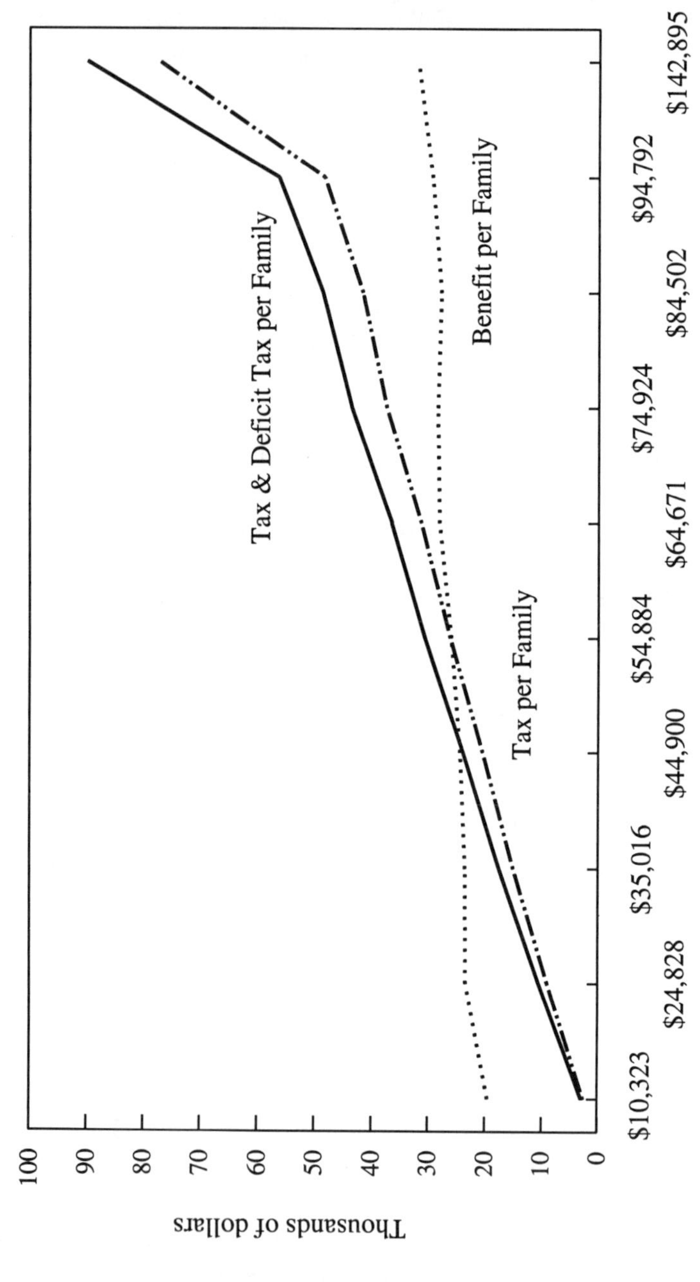

Fig 6.2: Government Spending and Tax Paid per Family by Income Level in Real Dollars, 1969, in 1990 Dollars (Thousands of Dollars)

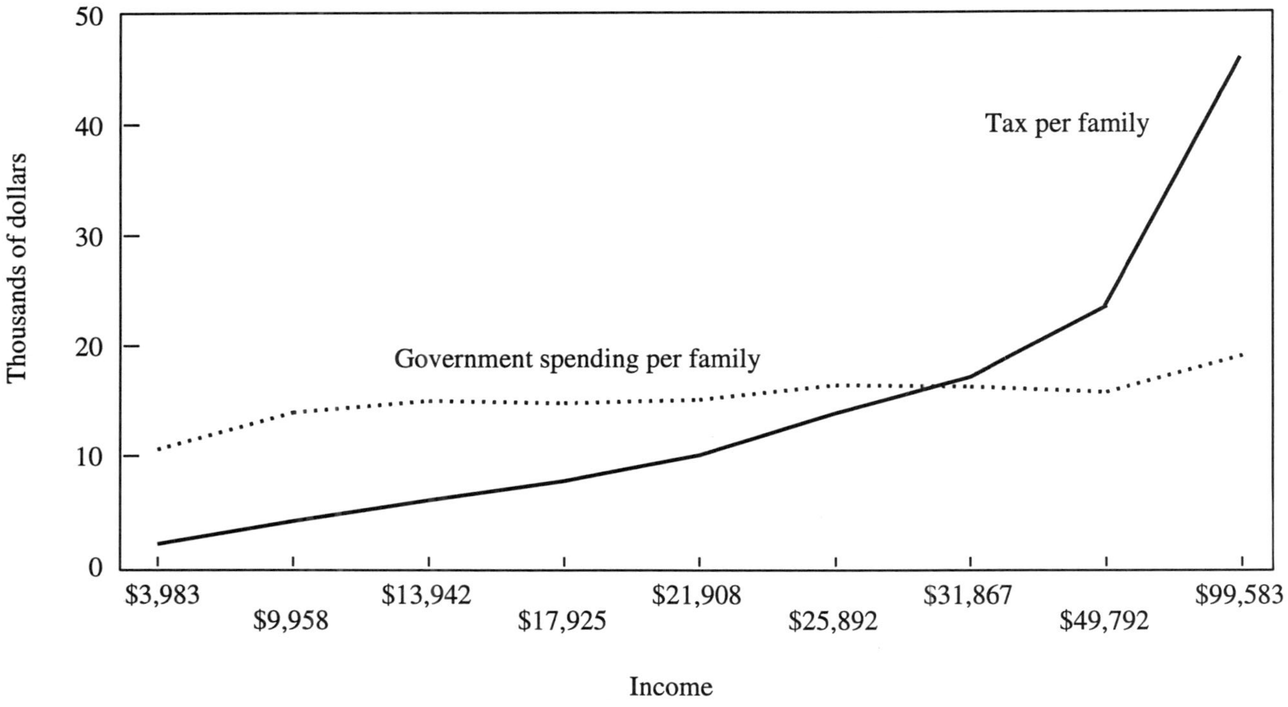

pointing to the spending areas that contribute most to the deficit and spending problem because it is precisely in those areas of spending that the net contributors are significant beneficiaries. Unless they have some assurance that the spending cuts will be matched by tax cuts which favour high income taxpayers, it is not rational for them to favour spending cuts either—at least not in the area of education and health care.

Second, reform of the system must begin on the side of taxation. A majority of taxpayers are net beneficiaries from the system of expenditure and taxation because the distribution of benefits from government is proportional and the associated tax burden is progressive. As long as this effective redistribution is possible there will be little support for spending cuts. Making the tax system more proportional would reduce the interest in and the possibility for the kind of redistribution that lies at the base of the current difficulties. Policies that would accomplish this proportionality include the flat rate income tax, which has been the subject of past Fraser Institute studies.

Chapter 6 Appendix: Tabular Material

Table 6.4a1: What Families in Different Income Groups on Average Get Out of Specific Government Expenditures, Newfoundland, 1990 (Dollars)

Income Group ('000s)	<20	20-30	30-40	40-50	50-60	60-70	70-80	80-90	90-100	>100
User Benefit Goods:										
Culture & Recreation	168	345	505	629	750	854	955	974	1,156	1,343
Health	3,724	4,291	3,996	4,205	4,484	4,719	4,630	4,736	4,829	4,558
Housing	410	361	352	325	298	286	281	276	273	266
Labour	53	195	326	463	647	813	913	988	1,024	1,282
Regional Planning & Development	51	98	114	130	163	174	227	260	356	482
Education	2,991	3,319	3,961	4,691	5,509	6,734	6,987	5,235	6,585	5,708
Resource Conservation & Industrial Development	810	1,115	1,282	1,393	1,616	1,706	1,989	2,109	2,640	4,170
of which: Trade & Industry	246	470	545	624	781	834	1,085	1,242	1,701	2,304
of which: Agriculture	69	0	35	0	0	0	0	0	0	998
of which: Other Resource Conservation & Industrial Development	496	645	703	770	836	873	904	868	940	868
Transportation & Communication	1,173	1,773	2,005	2,265	2,583	2,743	3,096	3,206	3,860	4,385

Table 6.4a1: What Families in Different Income Groups on Average Get Out of Specific Government Expenditures, Newfoundland, 1990 (Dollars)

Income Group ('000s)	<20	20-30	30-40	40-50	50-60	60-70	70-80	80-90	90-100	>100
Social Services (excl. CPP)	9,334	12,557	13,507	13,470	11,303	9,818	9,760	8,859	12,140	9,185
CPP/QPP	1,146	1,957	1,006	809	726	789	633	896	1,126	898
Sub total	19,859	26,010	27,054	28,382	28,080	28,638	29,470	27,539	33,989	32,277
Public Goods:										
Environment	427	555	605	662	719	751	778	747	809	747
General Services	1,508	1,962	2,138	2,342	2,543	2,656	2,751	2,641	2,860	2,643
Other (excl. interest charges)	383	498	543	595	646	675	699	671	727	671
Protection of Persons & Property	1,571	2,044	2,227	2,440	2,649	2,767	2,866	2,752	2,979	2,753
Research Establishments	105	136	149	163	177	185	191	184	199	184
Foreign Affairs & International Assistance	291	379	413	453	491	513	532	510	553	511
Sub total	4,286	5,575	6,075	6,655	7,226	7,546	7,817	7,504	8,126	7,509
Average Total	24,145	31,585	33,129	35,037	35,306	36,185	37,287	35,043	42,114	39,786
Average Tax	2,181	7,780	12,800	18,322	25,276	31,096	37,895	42,335	49,948	69,295
Average Net Benefits	21,964	23,805	20,330	16,715	10,030	5,089	-608	-7,292	-7,834	-29,509

Table 6.4a2: What Families in Different Income Groups on Average Get Out of Specific Government Expenditures, Prince Edward Island, 1990 (Dollars)

Income Group ('000s)	<20	20-30	30-40	40-50	50-60	60-70	70-80	80-90	90-100	>100
User Benefit Goods:										
Culture & Recreation	183	424	623	814	948	1,069	1,164	1,220	1,434	1,642
Health	2,604	2,938	3,074	3,685	3,551	3,788	4,044	3,765	3,759	3,596
Housing	452	394	340	292	294	293	280	291	283	318
Labour	89	321	498	702	888	963	1,052	997	1,192	1,091
Regional Planning & Development	28	53	71	87	98	105	149	177	194	302
Education	1,874	2,157	2,955	4,589	4,661	4,679	5,535	5,577	5,028	3,554
Resource Conservation & Industrial Development	971	1,754	2,217	2,564	2,710	3,274	3,483	3,598	5,025	6,799
of which: Trade & Industry	289	556	745	907	1,028	1,099	1,552	1,851	2,025	3,158
of which: Agriculture	179	499	660	642	668	1,053	739	642	1,821	2,590
of which: Other Resource Conservation & Industrial Development	503	699	812	1,015	1,014	1,122	1,192	1,104	1,179	1,051
Transportation & Communication	1,091	1,765	2,194	2,738	2,894	3,159	3,744	3,914	4,222	5,129

Table 6.4a2: What Families in Different Income Groups on Average Get Out of Specific Government Expenditures, Prince Edward Island, 1990 (Dollars)

Income Group ('000s)	<20	20-30	30-40	40-50	50-60	60-70	70-80	80-90	90-100	>100
Social Services (excl. CPP)	8,506	8,987	9,226	9,007	8,014	9,361	9,166	9,307	10,185	10,873
CPP/QPP	1,069	1,502	1,006	1,125	817	689	1,268	805	384	1,566
Sub total	16,867	20,295	22,206	25,603	24,874	27,380	29,885	29,652	31,706	34,872
Public Goods:										
Environment	209	290	337	422	421	466	495	458	490	436
General Services	1,530	2,125	2,469	3,086	3,080	3,411	3,621	3,355	3,583	3,193
Other (excl. interest charges)	331	460	535	668	667	739	784	727	776	692
Protection of Persons & Property	1,602	2,225	2,584	3,230	3,224	3,570	3,791	3,512	3,750	3,343
Research Establishments	51	71	82	103	103	114	121	112	119	106
Foreign Affairs & International Assistance	222	308	358	448	447	495	526	487	520	463
Sub total	3,945	5,480	6,365	7,956	7,942	8,794	9,338	8,651	9,238	8,234
Average Total	20,812	25,775	28,571	33,559	32,816	36,174	39,223	38,302	40,944	43,106
Average Tax	2,206	8,448	13,980	19,296	24,172	28,152	34,408	38,267	44,850	62,365
Average Net Benefits	18,606	17,327	14,591	14,264	8,644	8,022	4,814	36	-3,906	-19,259

Table 6.4a3: What Families in Different Income Groups on Average Get Out of Specific Government Expenditures, Nova Scotia, 1990 (Dollars)

Income Group ('000s)	<20	20-30	30-40	40-50	50-60	60-70	70-80	80-90	90-100	>100
User Benefit Goods:										
Culture & Recreation	171	368	607	751	889	1,030	1,094	1,224	1,465	1,582
Health	3,238	3,715	3,898	4,085	4,467	4,297	4,729	4,060	4,607	4,761
Housing	339	297	275	241	217	229	204	218	218	230
Labour	129	403	666	939	1,203	1,384	1,428	1,783	2,141	1,595
Regional Planning & Development	61	122	157	164	185	244	336	348	273	534
Education	1,947	2,392	3,038	3,916	4,766	4,038	4,958	2,803	5,768	5,875
Resource Conservation & Industrial Development	545	854	1,110	1,272	1,440	1,430	1,857	1,727	1,538	2,961
of which: Trade & Industry	178	356	462	481	541	715	984	1,019	800	1,566
of which: Agriculture	27	38	103	167	214	43	187	102	0	684
of which: Other Resource Conservation & Industrial Development	340	460	546	624	685	671	686	607	738	711
Transportation & Communication	841	1,334	1,658	1,861	2,065	2,262	2,582	2,487	2,485	3,245

Table 6.4a3: What Families in Different Income Groups on Average Get Out of Specific Government Expenditures, Nova Scotia, 1990 (Dollars)

Income Group ('000s)	<20	20-30	30-40	40-50	50-60	60-70	70-80	80-90	90-100	>100
Social Services (excl. CPP)	7,643	8,283	7,700	7,422	6,170	6,456	7,344	4,679	4,470	6,136
CPP/QPP	1,409	1,982	1,647	1,298	982	1,117	1,395	1,271	365	1,090
Sub total	16,322	19,750	20,757	21,949	22,384	22,488	25,926	20,601	23,328	28,010
Public Goods:										
Environment	356	482	573	655	719	704	719	637	774	745
General Services	1,578	2,135	2,534	2,897	3,180	3,116	3,183	2,817	3,425	3,298
Other (excl. interest charges)	292	395	468	536	588	576	588	521	633	610
Protection of Persons & Property	2,855	3,864	4,585	5,243	5,756	5,638	5,761	5,098	6,198	5,970
Research Establishments	103	139	165	189	207	203	208	184	223	215
Foreign Affairs & International Assistance	223	302	358	409	449	440	450	398	484	466
Sub total	5,406	7,318	8,683	9,928	10,900	10,677	10,909	9,654	11,736	11,304
Average Total	21,728	27,068	29,440	31,876	33,284	33,166	36,835	30,255	35,064	39,314
Average Tax	2,756	8,899	14,564	19,534	24,794	31,218	37,023	44,140	46,714	64,240
Average Net Benefits	18,973	18,169	14,876	12,342	8,490	1,947	-189	-13,884	-11,650	-24,925

Table 6.4a4: What Families in Different Income Groups on Average Get Out of Specific Government Expenditures, New Brunswick, 1990 (Dollars)

Income Group ('000s)	<20	20-30	30-40	40-50	50-60	60-70	70-80	80-90	90-100	>100
User Benefit Goods:										
Culture & Recreation	144	293	455	569	680	784	822	970	1,013	1,327
Health	3,393	3,922	3,818	4,005	4,004	4,193	4,163	4,598	4,718	4,239
Housing	324	283	259	226	230	213	197	200	204	216
Labour	58	188	354	497	607	738	744	1,018	978	1,202
Regional Planning & Development	49	95	124	142	159	211	210	222	251	518
Education	2,077	2,255	3,632	4,247	4,092	4,420	4,211	5,469	5,048	5,398
Resource Conservation & Industrial Development	616	856	1,113	1,168	1,312	1,600	1,747	1,695	1,848	2,450
of which: Trade & Industry	150	289	376	432	483	642	638	674	763	1,575
of which: Agriculture	84	83	140	71	151	273	408	260	314	163
of which: Other Resource Conservation & Industrial Development	383	484	598	665	679	684	701	762	771	711
Transportation & Communication	1,031	1,576	2,013	2,306	2,478	2,824	2,877	3,078	3,266	4,614

Table 6.4a4: What Families in Different Income Groups on Average Get Out of Specific Government Expenditures, New Brunswick, 1990 (Dollars)

Income Group ('000s)	<20	20-30	30-40	40-50	50-60	60-70	70-80	80-90	90-100	>100
Social Services (excl. CPP)	8,040	9,699	8,833	8,208	8,850	6,842	8,943	7,777	5,851	7,451
CPP/QPP	1,077	2,177	1,292	969	1,045	1,366	1,027	1,049	1,051	1,410
Sub total	16,810	21,344	21,893	22,337	23,457	23,190	24,942	26,076	24,227	28,825
Public Goods:										
Environment	245	310	382	425	434	437	448	487	493	454
General Services	1,324	1,676	2,068	2,301	2,349	2,368	2,425	2,636	2,668	2,459
Other (excl. interest charges)	372	471	581	646	660	665	681	740	749	691
Protection of Persons & Property	3,243	4,106	5,067	5,637	5,755	5,800	5,941	6,458	6,535	6,024
Research Establishments	110	139	171	191	195	196	201	218	221	204
Foreign Affairs & International Assistance	247	312	386	429	438	441	452	491	497	458
Sub total	5,540	7,013	8,655	9,629	9,831	9,907	10,148	11,031	11,164	10,290
Average Total	22,350	28,357	30,549	31,966	33,288	33,097	35,090	37,107	35,390	39,115
Average Tax	2,360	8,003	14,121	19,447	24,274	31,232	33,838	41,461	46,311	77,166
Average Net Benefits	19,990	20,354	16,428	12,518	9,014	1,865	1,252	-4,354	-10,920	-38,050

Table 6.4a5: What Families in Different Income Groups on Average Get Out of Specific Government Expenditures, Quebec, 1990 (Dollars)

Income Group ('000s)	<20	20-30	30-40	40-50	50-60	60-70	70-80	80-90	90-100	>100
User Benefit Goods:										
Culture & Recreation	182	279	420	517	654	775	909	1,009	1,104	1,468
Health	2,769	3,338	3,233	3,537	3,349	3,770	3,749	3,675	3,749	4,103
Housing	442	379	339	309	291	266	255	253	258	270
Labour	63	235	366	490	636	763	901	1,004	1,045	1,212
Regional Planning & Development	36	69	104	122	142	161	177	192	258	434
Education	1,852	2,095	2,834	3,383	3,770	4,605	4,413	5,185	3,414	4,364
Resource Conservation & Industrial Development	334	576	857	830	953	1,189	953	1,309	1,804	2,248
of which: Trade & Industry	89	170	255	301	349	395	433	471	633	1,064
of which: Agriculture	65	166	329	217	277	421	150	442	804	794
of which: Other Resource Conservation & Industrial Development	180	239	274	312	328	373	370	397	367	389
Transportation & Communication	680	1,036	1,373	1,597	1,793	2,041	2,158	2,322	2,638	3,695

Table 6.4a5: What Families in Different Income Groups on Average Get Out of Specific Government Expenditures, Quebec, 1990 (Dollars)

Income Group ('000s)	<20	20-30	30-40	40-50	50-60	60-70	70-80	80-90	90-100	>100
Social Services (excl. CPP)	7,377	8,225	6,957	6,762	5,950	6,009	5,185	4,968	4,991	5,017
CPP/QPP	926	1,626	1,329	1,357	1,009	1,077	1,157	462	925	1,135
Sub total	14,661	17,858	17,812	18,906	18,547	20,657	19,857	20,378	20,185	23,946
Public Goods:										
Environment	497	662	756	863	906	1,032	1,021	1,098	1,013	1,076
General Services	1,286	1,714	1,958	2,234	2,346	2,672	2,646	2,844	2,624	2,787
Other (excl. interest charges)	297	396	453	517	543	618	612	658	607	645
Protection of Persons & Property	1,123	1,497	1,710	1,951	2,049	2,333	2,310	2,483	2,291	2,433
Research Establishments	114	152	174	198	208	237	235	252	233	247
Foreign Affairs & International Assistance	208	278	317	362	380	433	429	461	425	452
Sub total	3,526	4,699	5,368	6,125	6,432	7,325	7,253	7,796	7,193	7,639
Average Total	18,187	22,557	23,180	25,031	24,980	27,982	27,110	28,174	27,378	31,586
Average Tax	2,222	8,896	15,349	20,980	27,491	33,054	38,773	44,335	51,931	78,690
Average Net Benefits	15,964	13,661	7,831	4,050	-2,511	-5,073	-11,662	-16,161	-24,553	-47,104

Table 6.4a6: What Families in Different Income Groups on Average Get Out of Specific Government Expenditures, Ontario, 1990 (Dollars)

Income Group ('000s)	<20	20-30	30-40	40-50	50-60	60-70	70-80	80-90	90-100	>100
User Benefit Goods:										
Culture & Recreation	162	272	409	548	674	797	894	1,008	1,135	1,446
Health	3,544	3,974	3,893	3,990	4,333	4,647	4,997	4,771	4,751	5,281
Housing	336	307	287	269	246	222	210	201	204	201
Labour	39	124	220	320	396	485	545	661	758	858
Regional Planning & Development	54	95	119	128	152	158	197	167	189	386
Education	2,520	1,860	2,310	3,051	3,883	4,453	4,656	4,919	4,963	5,132
Resource Conservation & Industrial Development	342	510	616	669	717	783	928	882	936	1,337
of which: Trade & Industry	95	167	210	226	268	278	348	294	333	680
of which: Agriculture	44	108	134	132	100	118	177	168	183	211
of which: Other Resource Conservation & Industrial Development	203	235	272	311	349	387	404	420	420	446
Transportation & Communication	613	818	986	1,110	1,266	1,364	1,536	1,491	1,578	2,224

Table 6.4a6: What Families in Different Income Groups on Average Get Out of Specific Government Expenditures, Ontario, 1990 (Dollars)

Income Group ('000s)	<20	20-30	30-40	40-50	50-60	60-70	70-80	80-90	90-100	>100
Social Services (excl. CPP)	7,833	8,112	6,625	5,342	5,434	5,434	5,518	3,838	4,832	4,784
CPP/QPP	1,305	2,163	1,812	1,347	1,274	1,350	1,332	754	841	1,248
Sub total	16,749	18,235	17,278	16,774	18,376	19,692	20,813	18,692	20,187	22,897
Public Goods:										
Environment	432	500	579	661	742	822	859	893	893	949
General Services	1,028	1,190	1,378	1,574	1,766	1,958	2,045	2,127	2,127	2,260
Other (excl. interest charges)	353	408	473	540	606	672	702	730	730	775
Protection of Persons & Property	1,583	1,834	2,124	2,425	2,722	3,017	3,152	3,277	3,278	3,482
Research Establishments	101	116	135	154	173	192	200	208	208	221
Foreign Affairs & International Assistance	213	247	286	326	366	406	424	441	441	469
Sub total	3,709	4,295	4,974	5,680	6,375	7,067	7,382	7,675	7,677	8,156
Average Total	20,458	22,529	22,252	22,453	24,750	26,759	28,194	26,367	27,864	31,053
Average Tax	2,584	9,467	15,555	20,693	26,411	30,651	37,554	40,585	46,792	78,811
Average Net Benefits	17,874	13,062	6,697	1,761	-1,661	-3,891	-9,360	-14,217	-18,928	-47,758

Table 6.4a7: What Families in Different Income Groups on Average Get Out of Specific Government Expenditures, Manitoba, 1990 (Dollars)

Income Group ('000s)	<20	20-30	30-40	40-50	50-60	60-70	70-80	80-90	90-100	>100
User Benefit Goods:										
Culture & Recreation	382	588	756	920	1,103	1,233	1,375	1,560	1,696	2,107
Health	3,656	4,272	4,369	4,361	4,606	4,354	4,494	5,085	4,699	5,281
Housing	343	296	269	225	213	210	198	200	207	219
Labour	59	178	306	453	559	644	726	832	892	876
Regional Planning & Development	106	200	233	265	317	350	370	414	558	946
Education	2,355	2,094	3,801	4,019	4,662	4,448	4,262	5,762	4,519	4,620
Resource Conservation & Industrial Development	871	1,301	1,430	1,712	1,714	1,779	1,837	2,673	1,951	3,556
of which: Trade & Industry	187	353	412	467	559	619	654	731	985	1,671
of which: Agriculture	490	712	718	914	793	800	818	1,524	566	1,484
of which: Other Resource Conservation & Industrial Development	194	236	300	331	363	360	365	419	400	401
Transportation & Communication	731	1,124	1,384	1,566	1,797	1,905	1,990	2,223	2,538	3,492

Table 6.4a7: What Families in Different Income Groups on Average Get Out of Specific Government Expenditures, Manitoba, 1990 (Dollars)

Income Group ('000s)	<20	20-30	30-40	40-50	50-60	60-70	70-80	80-90	90-100	>100
Social Services (excl. CPP)	7,373	7,897	7,265	4,917	5,851	5,566	5,711	5,765	4,284	6,039
CPP/QPP	1,182	2,047	1,822	1,113	1,231	1,105	1,024	1,080	1,505	1,400
Sub total	17,058	19,996	21,635	19,550	22,053	21,594	21,987	25,594	22,849	28,535
Public Goods:										
Environment	397	482	613	677	741	736	746	856	818	820
General Services	1,138	1,382	1,758	1,942	2,125	2,112	2,140	2,456	2,345	2,353
Other (excl. interest charges)	201	245	311	344	376	374	379	434	415	416
Protection of Persons & Property	1,620	1,968	2,503	2,765	3,026	3,007	3,047	3,496	3,338	3,350
Research Establishments	84	102	130	144	157	156	158	182	173	174
Foreign Affairs & International Assistance	232	281	358	395	432	430	435	500	477	479
Sub total	3,671	4,461	5,672	6,267	6,858	6,815	6,904	7,924	7,566	7,592
Average Total	20,729	24,457	27,307	25,816	28,911	28,409	28,891	33,517	30,415	36,127
Average Tax	2,597	9,156	13,674	19,284	24,810	29,481	34,160	38,950	47,532	72,906
Average Net Benefits	18,132	15,301	13,633	6,532	4,102	-1,073	-5,269	-5,432	-17,117	-36,779

Table 6.4a8: What Families in Different Income Groups on Average Get Out of Specific Government Expenditures, Saskatchewan, 1990 (Dollars)

Income Group ('000s)	<20	20-30	30-40	40-50	50-60	60-70	70-80	80-90	90-100	>100
User Benefit Goods:										
Culture & Recreation	337	542	712	849	978	1,122	1,260	1,421	1,460	1,936
Health	3,673	4,511	4,441	4,490	4,888	5,008	4,888	4,678	5,308	5,033
Housing	677	574	526	479	456	447	426	434	421	467
Labour	57	141	240	344	392	467	551	638	623	615
Regional Planning & Development	31	58	79	83	103	113	131	136	164	282
Education	2,887	2,669	3,174	3,353	4,181	4,931	5,733	4,571	5,039	4,648
Resource Conservation & Industrial Development	2,477	4,187	3,865	4,264	5,908	5,622	6,133	4,869	6,186	8,143
of which: Trade & Industry	158	298	410	430	534	585	675	702	850	1,458
of which: Agriculture	1,911	3,365	2,854	3,206	4,654	4,287	4,685	3,416	4,572	5,950
of which: Other Resource Conservation & Industrial Development	408	524	600	627	719	751	773	751	764	734
Transportation & Communication	794	1,282	1,594	1,700	2,023	2,197	2,388	2,466	2,729	3,852

Table 6.4a8: What Families in Different Income Groups on Average Get Out of Specific Government Expenditures, Saskatchewan, 1990 (Dollars)

Income Group ('000s)	<20	20-30	30-40	40-50	50-60	60-70	70-80	80-90	90-100	>100
Social Services (excl. CPP)	5,597	7,282	5,671	4,347	4,858	5,504	4,209	3,718	4,177	4,671
CPP/QPP	815	1,736	1,801	1,225	1,339	1,084	1,700	1,011	1,497	1,994
Sub total	17,346	22,981	22,103	21,133	25,124	26,495	27,419	23,941	27,604	31,639
Public Goods:										
Environment	391	501	574	600	688	718	739	718	731	703
General Services	1,331	1,708	1,957	2,045	2,344	2,447	2,518	2,447	2,489	2,394
Other (excl. interest charges)	257	330	378	395	453	473	487	473	481	463
Protection of Persons & Property	1,017	1,305	1,495	1,563	1,792	1,870	1,924	1,870	1,902	1,829
Research Establishments	124	159	183	191	219	228	235	228	232	223
Foreign Affairs & International Assistance	246	316	362	378	434	453	466	453	460	443
Sub total	3,366	4,321	4,950	5,172	5,930	6,189	6,369	6,189	6,296	6,054
Average Total	20,712	27,302	27,053	26,305	31,054	32,684	33,788	30,130	33,900	37,694
Average Tax	2,697	9,256	16,109	20,906	26,219	30,905	36,963	42,078	48,176	79,692
Average Net Benefits	18,015	18,046	10,945	5,399	4,835	1,779	-3,175	-11,947	-14,276	-41,998

Table 6.4a9: What Families in Different Income Groups on Average Get Out of Specific Government Expenditures, Alberta, 1990 (Dollars)

Income Group ('000s)	<20	20-30	30-40	40-50	50-60	60-70	70-80	80-90	90-100	>100
User Benefit Goods:										
Culture & Recreation	304	497	640	789	923	1,074	1,197	1,320	1,439	1,745
Health	3,375	4,006	3,745	4,192	4,628	4,536	4,551	4,413	4,703	4,911
Housing	515	446	409	373	321	327	296	286	275	309
Labour	65	174	293	374	463	563	627	726	772	912
Regional Planning & Development	59	102	125	172	198	236	267	284	363	566
Education	3,171	2,169	2,831	3,540	3,884	4,019	4,603	3,759	4,331	5,061
Resource Conservation & Industrial Development	2,151	2,511	3,280	3,730	3,892	3,856	4,206	3,511	4,411	4,378
of which: Trade & Industry	98	170	210	288	332	395	447	475	609	948
of which: Agriculture	852	988	1,443	1,541	1,495	1,342	1,533	914	1,488	1,070
of which: Other Resource Conservation & Industrial Development	1,201	1,353	1,628	1,901	2,066	2,120	2,226	2,121	2,314	2,361
Transportation & Communication	875	1,245	1,533	1,936	2,188	2,443	2,673	2,739	3,223	4,219

Table 6.4a9: What Families in Different Income Groups on Average Get Out of Specific Government Expenditures, Alberta, 1990 (Dollars)

Income Group ('000s)	<20	20-30	30-40	40-50	50-60	60-70	70-80	80-90	90-100	>100
Social Services (excl. CPP)	5,702	7,143	4,813	4,668	4,820	4,458	4,327	4,489	5,101	4,628
CPP/QPP	727	1,320	796	941	1,097	852	1,205	1,048	1,484	984
Sub total	16,944	19,613	18,466	20,712	22,414	22,365	23,951	22,575	26,101	27,713
Public Goods:										
Environment	433	487	586	685	744	764	802	764	834	851
General Services	1,071	1,206	1,451	1,695	1,841	1,890	1,984	1,891	2,063	2,105
Other (excl. interest charges)	352	396	477	557	605	621	652	621	677	691
Protection of Persons & Property	1,372	1,545	1,859	2,171	2,359	2,421	2,542	2,422	2,642	2,696
Research Establishments	150	169	203	238	258	265	278	265	289	295
Foreign Affairs & International Assistance	231	260	312	365	396	407	427	407	444	453
Sub total	3,608	4,063	4,889	5,710	6,204	6,366	6,686	6,371	6,949	7,091
Average Total	20,552	23,675	23,354	26,422	28,618	28,731	30,637	28,946	33,050	34,804
Average Tax	2,539	8,667	13,726	20,092	25,047	31,326	37,148	42,097	50,469	77,327
Average Net Benefits	18,013	15,009	9,629	6,330	3,571	-2,595	-6,511	-13,150	-17,419	-42,523

Table 6.4a10: What Families in Different Income Groups on Average Get Out of Specific Government Expenditures, British Columbia, 1990 (Dollars)

Income Group ('000s)	<20	20-30	30-40	40-50	50-60	60-70	70-80	80-90	90-100	>100
User Benefit Goods:										
Culture & Recreation	124	313	480	692	792	877	1,026	1,034	1,231	1,399
Health	3,379	3,966	3,709	3,825	4,126	4,632	4,371	4,843	5,144	4,928
Housing	167	144	141	126	111	105	102	105	96	106
Labour	44	106	175	262	327	342	445	461	486	609
Regional Planning & Development	44	81	115	119	135	178	172	206	266	329
Education	2,587	1,773	2,717	3,621	4,052	4,915	4,881	5,445	5,981	5,193
Resource Conservation & Industrial Development	488	742	822	847	940	1,130	1,165	1,416	1,630	1,542
of which: Trade & Industry	93	173	244	254	289	379	367	439	567	702
of which: Agriculture	59	172	118	73	51	105	141	277	346	132
of which: Other Resource Conservation & Industrial Development	336	397	459	520	601	645	658	700	717	708
Transportation & Communication	530	850	1,125	1,256	1,447	1,734	1,751	1,961	2,308	2,661

Table 6.4a10: What Families in Different Income Groups on Average Get Out of Specific Government Expenditures, British Columbia, 1990 (Dollars)

Income Group ('000s)	<20	20-30	30-40	40-50	50-60	60-70	70-80	80-90	90-100	>100
Social Services (excl. CPP)	6,295	8,155	6,023	4,832	5,218	5,964	4,416	5,300	5,700	5,573
CPP/QPP	1,006	2,226	1,469	1,183	1,181	1,529	661	958	1,172	1,176
Sub total	14,664	18,356	16,775	16,762	18,328	21,406	18,990	21,728	24,014	23,517
Public Goods:										
Environment	332	392	453	513	593	637	650	691	708	699
General Services	960	1,134	1,312	1,485	1,717	1,843	1,880	1,999	2,047	2,023
Other (excl. interest charges)	221	261	302	342	395	424	433	460	471	465
Protection of Persons & Property	1,195	1,413	1,634	1,849	2,139	2,296	2,342	2,490	2,550	2,520
Research Establishments	116	137	159	180	208	223	228	242	248	245
Foreign Affairs & International Assistance	209	247	286	324	374	402	410	436	446	441
Sub total	3,033	3,584	4,147	4,692	5,426	5,826	5,942	6,319	6,471	6,393
Average Total	17,697	21,940	20,922	21,455	23,754	27,232	24,932	28,047	30,484	29,910
Average Tax	2,738	8,896	15,478	20,311	25,592	30,457	35,513	40,051	47,995	70,398
Average Net Benefits	14,959	13,044	5,444	1,144	-1,838	-3,225	-10,581	-12,003	-17,510	-40,488

Table 6.5a1: What Families in Different Income Deciles on Average Get Out of Specific Government Expenditures, Newfoundland, 1990 (Dollars)

Decile	1	2	3	4	5	6	7	8	9	10
User Benefit Goods:										
Culture & Recreation	167	161	218	371	445	537	637	744	867	1,128
Health	3,417	3,615	4,468	4,287	3,918	4,128	4,252	4,391	4,647	4,739
Housing	440	406	362	365	358	341	324	298	290	271
Labour	39	56	98	208	283	356	460	645	820	1,087
Regional Planning & Development	37	55	76	98	110	122	133	158	191	335
Education	3,848	2,572	2,280	3,578	3,923	3,886	4,776	5,476	6,554	6,365
Resource Conservation & Industrial Development	861	729	924	1,120	1,207	1,368	1,415	1,579	1,782	2,818
of which: Trade & Industry	178	264	364	469	526	585	637	756	912	1,601
of which: Agriculture	173	0	0	0	0	57	0	0	0	316
of which: Other Resource Conservation & Industrial Development	510	465	560	651	682	726	778	823	871	901
Transportation & Communication	1,082	1,153	1,471	1,786	1,926	2,113	2,294	2,537	2,828	3,666

Table 6.5a1: What Families in Different Income Deciles on Average Get Out of Specific Government Expenditures, Newfoundland, 1990 (Dollars)

Decile	1	2	3	4	5	6	7	8	9	10
Social Services (excl. CPP)	5,438	10,474	14,299	12,167	12,189	14,394	13,608	11,148	9,830	9,726
CPP/QPP	429	1,549	1,973	1,919	1,057	1,137	823	716	739	877
Sub total	16,618	21,500	27,094	27,019	26,624	29,752	30,139	29,270	30,330	33,831
Public Goods:										
Environment	439	400	482	560	587	625	670	709	749	775
General Services	1,551	1,415	1,705	1,981	2,074	2,210	2,368	2,506	2,650	2,741
Other (excl. interest charges)	394	360	433	503	527	562	602	637	673	696
Protection of Persons & Property	1,616	1,475	1,777	2,063	2,161	2,303	2,467	2,611	2,760	2,856
Research Establishments	108	98	119	138	144	154	165	174	184	191
Foreign Affairs & International Assistance	300	274	330	383	401	427	458	484	512	530
Sub total	4,407	4,022	4,846	5,628	5,894	6,280	6,729	7,121	7,529	7,789
Average Total	21,025	25,522	31,940	32,647	32,519	36,032	36,869	36,392	37,858	41,620
Average Tax	1,457	2,238	4,227	8,170	11,132	14,150	18,254	25,021	32,279	51,645
Average Net Benefits	19,567	23,284	27,713	24,477	21,387	21,882	18,615	11,371	5,580	-10,025

Table 6.5a2: What Families in Different Income Deciles on Average Get Out of Specific Government Expenditures, Prince Edward Island, 1990 (Dollars)

Decile	1	2	3	4	5	6	7	8	9	10
User Benefit Goods:										
Culture & Recreation	179	118	230	324	476	571	701	834	1,033	1,368
Health	2,186	2,574	2,891	3,148	2,844	3,088	3,137	3,645	3,733	3,793
Housing	488	452	430	402	391	344	319	298	291	297
Labour	54	57	137	217	378	445	593	731	946	1,073
Regional Planning & Development	19	24	37	48	56	70	77	91	98	207
Education	2,976	955	1,693	1,848	2,462	2,743	3,270	4,430	5,118	4,780
Resource Conservation & Industrial Development	865	726	1,144	1,780	1,798	2,023	2,333	2,558	3,122	4,719
of which: Trade & Industry	202	250	383	497	581	732	808	951	1,028	2,161
of which: Agriculture	162	57	213	605	496	512	658	608	988	1,434
of which: Other Resource Conservation & Industrial Development	500	419	548	678	721	779	868	999	1,106	1,125
Transportation & Communication	960	916	1,289	1,638	1,841	2,119	2,361	2,776	3,047	4,253

Table 6.5a2: What Families in Different Income Deciles on Average Get Out of Specific Government Expenditures, Prince Edward Island, 1990 (Dollars)

Decile	1	2	3	4	5	6	7	8	9	10
Social Services (excl. CPP)	3,919	10,785	10,086	10,632	7,966	8,795	9,259	9,121	8,349	10,129
CPP/QPP	573	1,129	1,365	1,626	1,466	1,065	839	1,265	690	1,115
Sub total	12,218	17,736	19,302	21,663	19,677	21,262	22,889	25,748	26,427	31,735
Public Goods:										
Environment	208	174	228	281	300	323	360	415	459	467
General Services	1,521	1,274	1,666	2,059	2,192	2,367	2,637	3,036	3,360	3,418
Other (excl. interest charges)	329	276	361	446	475	513	571	658	728	740
Protection of Persons & Property	1,592	1,333	1,744	2,156	2,294	2,477	2,761	3,178	3,517	3,577
Research Establishments	51	42	55	69	73	79	88	101	112	114
Foreign Affairs & International Assistance	221	185	242	299	318	343	383	441	488	496
Sub total	3,921	3,285	4,296	5,310	5,651	6,103	6,800	7,828	8,663	8,812
Average Total	16,139	21,021	23,598	26,973	25,328	27,365	29,689	33,577	35,091	40,547
Average Tax	875	1,526	3,699	5,992	9,661	12,762	16,274	20,376	26,246	45,266
Average Net Benefits	15,265	19,495	19,899	20,981	15,667	14,602	13,416	13,201	8,845	-4,719

Table 6.5a3: What Families in Different Income Deciles on Average Get Out of Specific Government Expenditures, Nova Scotia, 1990 (Dollars)

Decile	1	2	3	4	5	6	7	8	9	10
User Benefit Goods:										
Culture & Recreation	170	121	234	326	472	616	739	860	1,035	1,384
Health	2,866	3,423	3,345	3,965	3,603	3,938	4,039	4,444	4,432	4,527
Housing	368	319	329	292	294	273	246	213	223	221
Labour	69	100	246	347	514	679	928	1,148	1,402	1,712
Regional Planning & Development	38	57	87	107	142	169	159	187	244	411
Education	3,271	1,293	1,238	2,358	2,561	3,167	3,901	4,471	4,773	4,604
Resource Conservation & Industrial Development	489	476	671	781	963	1,194	1,267	1,430	1,505	2,157
of which: Trade & Industry	111	168	256	312	417	495	466	549	714	1,203
of which: Agriculture	11	0	69	0	68	146	184	204	108	273
of which: Other Resource Conservation & Industrial Development	367	308	346	468	479	553	617	677	683	680
Transportation & Communication	781	776	978	1,294	1,451	1,712	1,831	2,055	2,275	2,813

Table 6.5a3: What Families in Different Income Deciles on Average Get Out of Specific Government Expenditures, Nova Scotia, 1990 (Dollars)

Decile	1	2	3	4	5	6	7	8	9	10
Social Services (excl. CPP)	3,980	9,863	8,836	9,204	7,361	7,975	7,332	6,430	6,530	5,681
CPP/QPP	761	1,720	1,660	2,416	1,587	1,689	1,244	1,093	995	1,186
Sub total	12,793	18,148	17,624	21,089	18,949	21,412	21,686	22,332	23,413	24,694
Public Goods:										
Environment	385	323	363	491	502	580	647	710	716	713
General Services	1,704	1,431	1,608	2,173	2,221	2,567	2,864	3,142	3,169	3,157
Other (excl. interest charges)	315	265	297	402	411	475	529	581	586	584
Protection of Persons & Property	3,084	2,590	2,910	3,932	4,020	4,645	5,183	5,686	5,735	5,714
Research Establishments	111	93	105	142	145	167	187	205	207	206
Foreign Affairs & International Assistance	241	202	227	307	314	363	404	444	448	446
Sub total	5,841	4,904	5,510	7,447	7,613	8,797	9,815	10,768	10,859	10,821
Average Total	18,634	23,052	23,134	28,535	26,562	30,209	31,501	33,100	34,272	35,515
Average Tax	973	2,229	5,481	7,323	11,554	15,239	19,057	24,073	31,635	50,991
Average Net Benefits	17,661	20,824	17,653	21,213	15,009	14,969	12,444	9,027	2,637	-15,476

Table 6.5a4: What Families in Different Income Deciles on Average Get Out of Specific Government Expenditures, New Brunswick, 1990 (Dollars)

Decile	1	2	3	4	5	6	7	8	9	10
User Benefit Goods:										
Culture & Recreation	224	159	304	431	626	811	969	1,137	1,357	1,831
Health	3,770	4,513	4,345	5,247	4,780	5,184	5,298	5,873	5,809	5,989
Housing	484	420	427	386	391	360	323	282	292	293
Labour	91	132	319	459	681	894	1,218	1,517	1,837	2,265
Regional Planning & Development	50	76	114	141	189	222	209	248	319	543
Education	4,302	1,705	1,608	3,120	3,397	4,169	5,117	5,908	6,256	6,091
Resource Conservation & Industrial Development	643	628	872	1,033	1,278	1,571	1,662	1,890	1,972	2,854
of which: Trade & Industry	145	221	333	414	553	651	611	726	936	1,592
of which: Agriculture	14	0	89	0	91	192	241	270	141	362
of which: Other Resource Conservation & Industrial Development	483	407	450	620	635	728	809	895	895	900
Transportation & Communication	1,028	1,024	1,270	1,713	1,926	2,254	2,401	2,716	2,981	3,722

Table 6.5a4: What Families in Different Income Deciles on Average Get Out of Specific Government Expenditures, New Brunswick, 1990 (Dollars)

Decile	1	2	3	4	5	6	7	8	9	10
Social Services (excl. CPP)	5,235	13,005	11,478	12,180	9,766	10,498	9,617	8,497	8,558	7,516
CPP/QPP	1,001	2,268	2,156	3,197	2,106	2,224	1,631	1,445	1,304	1,569
Sub total	16,828	23,930	22,894	27,907	25,140	28,185	28,445	29,512	30,685	32,673
Public Goods:										
Environment	271	193	264	324	351	403	426	433	439	472
General Services	1,468	1,045	1,432	1,755	1,900	2,180	2,307	2,344	2,376	2,555
Other (excl. interest charges)	412	293	402	493	534	612	648	658	667	718
Protection of Persons & Property	3,596	2,559	3,507	4,299	4,654	5,341	5,652	5,742	5,821	6,259
Research Establishments	122	87	119	145	157	181	191	194	197	212
Foreign Affairs & International Assistance	274	195	267	327	354	406	430	437	443	476
Sub total	6,142	4,371	5,990	7,344	7,949	9,123	9,655	9,808	9,943	10,692
Average Total	22,970	28,301	28,884	35,251	33,089	37,309	38,100	39,320	40,629	43,364
Average Tax	709	2,323	4,869	7,589	12,513	15,115	20,134	24,047	31,624	54,124
Average Net Benefits	22,261	25,977	24,015	27,663	20,575	22,194	17,966	15,273	9,005	-10,759

Table 6.5a5: What Families in Different Income Deciles on Average Get Out of Specific Government Expenditures, Quebec, 1990 (Dollars)

Decile	1	2	3	4	5	6	7	8	9	10
User Benefit Goods:										
Culture & Recreation	189	164	200	278	369	467	559	691	870	1,265
Health	2,129	3,143	3,270	3,219	3,369	3,200	3,607	3,460	3,684	3,932
Housing	464	441	410	383	345	330	294	290	259	262
Labour	22	62	122	238	317	441	529	668	862	1,117
Regional Planning & Development	25	37	54	66	99	109	125	149	169	334
Education	2,837	1,168	1,556	1,863	2,976	2,839	3,678	3,865	4,626	4,432
Resource Conservation & Industrial Development	269	348	408	556	814	750	952	963	1,131	1,907
of which: Trade & Industry	60	90	131	163	243	267	308	365	415	820
of which: Agriculture	16	98	79	162	294	204	315	263	341	699
of which: Other Resource Conservation & Industrial Development	192	161	198	230	277	279	329	334	374	387
Transportation & Communication	641	640	822	1,001	1,330	1,428	1,670	1,857	2,117	3,116

Table 6.5a5: What Families in Different Income Deciles on Average Get Out of Specific Government Expenditures, Quebec, 1990 (Dollars)

Decile	1	2	3	4	5	6	7	8	9	10
Social Services (excl. CPP)	4,340	9,382	9,039	8,125	7,034	6,844	6,661	5,620	5,572	5,142
CPP/QPP	114	1,062	1,731	1,558	1,541	1,256	1,241	1,111	1,058	911
Sub total	11,029	16,447	17,611	17,287	18,192	17,663	19,317	18,673	20,349	22,419
Public Goods:										
Environment	531	445	546	637	765	771	910	923	1,035	1,070
General Services	1,375	1,152	1,414	1,649	1,980	1,997	2,358	2,392	2,680	2,771
Other (excl. interest charges)	318	266	327	381	458	462	545	553	620	641
Protection of Persons & Property	1,201	1,006	1,235	1,440	1,729	1,744	2,059	2,089	2,340	2,420
Research Establishments	122	102	125	146	176	177	209	212	238	246
Foreign Affairs & International Assistance	223	187	229	267	321	324	382	388	434	449
Sub total	3,771	3,159	3,876	4,522	5,428	5,475	6,464	6,557	7,347	7,598
Average Total	14,800	19,605	21,487	21,809	23,621	23,138	25,781	25,230	27,696	30,017
Average Tax	408	2,051	4,989	8,886	13,195	18,138	22,547	29,099	37,113	63,854
Average Net Benefits	14,392	17,554	16,498	12,923	10,426	5,000	3,234	-3,868	-9,417	-33,838

Table 6.5a6: What Families in Different Income Deciles on Average Get Out of Specific Government Expenditures, Ontario, 1990 (Dollars)

Decile	1	2	3	4	5	6	7	8	9	10
User Benefit Goods:										
Culture & Recreation	165	162	274	405	526	642	760	918	1,111	1,493
Health	3,149	3,976	4,007	3,850	4,039	4,213	4,539	4,923	4,873	5,265
Housing	349	321	305	292	266	254	230	208	200	203
Labour	26	57	122	218	300	375	460	572	728	876
Regional Planning & Development	43	67	96	113	129	145	160	182	193	416
Education	3,048	1,873	1,913	2,299	3,100	3,628	4,072	4,684	5,310	4,930
Resource Conservation & Industrial Development	329	364	516	601	685	695	758	906	937	1,397
of which: Trade & Industry	76	119	169	199	228	256	283	321	341	733
of which: Agriculture	45	46	110	132	146	101	105	176	169	220
of which: Other Resource Conservation & Industrial Development	208	199	237	269	311	338	370	409	428	444
Transportation & Communication	585	651	826	960	1,111	1,224	1,337	1,502	1,599	2,313

Table 6.5a6: What Families in Different Income Deciles on Average Get Out of Specific Government Expenditures, Ontario, 1990 (Dollars)

Decile	1	2	3	4	5	6	7	8	9	10
Social Services (excl. CPP)	5,910	9,823	8,227	6,521	5,516	5,656	5,375	4,928	4,470	4,800
CPP/QPP	434	2,223	2,229	1,793	1,422	1,324	1,358	1,130	801	1,342
Sub total	14,038	19,517	18,517	17,052	17,094	18,157	19,049	19,953	20,222	23,035
Public Goods:										
Environment	442	422	504	571	661	719	788	870	911	943
General Services	1,053	1,006	1,200	1,361	1,574	1,713	1,876	2,071	2,168	2,247
Other (excl. interest charges)	361	345	412	467	540	588	644	711	744	771
Protection of Persons & Property	1,622	1,550	1,849	2,097	2,426	2,640	2,891	3,191	3,341	3,462
Research Establishments	103	98	117	133	154	168	184	203	212	220
Foreign Affairs & International Assistance	218	209	249	282	326	355	389	429	450	466
Sub total	3,799	3,630	4,332	4,911	5,681	6,183	6,771	7,475	7,826	8,109
Average Total	17,837	23,147	22,848	21,963	22,775	24,340	25,820	27,428	28,049	31,144
Average Tax	1,195	4,420	9,578	14,907	19,800	24,942	29,903	37,282	46,288	84,157
Average Net Benefits	16,642	18,727	13,271	7,056	2,975	-602	-4,083	-9,854	-18,239	-53,013

Table 6.5a7: What Families in Different Income Deciles on Average Get Out of Specific Government Expenditures, Manitoba, 1990 (Dollars)

Decile	1	2	3	4	5	6	7	8	9	10
User Benefit Goods:										
Culture & Recreation	375	370	464	623	744	843	1,019	1,178	1,351	1,922
Health	3,237	3,986	3,942	4,367	4,407	4,364	4,267	4,791	4,436	5,069
Housing	366	331	317	288	273	241	213	212	200	215
Labour	35	60	126	195	296	374	520	617	716	874
Regional Planning & Development	86	102	163	212	219	270	289	320	373	769
Education	3,822	1,439	1,573	2,184	3,597	4,074	4,207	4,864	4,424	4,764
Resource Conservation & Industrial Development	911	814	1,046	1,343	1,404	1,638	1,816	1,655	1,922	2,990
of which: Trade & Industry	151	180	287	374	387	476	510	565	659	1,357
of which: Agriculture	540	463	557	725	723	846	961	713	895	1,231
of which: Other Resource Conservation & Industrial Development	220	171	202	244	295	316	345	378	368	402
Transportation & Communication	717	675	931	1,178	1,334	1,527	1,676	1,855	1,996	3,059

Table 6.5a7: What Families in Different Income Deciles on Average Get Out of Specific Government Expenditures, Manitoba, 1990 (Dollars)

Decile	1	2	3	4	5	6	7	8	9	10
Social Services (excl. CPP)	4,322	10,153	7,907	7,776	7,396	6,180	4,445	6,191	5,466	5,704
CPP/QPP	415	1,371	1,875	2,296	1,732	1,636	1,001	1,293	946	1,420
Sub total	14,285	19,300	18,345	20,462	21,403	21,147	19,452	22,975	21,831	26,786
Public Goods:										
Environment	449	349	412	499	602	646	706	772	753	821
General Services	1,289	1,002	1,182	1,432	1,728	1,853	2,024	2,213	2,159	2,355
Other (excl. interest charges)	228	177	209	253	306	328	358	391	382	417
Protection of Persons & Property	1,835	1,427	1,683	2,039	2,460	2,638	2,882	3,151	3,073	3,353
Research Establishments	95	74	87	106	128	137	150	164	160	174
Foreign Affairs & International Assistance	262	204	241	291	352	377	412	450	439	479
Sub total	4,158	3,234	3,815	4,622	5,576	5,979	6,531	7,140	6,965	7,598
Average Total	18,444	22,534	22,159	25,084	26,979	27,126	25,982	30,116	28,796	34,384
Average Tax	1,040	2,557	6,480	10,018	12,729	17,461	22,198	26,849	33,657	61,159
Average Net Benefits	17,404	19,977	15,679	15,066	14,250	9,665	3,785	3,266	-4,861	-26,775

Table 6.5a8: What Families in Different Income Deciles on Average Get Out of Specific Government Expenditures, Saskatchewan, 1990 (Dollars)

Decile	1	2	3	4	5	6	7	8	9	10
User Benefit Goods:										
Culture & Recreation	298	310	431	533	646	744	852	983	1,193	1,691
Health	3,143	4,027	4,088	4,450	4,507	4,405	4,389	5,015	4,898	5,010
Housing	709	665	635	570	553	518	480	451	442	446
Labour	37	48	96	140	195	258	350	396	511	621
Regional Planning & Development	25	28	42	56	69	86	83	101	121	217
Education	4,723	1,851	1,843	2,810	2,893	3,290	3,270	4,335	5,180	4,766
Resource Conservation & Industrial Development	2,577	2,199	2,729	4,221	4,427	3,682	4,379	5,829	5,730	6,814
of which: Trade & Industry	131	146	216	289	357	444	431	525	625	1,122
of which: Agriculture	1,996	1,685	2,092	3,406	3,503	2,626	3,332	4,575	4,348	4,943
of which: Other Resource Conservation & Industrial Development	451	369	420	525	567	612	617	729	756	749
Transportation & Communication	768	730	952	1,264	1,450	1,678	1,694	2,017	2,281	3,238

Table 6.5a8: What Families in Different Income Deciles on Average Get Out of Specific Government Expenditures, Saskatchewan, 1990 (Dollars)

Decile	1	2	3	4	5	6	7	8	9	10
Social Services (excl. CPP)	2,478	7,883	7,194	7,263	6,165	5,517	4,056	5,175	4,705	4,309
CPP/QPP	167	823	1,674	1,771	1,743	1,791	1,163	1,277	1,370	1,614
Sub total	14,926	18,563	19,684	23,077	22,647	21,969	20,717	25,579	26,430	28,727
Public Goods:										
Environment	431	353	402	503	543	586	590	697	723	716
General Services	1,469	1,202	1,369	1,713	1,850	1,995	2,011	2,376	2,464	2,441
Other (excl. interest charges)	284	232	265	331	358	386	389	459	476	472
Protection of Persons & Property	1,123	918	1,046	1,309	1,413	1,525	1,537	1,816	1,883	1,865
Research Establishments	137	112	128	160	173	186	188	222	230	228
Foreign Affairs & International Assistance	272	222	253	317	342	369	372	440	456	452
Sub total	3,715	3,040	3,464	4,331	4,678	5,046	5,086	6,011	6,233	6,174
Average Total	18,641	21,603	23,148	27,408	27,326	27,016	25,803	31,589	32,663	34,901
Average Tax	983	2,380	5,521	8,912	12,892	17,867	21,100	26,052	33,939	62,549
Average Net Benefits	17,658	19,223	17,627	18,496	14,434	9,148	4,703	5,538	-1,276	-27,648

Table 6.5a9: What Families in Different Income Deciles on Average Get Out of Specific Government Expenditures, Alberta, 1990 (Dollars)

Decile	1	2	3	4	5	6	7	8	9	10
User Benefit Goods:										
Culture & Recreation	235	346	453	567	651	802	923	1,098	1,307	1,698
Health	2,777	3,955	3,755	4,023	3,824	4,170	4,641	4,406	4,623	4,873
Housing	548	487	470	423	400	374	324	319	286	300
Labour	38	78	145	224	304	384	465	574	701	896
Regional Planning & Development	49	62	89	115	134	171	198	248	291	530
Education	3,945	2,263	2,585	2,449	2,919	3,565	3,876	3,968	4,158	4,985
Resource Conservation & Industrial Development	2,016	2,188	2,439	3,083	3,039	3,779	3,899	3,937	4,000	4,306
of which: Trade & Industry	82	103	150	192	224	287	332	416	488	887
of which: Agriculture	735	937	940	1,421	1,145	1,584	1,496	1,436	1,293	1,053
of which: Other Resource Conservation & Industrial Development	1,199	1,148	1,349	1,470	1,670	1,907	2,072	2,085	2,220	2,366
Transportation & Communication	792	891	1,162	1,382	1,596	1,944	2,192	2,496	2,814	4,048

Table 6.5a9: What Families in Different Income Deciles on Average Get Out of Specific Government Expenditures, Alberta, 1990 (Dollars)

Decile	1	2	3	4	5	6	7	8	9	10
Social Services (excl. CPP)	3,425	7,856	7,128	6,142	4,874	4,547	4,844	4,301	4,599	4,729
CPP/QPP	169	1,097	1,306	1,189	860	879	1,085	1,004	1,010	1,175
Sub total	16,010	21,410	21,972	22,682	21,637	24,395	26,347	26,287	27,790	31,844
Public Goods:										
Environment	432	414	486	530	602	687	746	751	800	853
General Services	1,069	1,023	1,203	1,311	1,489	1,701	1,847	1,859	1,979	2,109
Other (excl. interest charges)	351	336	395	430	489	559	607	611	650	693
Protection of Persons & Property	1,369	1,311	1,541	1,679	1,907	2,178	2,366	2,381	2,535	2,702
Research Establishments	150	143	169	184	209	238	259	261	277	296
Foreign Affairs & International Assistance	230	220	259	282	320	366	398	400	426	454
Sub total	3,600	3,447	4,053	4,416	5,016	5,729	6,222	6,263	6,667	7,107
Average Total	19,610	24,857	26,024	27,097	26,653	30,124	32,570	32,550	34,456	38,951
Average Tax	1,152	3,102	6,867	10,971	14,752	20,330	25,193	32,961	41,931	72,678
Average Net Benefits	18,458	21,755	19,158	16,126	11,901	9,794	7,376	-411	-7,475	-33,727

Table 6.5a10: What Families in Different Income Deciles on Average Get Out of Specific Government Expenditures, British Columbia, 1990 (Dollars)

Decile	1	2	3	4	5	6	7	8	9	10
User Benefit Goods:										
Culture & Recreation	91	124	233	365	513	672	788	880	1,057	1,357
Health	2,843	3,860	3,863	3,667	3,778	3,903	4,008	4,587	4,599	5,008
Housing	177	160	153	144	142	124	112	106	103	104
Labour	28	41	84	132	181	258	322	347	462	578
Regional Planning & Development	36	45	66	90	120	117	130	174	187	323
Education	4,255	1,620	1,220	2,099	2,767	3,835	3,831	4,844	5,265	5,288
Resource Conservation & Industrial Development	493	506	551	775	856	846	928	1,126	1,251	1,594
of which: Trade & Industry	78	97	140	192	255	250	278	372	400	690
of which: Agriculture	26	119	50	182	136	68	68	107	170	198
of which: Other Resource Conservation & Industrial Development	389	290	362	401	465	529	582	647	682	707
Transportation & Communication	517	506	715	914	1,165	1,252	1,398	1,720	1,856	2,622

Table 6.5a10: What Families in Different Income Deciles on Average Get Out of Specific Government Expenditures, British Columbia, 1990 (Dollars)

Decile	1	2	3	4	5	6	7	8	9	10
Social Services (excl. CPP)	3,296	8,767	8,678	6,443	6,286	5,032	5,009	5,692	4,787	5,719
CPP/QPP	216	1,409	2,248	1,807	1,535	1,191	1,036	1,532	813	1,180
Sub total	11,951	17,039	17,810	16,435	17,343	17,231	17,562	21,008	20,380	23,773
Public Goods:										
Environment	384	286	357	396	459	522	575	639	674	698
General Services	1,111	829	1,034	1,145	1,329	1,512	1,664	1,850	1,949	2,021
Other (excl. interest charges)	256	191	238	263	306	348	383	425	448	465
Protection of Persons & Property	1,384	1,032	1,288	1,426	1,656	1,883	2,073	2,304	2,428	2,517
Research Establishments	135	100	125	139	161	183	202	224	236	245
Foreign Affairs & International Assistance	242	181	225	250	290	330	363	403	425	441
Sub total	3,513	2,619	3,267	3,618	4,201	4,777	5,258	5,845	6,160	6,386
Average Total	15,464	19,658	21,077	20,053	21,543	22,008	22,820	26,854	26,540	30,159
Average Tax	1,158	3,038	6,385	11,136	16,232	19,841	25,008	30,298	38,050	66,297
Average Net Benefits	14,306	16,619	14,692	8,917	5,311	2,167	-2,187	-3,444	-11,510	-36,138

Appendix A: Glossary

Culture and Recreation:

Spending on culture and recreation includes expenditure on archives, historic sites, art galleries, libraries, centres for the performing arts, cinematography, zoos, stadiums, community centres, swimming pools, parks and playgrounds, amateur sports, and other miscellaneous leisure activities. Also included are the administrative costs of departments and agencies whose activites fall under culture and recreation, grants in aid of culture and recreation, and expenditures on facilities.

Education:

Outlays on elementary and secondary education, post-secondary education, and other related activities fall under this function. Elementary and secondary education spans from kindergarten to senior matriculation including technical and vocational training given at these levels, native schools, and schools for the handicapped. Other outlays included in elementary and secondary education are expenses on general administration, equipment, supplies, the registry of teachers, and the construction of buildings.

Post-secondary education comprises expenditures on universities, other post-secondary institutions (teachers' colleges, advanced technical instiitiutes, junior colleges, music conservatories, schools specializing in the instruction and training of artists, and nursing education provided by colleges and universities), bursaries and scholarships.

Other activities related to education include spending on the general administration of the education department, research activities related to education, official languages training, and the teacher apprenticeship program.

Environment:

Expenditure on the environment encompasses all spending pertaining to water purification and supply, sewage and waste garbage collection and disposal, pollution control, and other miscellaneous related activities.

Foreign Affairs and International Assistance:

Expenditures related to the formal relations of Canada with other sovereign states fall under foreign affairs and international assistance. This category also includes contributions made with the purpose of stimulating economic development and improving social conditions in foreign countries.

General Government Services:

Four categories fall under this function. The first, executive and legislative, covers expenses related to political and law enactment, the Govenor General, the Lieutenant Govenor, the Prime Minister, the Premiers, Members of Parliament, Members of the provincial Legislative Assemblies, maintenance of the legislatures and other related activities.

The second category, administrative, comprises all spending on administration that cannot be allocated to more specific sub-functions.

The third accounts for contributions to government-operated and non-government-operated pension plans.

The last is a residual category for expenditures of a general nature that cannot be allocated to more specific functions. This covers outlays on general insurance, general accident and damage claims, fire and liability insurance, court litigations, general purpose grants to organizations and individuals that cannot be more specifically allocated, inter-government services, conventions, et cetera.

General Purpose Transfers:

General purpose transfers takes into account all forms of general purpose transfers paid to other levels of government. At the federal level this includes statutory subsidies, federal corporation income tax on privately owned public utilities, payments in respect of reciprocal taxation, equalization payments, grants in lieu of taxes, and other miscellaneous general purpose transfers. At the provincial level this includes grants in lieu of taxes and other miscellaneous general purpose transfers.

Health:

Included under health are expenditures on hospital, medical, and preventive care. Hospital care encompasses expenditures on all types of hospital services in both general and specialized hospitals, including government hospitals, with the exception of national defence and veterans' hospitals and transfers to private hospitals. It also covers expenditures related to nursing schools attached to hospitals unless under the responsibility of the Department of Education.

Medical care covers outlays on general medical care including dental and out-patient services. Preventive care provides for spending on the prevention of diseases and the mitigation of their effects. It covers public health clinics, communicable disease control services, health, food and drug inspection services, nursing, nutrition and hygene advisory programs and research, and research on disease.

Other outlays covered by health are expenditures on certain rehabilitation programs, the administration of the health department, collection of health statistics, clinics treating the mentally retarded, laboratory and diagnostic services, and grants to health organizations.

Housing:

Housing covers outlays pertaining to the improvement of the housing stock, the operation and the maintenance of government rental housing, research, general administration of departments and agencies with housing related activities, other expenses related to housing (such as transfer payments to owners of rental housing so that they can offer affordable housing and transfer payments to persons, corporations or other to aid in augmenting the existing housing stock), and home-buyer assistance.

Interest Payments:

This covers interest payments resulting from government borrowings charges, other than administrative, pertaining to servicing of the public debt.

Labour:

Labour accounts for spending related to labour, employment, immigration, and special retraining services. Labour and employment covers outlays regarding the development and promotion of labour relations and fair employment conditions. It also covers the costs of employment agencies such as the National Employment Service and other similar government agencies and institutions, as well as outlays incurred in the application of employment standards and minimum wage laws.

Immigration accounts for spending on the promotion of immigration and assistance to immigrants.

Special retraining services covers outlays made to upgrade labour skills. The major program along these lines is the Federal Manpower Training Program.

Administrative expenditures of government departments whose activities fall under labour are also included.

Resource Conservation and Industrial Development:

Expenditures on agriculture, fish and game, forestry, mines, oil and gas, trade and industry, tourism, and water are included under natural resources. Agriculture is comprised of outlays pertaining to agricultural research and development, drainage and irrigation of farmland, protection, inspection and quality control, the control, regulation, promotion, and marketing of farm products, as well as subsidies, grants, and bonuses in support of agricultural organizations.

Fish and game expenses include outlays on research in fish and wildlife pathology, control and regulation of fishing and hunting activities, and subsidies and bonuses to commercial fishers and hunters.

Forestry expenses cover outlays on the inspection and survey of fire control, forest resources and ranging, reforestation, research into tree diseases, marketing of forest products, and grants to forestry oriented organizations.

Mines covers spending on the control, regulation, construction, and promotion of mining, geological, and mineralogicial survey and research, bonuses, and subsidies in support of mining activities.

Oil and gas includes expenditures on research, exploration, and development of oil and gas resources, along with outlays on the construction of field roads, promotion of oil and gas products, and compensation payments to refineries paying world prices for imported oil or oil derived from the tar sands.

Under trade and industry are found outlays pertaining to the promotion, protection, and development of general industrial and commercial activities; included are the expenditures of the Corporate Affairs Branch of the federal department of Consumer and Corporate Affairs, the Tariff Board, the Foreign Investment Review Agency, as well as expenditures on industrial parks and assistance of industrial development, and the outlays of provincial programs such as the registry of companies and corporate affairs.

Outlays on tourist bureaus, camping sites, and the promotion of tourism and convention facilities fall under tourism.

Water includes outlays related to hydraulic survey and research, the control and regulation of dams, hydraulic power installations, and flood control measures.

Other natural resource outlays include administrative expenditures of government departments related to the forementioned categories and general outlays on resource conservation.

Other:

This function serves as a residual for all expenditures that cannot be correctly identified as belonging to any one particular function. At the federal and provincial levels this includes transfer payments to their own enterprises.

Protection of Persons and Property:

This function is composed of seven sub-functions. The first, national defence, covers outlays on the armed forces, installations, military colleges, and military bases—including hospitals and schools on military bases and defence reserves.

The second, courts of law, encompasses outlays on all aspects of the judicial system from the Supreme Court to Family Court, and from prosecutors to jurors.

The third, correction and rehabilitation, accounts for spending on the incarceration and rehabilitation of all convicted and sentenced individuals in penitentiaries, jails, and other detention establishments, as well as outlays on probation services.

The fourth, policing, covers all expenditures pertaining to the maintenance of law and order; this includes the police force, which comprises the formation, maintenance, and equipment of police forces, specialized training establishments, transportation and communications, laboratory equipment, and outlays on forensic science.

The fifth sub-function, firefighting, includes outlays on the prevention, investigation, and extinction of fires.

Regulatory measures covers spending on a variety of services provided to protect the individual or groups of individuals and property against negligence, exploitation, and abuse. Where the purpose of the program is to protect a specific industry or activity it is classified under the same function as the industry or activity.

The seventh sub-function, other, covers outlays for special measures taken to handle emergency situations and for permanent organizations established to deal with such contingencies.

Regional Planning and Development:

Regional development comprises expenditures on planning and zoning, community development, urbarn renewal, and land rehabilitation.

Research Establishments:

This function comprises expenditures on research councils and organizations such as the National Research Council and Atomic Energy of Canada whose major activities are pure or applied science research.

Social Services:

Social services is comprised of social welfare and social security. Social welfare spending encompasses outlays on general assistance programs such as those for the old-aged, unemployed, needy persons, blind, and disabled, outlays related to welfare agencies, and the provision of services to the elderly and children, and legal aid and homes for the elderly. Other social welfare outlays are non-statutory payments to victims of natural disasters and payments whose amounts are indeterminate, such as criminal injury compensation, as well as administrative costs and other miscellaneous expenditures.

Social security covers contributions to the Canada Pension Plan and the Quebec Pension Plan (where the government is the employer), outlays on non-contributory plans such as Old Age Security, labour force plans, unemployment insurance and workers' compensation, family allowance, including supplementary family allowance payments made by the province of Quebec, and veterans' benefits, which encompasses all expenses related to veterans' services including the cost of administration, pensions, and grants.

Transportation and Communications:

There are six sub-functions which comprise the function transportation and communications. The first of these, air, at the federal level consists of outlays on navigational, air traffic, and other related services, as well as the costs involved in operating subsidy payments to regional air carriers and municipal airports; at the provincial level it includes outlays on non-commercial operations of air services.

The second one, road, consists of expenditures on highways, secondary roads, boulevards, avenues, bridges, over- and under-passes, tunnels, ferries, maintenance (such as the removal of snow and other debris), and costs related to traffic control and parking.

The third, rail, accounts for outlays on research and the improvement and implementation of policies and programs, as well as subsidy payments to passenger service infrastructure and freight assistance in certain geographical regions.

The sub-function water accounts for outlays on navigational channels, canals, harbours, wharfs, ferries, the Coast Guard, and some northern transportation services.

The fifth sub-function, telecommunications, consists of expenditures on research, planning, and development of telecommunications requirements; included are expenditures on the Canadian Radio Television and Telecommunications Commission and other communications systems.

The final sub-function is a residual category for the remaining transport and communications outlays that cannot be identified as to belong to any one forementioned sub-function.

Appendix B: Methodology

Data

THE IDEAL DATA FOR THIS STUDY on government spending are annual expenditures classified by function, economic classification, and province for all three levels of government, federal, provincial, and local. Further requirements are that the data be consistent over time and that they be comparable across provinces. Statistics Canada's Financial Management System, compiled by the Public Institutions Division, has the data that best suit our needs. The Financial Management System's main objective is to ensure consistent and uniform data dealing with government financial transactions. The system incorporates not only government departments, but also regulatory and special funds, which perform functions similar to departments, but excludes the Canada Pension Plan.

Federal, Provincial, and Municipal Government Expenditure data, Statistics Canada 68-211, 68-207, and 68-204 respectively, are given both by function, on health care, education, and trade and industry, and by economic classification:

- goods and services
- salaries and wages
- other
- transfer payments to:
  - provincial governments

- local governments
- persons and noncommercial institutions
- business
- non-residents

Whereas provincial and municipal data are given by province, federal data are given on a national basis and must be apportioned by province; intergovernmental transfer payments are nevertheless given on a provincial basis.

Actual figures, including intergovernmental transfer payments, are available for the years 1970/71 to 1984/85 for both provincial and municipal government expenditures and up to 1986/87 for federal government expenditures. Detailed data by function are available for federal, provincial and municipal governments from the Public Institutions Division up to 1991/92; estimates for federal, provincial, and municipal government spending by function and economic classification are available for 1985/86 to 1987/88. A historical revision of government expenditure by function is available for the years 1965/66 to 1991/92 in Public Finance Historical Data 1965/66-1991/92 (catalogue 68-512); consolidated government expenditure is also given for the years up to 1990/91. Using both consolidated expenditure data and non consolidated data, we are able to estimate inter-governmental transactions (transfer payments and sales of goods and services) by function. Using this information, data on transfer payments to other levels of government found in the Provincial Economic Accounts (catalogue 13-213), detailed data available on federal government transfers under the Established Programs Financing and Canada Assistance Plan, and by analysing past values of transfer payments and their relations to total expenditure by function, we are able to estimate transfers to other levels of government by function for the years 1988/89 to 1990/91.

The following section looks at each individual function, and details the bases for provincial and territorial distribution of federal government spending.

Culture and Recreation

Culture and recreation is composed of three functions:

i. Recreation—covers outlays on stadiums, community centres, swimming pools, parks and playgrounds, et cetera.

ii. Culture—expenditures on archives, historic sites, art galleries, libraries, centres for the performing arts, zoos, et cetera.

iii. Other—administrative expenditures of departments and agencies whose activities fall under culture and recreation as well as expenditure on cinematography, amateur sport, and other miscellaneous activities.

The three levels of government have outlays corresponding to all three sub-functions.

Federal government expenditures under culture and recreation on salaries and wages, other goods and services, and transfers to persons and business are allocated to the provinces/territories by a series on salaries and wages paid by the federal government by province/territory within Canada or outside Canada. Any amount that is attributed outside Canada is then distributed to the provinces/territories according to their share of the population. The categories, other goods and services and transfers to persons and business are found to be highly correlated with salaries and wages. Thus, we assume that there is a fixed coefficient between salaries and wages and other goods and services on the one hand, and salaries and wages and transfers to persons and business on the other, thereby permitting these two categories to also be allocated according to the series on salaries and wages and population.

Education

The following sub-functions identify the major components of education:

i. Elementary and secondary education—covers outlays on kindergarten to senior matriculation including technical and vocational training given at these levels, native schools, schools for the handicapped, and expenses on general administration, equipment and supplies, registry of teachers, and the construction of buildings.

ii. Post-secondary education—includes outlays on universities, other post-secondary institutions, bursuries, and scholarships.

iii. Other—accounts for expenditures on the general administration of the education department, research activities related to education, the teacher apprenticeship training program, language training, et cetera.

Both federal and provincial government expenditures fall under all three sub-functions. Municipal government spending falls entirely under elementary and secondary education.

Federal spending on education is allocated by province/territory according to data on federal government direct expenditure on education obtained from a Statistics Canada publication, Financial Statistics of Education (catalogue 81-208). The sub-functions, elementary and secondary education, and other—which is small—are distributed according to data on elementary and secondary school education found in table 9 (op. cit., "Expenditure on Elementary and Secondary Education by Direct Source of Funds Canada and the Provinces"), and post-secondary education is allocated according to data on post-secondary, university, and non-university education taken from table 23 (op. cit., "Expenditure on Post-Secondary, Non-University and University, by Direct Source of Funds Canada and the Provinces").

Federal government transfers on education to other levels of government go nearly entirely to post-secondary education. The series on post-secondary education grants taken from Statistics Canada (catalogue 13-213, table 17, "Current Transfers to Other Levels of Government") is used to distribute federal government transfers on education to other levels of government.

Environment

Spending on the environment encompasses all spending pertaining to water purification and supply, sewage and waste garbage collection and disposal, pollution control, and other miscellaneous related activities.

All three levels of government spend on the environment. Federal outlays are distributed across the provinces/territories according to their share of the population.

Foreign Affairs and International Assistance

The federal government is the only level of government that has outlays on foreign affairs and international assistance. These are allocated to the provinces/territories according to their shares of the population.

General Government Services

Below are the classifications comprising general government services:

i. Executive and legislative—covers outlays related to political and law enactment, governor general, lieutenant governor, Prime Minister, Premiers, Members of Parliament, Members of the Legislative Assembly, maintenance of legislatures, et cetera.

ii. Administrative—comprises all spending on administration that cannot be allocated to a more specific sub-function.

iii. Pension plans—accounts for contributions to pension plans that are not operated by government, and payments under government-operated pension plans.

iv. Other—includes outlays on general insurance, inter-government services, conventions, et cetera.

Federal salaries and wages and other goods and services are allocated to the provinces/territories by a series on salaries and wages paid by the federal government by province/territory within Canada or outside Canada. Any amount that is attributed outside Canada is then distributed to the provinces/territories according to their shares of the population. We assume that there exists a fixed coefficient between salaries and wages, and other goods and services. The latter two are found to have a high correlation coefficient, 0.975. The other major entry, transfers to persons and non-commercial institutions, of which the largest component is government pension plan contributions, is apportioned by province according to the above series on salaries and wages and population. Pension contributions are related to salaries and wages.

Health

The four entries under health are:

> i. Hospital care—encompasses expenditures on all types of hospital services in both general and specialized hospitals. Included are government-owned hospitals excluding national defence and veterans' hospitals. Transfers to private hospitals are also covered in this sub-function.
>
> ii. Medical care—covers outlays on general medical care programs including dental and out-patient services.
>
> iii. Preventive care—provides for spending on the prevention of diseases and the mitigation of their effects. Included in this sub-function are expenditures on public health clinics, communicable disease control, health inspection services, nutrition and hygene programs, and research.
>
> iv. Other—covers outlays on certain rehabilitation programs, health department administration, collection of health statistics, clinics treating the mentally retarded, grants to health organizations, et cetera.

The federal, provincial, and municipal governments' health expenditures fall under all four sub-functions.

The series on the federal government's direct health expense by region obtained from a study undertaken by Health and Welfare Canada, National Health Expenditures in Canada 1975-1987 (table 77) is used to allocate federal government health expenditures net of transfer payments to other levels of government across provinces/territories. Series on federal health expenditures under the Established Programs Financing (EPF) and the Canada Assistance Plan (CAP) obtained from the *Green Book Tables—Provincial Government Health Expenditure and Related Federal Contributions Canada, the Provinces and the Territories, 1974/75 to 1990/91* (Health and Welfare Canada, July 1993) are used to distribute transfer payments on health to other levels of government across the provinces/territories.

Housing

The housing function comprises the following two sub-functions:

i. General assistance—covers expenditures pertaining to the improvement of the housing stock, the operation and maintenance of rental housing, research, general administration, and other expenses related to housing.

ii. Home-buyer assistance—provides for outlays paid to qualified persons to aid them in purchasing houses.

Federal and provincial government spending on housing falls under both sub-categories, while municipal governments' outlays fall entirely under general assistance.

Federal outlays are regionally distributed by three series. The first is a series on salaries and wages paid by the federal government by province/territory within Canada or outside Canada. Any amount that is attributed outside Canada is then distributed to the provinces/territories according to their shares of the population. The second, a series on transfers to business, specifically subsidies and capital assistance to non-agricultural and non-petroleum business, distributes transfers to business by province/territory. The latter series is taken from Statistics Canada, Provincial Economic Accounts (catalogue 13-213, table 14, "Government Transfer Payments to Business"). The third is a series on federal subsidies paid under the National Housing Agreement by region. It is used to allocate transfers to persons.

Interest Payments

Federal interest payments are allocated by province/territory by the series on federal interest payments obtained from Statistics Canada, Provincial Economic Accounts (catalogue 13-213, table 4, "Federal Government Revenue and Expenditure").

Labour

There are four sub-functions under labour:

> i. Labour and employment—covers outlays regarding the development and promotion of labour relations and fair employment conditions. This encompasses all government agencies and institutions pertaining to the application of employment standards, minimum wage laws, and national employment services.
>
> ii. Immigration—accounts for spending on the promotion of immigration and assistance to immigrants.
>
> iii. Other—includes administration expenditures of the departments providing services detailed in the labour function.
>
> iv. Special retraining services—covers expenditures made to upgrade labour skills, chiefly expenditures under the Federal Manpower Training Program.

Both Federal and Provincial Governments have expenditures that are included under all four sub-functions. Municipal governments have no labour spending.

Federal labour and employment and other are allocated by province according to a series on salaries and wages paid by federal government by province/territory, within Canada and outside Canada. Any amount apportioned outside Canada is re-allocated to the provinces/territories according to their shares of the population. Since salaries and wages are highly correlated with both other goods and services and transfers to persons and business, we assume that there exists a fixed coefficient between both salaries and wages and other goods and services, and transfers to persons and business. Special retraining services are allocated to the provinces/territories according their shares of the population. Immigration is distributed by the series from Statistics Canada, Destination of Immigrants (catalogue 11-010, table 11.3, "Immigration, by province of destination").

Other

This function serves as a residual category for all expenditures that cannot by correctly identified as belonging to any one particular function. Transfer payments to their own enterprises are included at the federal and provincial levels.

Federal government data on capital assistance obtained from the Provincial Economic Accounts (13-213) distributes transfers to own enterprises across the provinces/territories. Any "other" expenditures are allocated by province/territory according to the distribution of total federal government spending net of "other".

Protection of Persons and Property

Protection of persons and property is composed of seven sub-functions:

i. National defence—covers outlays on the armed forces, military bases, installations, military colleges, hospitals, et cetera.

ii. Courts of law—encompasses outlays on all aspects of the judicial system from the Supreme Court to family court, from prosecutors to jurors.

iii. Correction and rehabilitation—accounts for spending on all penitentiaries, jails, and other detention establishments, as well as on probation services.

iv. Policing—covers expenditures pertaining to the maintenance of law and order by police personnel; expenditure on forensic science is also included.

v. Firefighting—includes outlays on the prevention, investigation, and extinction of fires.

vi. Regulatory measures—encompasses spending on a variety of services provided to protect the individual or group of individuals and property against negligence, exploitation, and abuse.

vii. Other—covers outlays for special measures taken to handle emergency situations and for permanent organizations established to deal with such contingencies.

Municipal governments' expenses fall under courts of law, policing, firefighting, regulatory measures, and other. The provincial governments' outlays include, as well, correction and rehabilitation; the federal government's outlays include all seven sub-functions.

Defence is the major entry under federal protection of persons and property and is regionally allocated according to data found in the Canada Yearbook (11-402E) on National Defence expenditures by the federal government by region. The series on federal government expenditure on salaries and wages and on population by region are used to distribute the remaining expenditures under protection of persons and property by province/territory. Salaries and wages from the sub-functions other than National Defence on average consist of 65 per cent of the outlays on protection of persons and property net of national defence.

Research Establishments

Both federal and provincial governments spend on research establishments. These are expenditures on research councils and organizations, such as the National Research Council and Atomic Energy of Canada whose major activities are pure or applied science research.

Salaries and wages and other goods and services are regionally allocated by the series on federal payments on salaries and wages across areas and by the series on population. Transfer payments to persons and business are distributed across the provinces/territories according to a series on transfers to persons in the form of scholarships and grants (catalogue 13-213, table 13, "Government Transfer Payments to Persons"). Since transfer payments to business are negligible under this function, it is regionally allocated by the same series as transfer payments to persons.

Regional Planning and Development

Regional planning and development consists of expenditures on planning and zoning, community development, urban renewal, and land rehabilitation, and expenditures by departments and agencies such as the National Capital Commission, the Department of Regional Industrial Expansion—DRIE (the Department of Regional Economic Expansion—DREE), and the Department of Municipal Affairs.

All three levels of government spend on regional planning and development. At the federal level, salaries and wages and other goods and services are distributed across the provinces/territories by a series on the value added in manufacturing activity in each province/territory (catalogue 31-203). Transfers to business are regionally allocated by a series on federal government transfer payments to business (non-agricultural and non-petroleum) (catalogue 13-213, table 16, "Transfer Payments to Business").

Resource Conservation and Industrial Development

Outlays on resource conservation and industrial development are:

i. Agriculture—outlays pertaining to agricultural research and development, drainage and irrigation of farmland, protection, inspection and quality control, and the control, regulation, promotion, and marketing of farm products, as well as subsidies, grants, and bonuses in support of agricultural organizations.

ii. Fish and game—covers expenditures on research in fish and wildlife pathology, control and regulation of fishing and hunting activities, and subsidies and bonuses to commercial fishers and hunters.

iii. Forests—provides for outlays on the inspection and survey of fire control, forest resources and ranging, as well as on research pertaining to tree diseases, reforestation, marketing of forest products, and grants.

iv. Mines—outlays pertaining to the control, regulation, construction, and promotion of mining.

v. Oil and gas—includes expenditures on research, exploration and development, construction of field roads, promotion of oil and gas products, and compensation payments to refineries paying world prices for imported oil or oil derived from tar sands.

vii. Tourism—outlays on tourist bureaus, camping sites, and the promotion of tourism and convention facilities.

viii. Trade and industry—expenditure on the promotion, protection, and development of general industrial and commercial activities, outlays on relevant departments and agencies, and grants and subsidies. Also included are expenditures of the Corporate Affairs Branch of the federal department of Consumer and Corporate Affairs, the Tariff Board, and the Foreign Investment Review Agency, and at the provincial level the registry of companies, corporate affairs, et cetera. Also included are expenditures on industrial parks and assistance of industrial development.

ix. Water—outlays related to the control and regulation of dams, hydraulic power installations, and flood control measures.

x. Other resource conservation and industrial development—includes administrative expenditures of government departments whose activities are related to more than one sub-function, and general outlays on resource conservation.

Federal and provincial governments have outlays corresponding to all ten sub-functions; the municipal governments' outlays are on other resource conservation and industrial development and trade and industry.

Agriculture is distributed regionally according to the distribution of farm land across the country. Federal government expenditure on forestry is allocated regionally according to the distribution of forest land across the provinces/territories. Spending on mining is distributed by province/territory by a series on the marketable product from mining by province/territory. Fish, game, and other resource conservation and industrial development are allocated by federal government payments of salaries and wages by province/territory, within Canada and outside Canada. That amount allocated outside Canada is then attributed to the provinces/territories according to their shares of the population. The basis for distributing the entire amount spent on fish, game, and other by the series on salaries and wages and population is that there is a correlation coefficient of 0.96 between the sum of salaries and wages on the remaining sub-functions and other goods and services and a coefficient of 0.87 between the sum of salaries and wages and the sum of transfers to persons and business.

Federal outlays on oil and gas are regionally allocated as follows. Salaries and wages and other goods and services are distributed across the provinces/territories by a series on oil and gas production across Canada. Both transfer payments to business and to persons (transfer payments to persons are negligible) are distributed according to a series on transfer payments to business constructed from the following data (catalogue 13-213, Table 14, "Transfer Payments to Business"):

- Payments to importers of crude oil and petroleum products
- Petroleum Compensation Fund payments
- Petroleum Incentives Program

Trade and industry and tourism salaries and wages and other goods and services are distributed across the provinces/territories by a series on the value added in manufacturing activity in each province/territory (catalogue 31-203). Transfer payments to business falling under trade and industry and tourism are distributed according to a series on federal government transfers to non-agricultural and non-petroleum business (catalogue 13-213, "Government Transfer Payments to Business").

Social Services

Social services has two sub-functions, social welfare and social security, which are further subdivided as follows:

Social Welfare

i. Social welfare assistance—covers outlays on general assistance programs, such as those for old age, the unemployed, needy persons, the blind, and the disabled.

ii. Social welfare services—outlays related to welfare agencies and the provision of services to the elderly and children, legal aid, homes for the elderly, et cetera.

iii. Ex-gratia pensions and allowances—these are non-statutory payments to victims of natural disasters and payments whose amounts are indeterminate, such as criminal injury compensation.

iv. Other—includes administrative and other expenditures which do not fit into the above three categories.

Social Security

i. Contribution plans—covers outlays pertaining to plans such as the Canada Pension Plan and the Quebec Pension Plan. Note that revenues and expenditures of the Canada Pension Plan are no longer included. Any CPP outlays pertain to the federal government's contribution as an employer.

ii. Non-contributory plans—includes spending related to plans such as Old Age Security.

iii. Labour force plans—accounts for outlays related to unemployment insurance and workers' compensation schemes.

iv. Family allowance—provides for payments made under the federal government Family Allowance Program and the supplementary family allowance payments made by the province of Quebec.

v. Veterans' benefits—encompasses all outlays related to veterans services including administrative cost, pensions and grants.

Municipal government expenditures are limited to social welfare, social welfare assistance and other. The provincial governments have entries under social welfare services and ex-gratia pensions and allowances. Non-contributory plans and veterans' benefits are the domain of the federal government.

Numerous series are used to distribute the federal outlays across the provinces/territories. Salaries and wages and other goods and services, which are highly correlated, are allocated by a series on federal government payments of salaries and wages by province/territory, within Canadà and outside Canada. Any amount allocated outside Canada is then attributed to the provinces/territories according to their shares of the population. Distributive series on the universal pension plan (CPP/QPP) (catalogue 86-507), old age security (catalogue 86-509), unemployment insurance (catalogue 86-506), family allowance (catalogue 86-508), and veterans' benefits (catalogue 13-213, "Government Transfer Payments to Persons": WWI & WWII pensions and war veterans' allowances) are used to allocate their corresponding transfer payments to persons. Workers' compensation and social welfare other are distributed according to the provincial distribution of the sum of the above distributed social services transfer payments to persons.

Transportation and Communications

Transportation and communications is comprised of six sub-functions:

i. Air—at the federal level this entry consists of outlays on navigational, air traffic, and other related services, as well as the costs involved in operating subsidy payments to regional air carriers and municipal airports. Included at the provincial level are outlays on non-commercial operations of air services.

ii. Road—expenditures on highways, secondary roads, boulevards, avenues, bridges, over- and under-passes, tunnels, ferries (operated by the highway departments), and maintenance such as removal of snow and other debris on roads.

iii. Rail—outlays on research, improvement, and implementation of policies and programs, as well as subsidy payments to passenger service infrastructure and freight assistance in certain geographical regions.

iv. Water—expenditures on navigational channels, canals, harbours, wharfs, ferries, the Coast Guard, and some northern transportation services.

v. Telecommunications—outlays on research, planning, and development of telecommunications requirements, as well as expenditures on the Canadian Radio-television and Telecommunications Commission and other commmunications systems.

vi. Other—residual expenditures on transportation and communications, which cannot be identified as to belong to any one particular sub-function.

The federal and provincial governments have entries under all six sub-functions, and municipal governments' outlays are on either road or other.

Federal salaries and wages and other goods and services, which are found to be highly correlated, and transfer payments to persons, which are neglible, are regionally allocated according to a series on federal government payments of salaries and wages by province/territory, within Canada and outside Canada. Any amount allocated outside Canada is then attributed to the provinces/territories according to their shares of the population. Transfers to business are distributed by a series on federal government subsidies and capital assistance directed to non-agricultural and non-petroleum business (catalogue 13-213, "Government Transfer Payments to Business").

General Purpose Transfers

This function includes all forms of general purpose transfer payments paid to other levels of government. At the federal level this category includes statutory subsidies, federal corporation income tax on privately owned public utilities, payments in respect of reciprocal taxation, equalization payments, grants in lieu of taxes, and other miscellaneous general purpose transfers. The provincial level includes grants in lieu of taxes and other miscellaneous general purpose transfers.

Federal government transfers to own enterprises are distributed to the provinces/territories by a series on capital assistance (catalogue 13-213, table, "Government transfer payments to business").

Funding versus spending

This study makes an important distinction between spending (expenditure) on a category and the funding of that category. The source of all revenues for every level of government is, of course, the taxpayer. However, our objective is to analyse how the various levels of government allocate the money they receive from taxpayers. Spending on a category by a level of government is just that: the provincial government of Newfoundland spent $379.85 million on education in the fiscal year 1980/1981. It does not convey any information as to which levels of government financed those $379.85 million. We estimate that the funding breakdown was as follows: the provincial government financed $231.35 million from own revenue sources, that is tax revenue, other revenue such as investment income and sales of goods and services, and from issuing debt, and the federal government financed $148.5 million.

Funding by a level of government on a function is defined as that level of government's spending on the category less any transfer payments from other levels of government directed to the category. In the above discussion, federal transfer payments to the provincial government are of two types: specific and general. Specific transfer payments are earmarked for expenditure on a particular category whereas general transfer payments are used at the discretion of the recipient government.

Two assumptions are made in order to distribute general transfer payments across functions. First, we assume that the recipient government, the provincial government in this case, makes no distinction between a dollar received from its tax collection and a dollar received as a general transfer. Consequently, we assume that general transfer payments are allocated across categories in the same proportion as the recipient government decides to spend across functions. In the analysis, the recipient government's decision to spend on a functions is estimated as spending net of specific transfer payments on the function.

We make a further assumption with regards to specific transfer payments. The sum of specific transfer payments from various levels of government on a function is assumed to be less than or equal to the amount spent on the function by the recipient government. Although transfer payments shown in the transferor's records should be the same as the amounts received, this is often not the case. This is due to the absence of uniform accounting practices, different year ends, and difficulties in allocating transfers to particular functions. Statistics Canada allocates transfer payments on the basis of real or apparent intent of the transferor.

Distribution of total spending by income groups

The study also addresses the issue of on whose behalf is government spending incurred. Government spending is distributed across families using distributive series derived from two Statistics Canada surveys, the Survey of Consumer Finance and the Family Expenditure Survey. The Survey of Consumer Finances covers 45,580 individual families (each is weighted so as to obtain the total number of families in the ten provinces), and details familiy characteristics and income. The Family Expenditure Survey gives information on family expenditure for 4,856 families.

Three series are derived from the Family Expenditure Survey: consumption of automotive fuel, recreation expenditure, and total consumption. An equation is estimated for each, using ordinary least squares. Since the definition of the head of the family differs between the surveys, the head of the family in the Family Expenditure Survey is redefined to be consistent with the definition used in the Survey of Consumer Finances.

The independent variables are:

- Income
- Income squared
- Education of the family's head (6 categories, 5 variables)
- Occupation of the family's head (13 categories, 12 variables)
- Housing (e.g., homeowner with mortgage) (5 categories, 4 variables)
- Family size
- Age of the head of the family

The estimated coefficients are then applied to the Survey of Consumer Finance data to obtain each family's consumption of auto fuel, recreation expenditure, and total consumption. These values are then used to derive distributive series across families.

Culture and Recreation

We assume that culture and recreation expenditures are made on behalf of those people who consume culture and recreation services. Thus, these expenditures should be allocated directly to them. Expenditures are distributed across families by the series, "Consumption of Recreation," derived from the Family Expenditure Survey, which covers everything from movies and ballets to camping equipment and stereos.

Education

Education is broken down into elementary and secondary and post-secondary. Essentially, we assume that education expenditures are made on behalf of students. All expenditures are assigned to families who have members receiving educational services. Elementary and secondary expenditures are distributed to families that have children between the ages of five and seventeen. The series used comes from the Survey of Consumer Finances. Post-secondary education is not as easily allocated. It is clear that on average those who attend a post-secondary institution have higher life-time earnings. However, students have below normal yearly incomes during their studies. Thus, allocating expenditures directly to students—sorted by their annual incomes—gives the impression of redistributing to the poor or low income groups, which is clearly not the case. Since we cannot in any ad hoc way use lifetime income data for one category and not for the others, the best series for this sub-function is the series on those attending post-secondary institutions based on data found in the Survey of Consumer Finances.

General Services

Under general government services no one specific group can be identified and thus they are distributed proportionately across individuals. The series on individuals is obtained from the Survey of Consumer Finances.

Health

While we recognize that there is some type of public good aspect to hospital expenditures, specific groups can be identified: those people who use hospital and medical services. Thus we assume that expenditures on health are made on behalf of those who consume health services, and furthermore, the expenditures are allocated to groups in proportion to the costs of providing the services they consume. Health is allocated by a series on families' expenditures on hospital expenditures and expenditures on general practicioners. This series is derived from two series. The first is obtained from a series on hospital expenditures by income class, which is derived by combining hospital expenditure by age group from Statistics Canada, catalogue 83-522E, "An Analysis of Hospital Expenditures in Canada", with population data from the Survey of Consumer Finances. The second is obtained by combining expenditure by adult or child on general practicioners by income class of the family with population data from the Survey of Consumer Finances.

Housing

No final policy has been adopted for housing; for the time being, housing expenditures are distributed by the series "Other Government Transfer Payments" from the Survey of Consumer Finances.

Labour

We assume that expenditures in this category are made on behalf of labour and thus are allocated directly to labour. Until a more appropriate series on wages is found we will use a series on wages and salaries from the Survey of Consumer Finances. As far as these expenditures are made to trainees and the unemployed, this series will understate expenditures made on behalf of the lower income groups.

Environment, Foreign Affairs and International Assistance, Other, Protection of Persons and Property, Research Establishments, Resource Conservation and Industrial Development net of Agriculture, Tourism, and Trade and Industry

The expenditures in these categories are essentially ones where specific groups cannot be identified. Included are categories that approach the definition of public goods, such as national defence, and groups that are clearly not public goods but for which no obvious way of allocating them exists. Thus, these expenditures are allocated proportionately across individuals. The series on individuals is based on data from the Survey of Consumer Finances.

Regional Planning and Development and Resource Conservation and Industrial Development (specifically Agriculture, Tourism, and Trade and Industry)

To the extent that these expenditures go directly into private hands, that portion should be allocated directly to business. Expenditures on agriculture are assumed to be made on behalf of farmers and thus are allocated directly to them. We distribute the expenditures equally across families reporting net farm self-employed income. The series is derived from the Survey of Consumer Finances.

Regional planning and development chiefly covers municipal public works and could be distributed on a per household basis. Trade and industry is a more direct help to business and could thus be distributed by a series on dividends. Fifty percent of the sum of regional planning and development and trade and industry (including tourism) is allocated by capital income and the remaining fifty percent is allocated across families by the series on total consumption. The first series come from the Survey of Consumer Finances and the second is derived from the Family Expenditure Survey.

Social Security

For all social security expenditures we assume that the expenditures are made on behalf of those who receive the transfers. We allocate the expenditures directly to the recipients in proportion to the amounts they receive. Five series are obtained from the Survey of Consumer Finances. These series are: Canada and Quebec pension plans, family allowance, old age security payments, unemployment insurance, and total government transfer payments.

Transportation and Communications

Expenditures under transportation and communications are broken down into two categories: highway and other. Highway expenditures are on highways, roads, and road maintenance. Other expenditures are on air, rail, water, et cetera. In allocating these expenditures we tried to identify those groups that benefit from these expenditures and assumed that it was on those groups' behalf that the expenditures were made.

Four groups are identified under the sub-function highway. Two per cent of highway expenditures are allocated to national defence as that is approximately the expenditure on defence as a percentage of Gross Domestic Product; this is a purely arbitrary rule as a criteria for allocation. National defence, being a public good, is distributed proportionately across individuals. Two other groups are non-users and road-users for which we follow Gillespie's method and allocate one third to non-users and two thirds to road-users. We assume that the non-user group that benefits are property owners, that is their property values are enhanced by access to roadways. This allocation is distributed by a series on capital income (this is the allocator of property taxes in our tax study) derived from the Family Expenditure Survey. The other group road-users can be further sub-divided into two groups: those who benefit from the lower prices of goods transported via roads and those who consume road services to travel, to go to work, et cetera. One third of the two thirds set aside for road-users is allocated to those benefiting from the lower price of transported goods by a series on total consumption from the Family Expenditure Survey. The remainder is allocated to consumption of road services, which is proxied by the consumption of automotive fuel. This series is derived from the Family Expenditure Survey. Other transportation is distributed equally across individuals.

Appendix C: Tabular Material

Note: Figures may not add up due to rounding.

Table C.1a: Federal Funding of Spending on Culture and Recreation (Millions of Dollars)

Year	Nfld	PEI	NS	NB	Que	Ont	Man	Sask	Alta	BC	Terr	Cda
1970	3	1	7	4	28	53	11	4	7	10	2	131
1975	14	3	24	12	91	163	20	13	24	35	5	403
1980	18	5	46	22	145	224	31	20	42	56	14	623
1985	27	10	67	34	221	353	47	27	72	92	19	968
1988	36	11	85	40	259	420	57	38	84	115	36	1,180
1990	36	12	93	48	285	482	66	44	92	128	16	1,302

Table C.1b: Provincial Funding of Spending on Culture and Recreation (Millions of Dollars)

Year	Nfld	PEI	NS	NB	Que	Ont	Man	Sask	Alta	BC	Terr	Cda
1970	2	1	2	5	37	61	10	6	11	14	1	150
1975	20	2	9	10	171	166	28	13	57	63	1	540
1980	16	4	24	21	223	274	30	38	187	86	5	909
1985	21	5	25	31	356	421	59	63	303	205	9	1,499
1988	25	5	38	30	368	565	61	71	255	141	9	1,568
1990	30	10	47	47	419	578	99	104	240	214	49	1,836

Table C.1c: Municipal Funding of Spending on Culture and Recreation (Millions of Dollars)

Year	Nfld	PEI	NS	NB	Que	Ont	Man	Sask	Alta	BC	Terr	Cda
1970	1	1	3	3	60	147	12	11	31	36	0	304
1975	11	1	7	13	174	356	51	31	90	117	2	855
1980	9	2	16	15	346	556	54	64	293	210	4	1,571
1985	19	4	38	27	475	883	78	89	273	313	19	2,218
1988	29	5	51	27	568	1,041	94	113	348	365	16	2,656
1990	30	7	66	31	697	1,390	198	141	450	453	16	3,478

Table C.1d: Total Funding of Spending on Culture and Recreation (Millions of Dollars)

Year	Nfld	PEI	NS	NB	Que	Ont	Man	Sask	Alta	BC	Terr	Cda
1970	5	3	13	12	125	261	33	21	49	60	3	584
1975	44	6	40	35	436	685	100	57	171	215	8	1,797
1980	44	11	85	58	714	1,054	116	121	522	353	24	3,103
1985	67	19	131	92	1,052	1,656	184	180	648	610	46	4,685
1988	90	21	174	98	1,195	2,025	213	221	687	621	60	5,404
1990	97	29	206	125	1,401	2,450	363	288	782	794	81	6,617

Table C.1e: Federal Government Expenditure on Culture and Recreation (Millions of Dollars)

	Nfld	PEI	NS	NB	Que	Ont	Man	Sask	Alta	BC	Terr	Cda
Gross expenditure	2	1	6	3	20	50	10	4	7	10	1	113
Transfer to provincial government	0	0	0	0	0	0	5	0	0	0	0	5
Transfer to municipal government	0	0	0	0	0	0	0	0	0	0	0	0
Net expenditure 1970	2	1	6	3	20	50	5	4	7	10	1	108
Gross expenditure	7	2	19	9	67	156	15	12	22	33	2	346
Transfer to provincial government	0	0	0	0	0	0	0	0	0	0	0	1
Transfer to municipal government	0	0	0	0	0	0	0	0	0	0	0	0
Net expenditure 1975	7	2	19	9	67	156	15	12	22	33	2	345
Gross expenditure	11	3	37	17	115	215	24	18	40	55	4	538
Transfer to provincial government	0	0	0	0	0	0	0	0	0	0	0	0
Transfer to municipal government	0	0	0	0	0	0	0	0	0	0	0	0
Net expenditure 1980	11	3	37	17	115	215	24	18	40	55	4	538

Table C.1e: Federal Government Expenditure on Culture and Recreation (Millions of Dollars)

	Nfld	PEI	NS	NB	Que	Ont	Man	Sask	Alta	BC	Terr	Cda
Gross expenditure	18	7	59	27	174	339	39	27	66	88	7	852
Transfer to provincial government	0	0	0	0	2	0	0	0	0	0	0	4
Transfer to municipal government	0	0	0	0	0	0	0	0	2	0	0	3
Net expenditure 1985	18	7	59	27	173	339	39	27	63	88	7	846
Gross expenditure	24	8	72	34	210	404	46	32	78	111	27	1,044
Transfer to provincial government	1	0	0	0	0	0	0	0	1	3	19	24
Transfer to municipal government	0	0	0	0	0	4	0	0	1	2	0	7
Net expenditure 1988	23	8	72	34	210	400	46	32	76	106	7	1,013
Gross expenditure	27	9	81	38	243	464	52	36	88	123	16	1,176
Transfer to provincial government	0	0	0	0	0	0	0	0	0	1	7	9
Transfer to municipal government	0	0	0	0	0	1	0	0	0	1	0	2
Net expenditure 1990	27	9	81	38	243	463	52	36	87	122	9	1,165

Table C.1f: Provincial Government Expenditure on Culture and Recreation (Millions of Dollars)

	Nfld	PEI	NS	NB	Que	Ont	Man	Sask	Alta	BC	Terr	Cda
Gross expenditure	2	1	3	5	37	57	15	6	9	11	2	148
Transfer to municipal government	0	0	0	0	3	1	0	0	1	1	0	7
Net expenditure 1970	2	1	3	5	34	56	15	6	8	10	1	142
Gross expenditure	25	3	14	8	166	134	32	13	54	56	3	507
Transfer to municipal government	0	0	4	0	9	16	0	0	21	15	0	67
Net expenditure 1975	25	3	9	8	156	118	32	12	32	41	3	440
Gross expenditure	21	6	28	18	232	238	31	31	177	72	16	870
Transfer to municipal government	0	0	4	0	37	15	4	4	10	11	0	86
Net expenditure 1980	21	6	24	18	195	222	28	27	166	62	16	784
Gross expenditure	26	7	27	23	374	346	57	53	285	193	20	1,410
Transfer to municipal government	0	0	7	0	55	31	6	5	88	0	0	192
Net expenditure 1985	25	7	20	23	319	315	51	48	197	193	20	1,218

Table C.1f: Provincial Government Expenditure on Culture and Recreation (Millions of Dollars)

	Nfld	PEI	NS	NB	Que	Ont	Man	Sask	Alta	BC	Terr	Cda
Gross expenditure	32	6	46	18	383	451	60	62	231	129	32	1,451
Transfer to municipal government	0	0	10	1	54	66	12	3	54	0	5	205
Net expenditure 1988	32	6	36	17	329	385	48	59	177	129	28	1,246
Gross expenditure	34	12	53	35	424	485	93	93	214	196	52	1,690
Transfer to municipal government	0	0	2	0	11	13	3	1	11	0	1	42
Net expenditure 1990	34	12	51	34	413	472	90	92	203	196	51	1,648

Table C.1g: Municipal Government Expenditure on Culture and Recreation (Millions of Dollars)

Year	Nfld	PEI	NS	NB	Que	Ont	Man	Sask	Alta	BC	Terr	Cda
1970	0.83	0.59	3.55	4.64	71.05	154.77	12.65	10.66	34.23	40.33	0.63	333.92
1975	12.43	1.36	12.16	17.28	212.63	410.98	53.07	32.63	116.52	140.53	2.56	1,012.12
1980	11.68	2.55	24.73	23.10	404.52	617.13	63.97	76.36	316.38	236.34	4.26	1,781.02
1985	23.95	5.08	50.93	42.56	560.52	1,001.80	94.53	104.84	387.34	329.79	19.82	2,621.14
1988	35.37	6.29	66.27	46.99	656.52	1,240.59	119.23	129.61	433.41	385.82	24.97	3,145.06
1990	36.55	8.44	74.52	52.50	745.44	1,515.80	220.42	159.51	491.97	476.94	21.57	3,803.67

Table C.2a: Federal Funding of Spending on Education (Millions of Dollars)												
Year	Nfld	PEI	NS	NB	Que	Ont	Man	Sask	Alta	BC	Terr	Cda
1970	47	19	47	59	445	206	74	57	78	56	14	1,102
1975	70	20	112	96	631	328	95	58	96	61	32	1,599
1980	155	40	197	175	1,043	786	198	136	176	256	56	3,217
1985	234	55	283	276	1,448	1,184	323	226	360	448	96	4,934
1988	299	62	335	303	1,437	1,304	405	291	501	536	138	5,611
1990	259	55	296	276	1,258	1,111	378	304	457	497	12	4,903

Table C.2b: Provincial Funding of Spending on Education (Millions of Dollars)												
Year	Nfld	PEI	NS	NB	Que	Ont	Man	Sask	Alta	BC	Terr	Cda
1970	48	2	89	94	734	1,336	120	97	425	278	13	3,237
1975	167	33	152	191	1,829	2,425	244	237	720	650	14	6,661
1980	231	45	272	261	4,005	3,150	264	338	1,285	874	26	10,751
1985	311	58	537	370	5,232	6,485	664	601	2,078	1,648	61	18,046
1988	392	75	594	497	6,168	6,762	747	556	2,325	1,872	71	20,058
1990	526	101	657	619	7,205	7,379	892	744	2,404	3,429	225	24,181

Table C.2c: Municipal Funding of Spending on Education (Millions of Dollars)

Year	Nfld	PEI	NS	NB	Que	Ont	Man	Sask	Alta	BC	Terr	Cda
1970	1	6	47	0	318	810	82	76	130	188	0	1,657
1975	3	0	63	0	366	920	165	104	187	394	0	2,201
1980	11	0	116	0	421	1,886	220	171	440	717	5	3,989
1985	19	6	66	0	418	3,122	136	292	601	374	1	5,033
1988	24	0	217	0	343	4,335	230	335	520	514	1	6,519
1990	27	0	167	0	0	5,041	187	292	576	753	0	7,044

Table C.2d: Total Funding of Spending on Education (Millions of Dollars)

Year	Nfld	PEI	NS	NB	Que	Ont	Man	Sask	Alta	BC	Terr	Cda
1970	95	26	183	153	1,497	2,352	275	230	633	523	27	5,996
1975	240	53	327	287	2,826	3,673	504	398	1,003	1,105	46	10,462
1980	397	85	586	436	5,469	5,822	683	645	1,901	1,847	87	17,957
1985	564	119	887	646	7,097	10,791	1,124	1,118	3,039	2,470	158	28,013
1988	714	138	1,146	800	7,948	12,401	1,383	1,181	3,346	2,922	210	32,188
1990	812	156	1,120	895	8,463	13,532	1,457	1,340	3,437	4,679	237	36,128

Table C.2e: Federal Government Expenditure on Education (Millions of Dollars)

	Nfld	PEI	NS	NB	Que	Ont	Man	Sask	Alta	BC	Terr	Cda
Gross expenditure	18	18	18	28	265	184	57	46	71	54	5	765
Transfer to provincial government	14	16	11	20	196	152	37	29	55	38	1	568
Transfer to municipal government	0	0	0	0	0	1	1	1	1	0	0	5
Net expenditure 1970	3	2	7	9	69	31	20	16	14	17	4	191
Gross expenditure	10	3	36	18	351	266	51	42	77	49	3	906
Transfer to provincial government	6	2	28	13	312	204	21	13	45	17	2	663
Transfer to municipal government	0	0	0	0	1	0	1	0	1	0	0	3
Net expenditure 1975	4	1	7	5	37	62	30	29	32	31	2	240
Gross expenditure	50	14	85	76	508	736	135	123	163	250	6	2,146
Transfer to provincial government	47	10	73	68	436	664	88	79	117	198	5	1,784
Transfer to municipal government	0	0	0	0	3	0	4	2	1	0	0	9
Net expenditure 1980	4	4	12	8	69	72	43	43	46	51	1	353

Table C.2e: Federal Government Expenditure on Education (Millions of Dollars)

	Nfld	PEI	NS	NB	Que	Ont	Man	Sask	Alta	BC	Terr	Cda
Gross expenditure	69	21	127	122	776	1,111	236	223	318	439	9	3,452
Transfer to provincial government	64	15	96	106	630	898	120	125	213	335	7	2,609
Transfer to municipal government	0	0	0	0	0	0	0	0	1	0	0	1
Net expenditure 1985	5	6	31	16	146	213	115	99	105	104	2	842
Gross expenditure	79	19	141	109	639	1,217	258	245	460	523	12	3,702
Transfer to provincial government	72	16	113	90	460	963	139	128	337	405	11	2,733
Transfer to municipal government	0	0	0	0	0	0	0	0	0	0	0	0
Net expenditure 1988	8	3	28	19	179	254	119	117	123	118	2	969
Gross expenditure	73	18	130	102	563	1,022	254	244	429	483	11	3,329
Transfer to provincial government	67	15	104	84	395	781	127	120	303	366	10	2,371
Transfer to municipal government	0	0	0	0	0	0	0	0	0	0	0	0
Net expenditure 1990	7	3	26	18	168	241	127	125	125	116	2	958

Table C.2f: Provincial Government Expenditure on Education (Millions of Dollars)

	Nfld	PEI	NS	NB	Que	Ont	Man	Sask	Alta	BC	Terr	Cda
Gross expenditure	91	19	127	144	1,065	1,478	168	136	477	299	23	4,026
Transfer to municipal government	0	10	66	0	757	886	93	80	196	170	1	2,259
Net expenditure 1970	91	8	61	144	308	592	75	56	281	129	22	1,768
Gross expenditure	233	52	251	281	2,361	2,591	302	262	774	651	45	7,802
Transfer to municipal government	0	29	145	0	1,461	1,575	145	154	378	441	4	4,333
Net expenditure 1975	233	22	105	281	900	1,016	157	108	396	210	41	3,469
Gross expenditure	380	81	418	429	4,949	3,709	392	408	1,396	1,027	80	13,268
Transfer to municipal government	0	52	248	0	3,178	2,199	222	258	648	467	3	7,274
Net expenditure 1980	380	30	170	429	1,771	1,510	170	150	748	559	77	5,993
Gross expenditure	536	106	780	631	6,507	7,145	854	691	2,279	1,973	155	21,655
Transfer to municipal government	0	75	492	0	4,158	3,375	571	404	1,207	1,224	13	11,517
Net expenditure 1985	536	32	288	631	2,349	3,770	283	288	1,072	749	142	10,139

Table C.2f: Provincial Government Expenditure on Education (Millions of Dollars)

	Nfld	PEI	NS	NB	Que	Ont	Man	Sask	Alta	BC	Terr	Cda
Gross expenditure	677	135	878	781	7,406	7,269	1,003	688	2,658	2,264	207	23,965
Transfer to municipal government	0	87	570	0	4,771	4,088	641	439	1,351	1,380	19	13,346
Net expenditure 1988	677	48	308	781	2,635	3,181	362	249	1,307	884	188	10,618
Gross expenditure	773	153	911	876	8,295	7,849	1,124	885	2,697	3,771	235	27,569
Transfer to municipal government	0	96	675	0	5,470	4,841	760	520	1,600	1,634	20	15,616
Net expenditure 1990	773	57	235	876	2,826	3,007	365	365	1,097	2,137	215	11,952

Table C.2g: Municipal Government Expenditure on Education (Millions of Dollars)

Year	Nfld	PEI	NS	NB	Que	Ont	Man	Sask	Alta	BC	Terr	Cda
1970	1.00	16.48	114.71	0.00	1,120.98	1,729.60	180.63	157.99	338.38	376.85	0.95	4,037.56
1975	3.40	29.71	214.51	0.00	1,888.90	2,594.63	317.03	261.06	575.56	863.87	3.95	6,752.63
1980	13.13	51.56	403.93	0.00	3,628.61	4,240.08	470.03	451.66	1,107.25	1,235.86	8.85	11,610.95
1985	22.97	81.33	568.59	0.00	4,601.74	6,808.00	725.09	732.17	1,861.38	1,617.13	13.28	17,031.68
1988	29.36	86.91	809.76	0.00	5,135.22	8,965.58	901.86	815.18	1,916.62	1,920.43	20.49	20,601.40
1990	32.70	95.97	858.74	0.00	5,469.54	10,283.22	966.16	849.96	2,214.83	2,425.99	20.46	23,217.56

Table C.3a: Federal Funding of Spending on the Environment (Millions of Dollars)

Year	Nfld	PEI	NS	NB	Que	Ont	Man	Sask	Alta	BC	Terr	Cda
1970	1	1	1	0	2	2	0	0	0	0	1	9
1975	11	2	13	10	84	120	14	10	24	33	4	326
1980	16	2	16	14	115	132	17	13	35	35	3	399
1985	25	3	18	20	190	164	21	20	43	49	3	556
1988	30	5	27	24	204	213	26	25	55	63	5	675
1990	33	7	32	29	232	283	34	31	69	86	3	840

Table C.3b: Provincial Funding of Spending on the Environment (Millions of Dollars)

Year	Nfld	PEI	NS	NB	Que	Ont	Man	Sask	Alta	BC	Terr	Cda
1970	2	1	1	3	21	25	1	0	4	6	1	66
1975	14	3	7	12	80	297	5	5	64	20	2	509
1980	24	1	18	21	127	341	11	22	315	101	1	982
1985	31	2	14	36	619	403	22	36	204	140	1	1,508
1988	37	4	26	37	506	680	23	46	316	179	9	1,861
1990	52	9	33	47	493	699	36	56	289	247	21	1,981

Table C.3c: Municipal Funding of Spending on the Environment (Millions of Dollars)

Year	Nfld	PEI	NS	NB	Que	Ont	Man	Sask	Alta	BC	Terr	Cda
1970	2	0	16	7	119	186	21	20	50	59	1	481
1975	13	5	32	34	252	410	35	35	134	119	6	1,076
1980	28	3	38	17	507	600	61	61	325	218	14	1,873
1985	25	4	59	28	674	886	87	89	257	172	22	2,302
1988	40	2	90	26	777	1,247	120	111	255	210	25	2,905
1990	35	1	138	26	1,568	1,826	195	138	303	374	31	4,635

Table C.3d: Total Funding of Spending on the Environment (Millions of Dollars)

Year	Nfld	PEI	NS	NB	Que	Ont	Man	Sask	Alta	BC	Terr	Cda
1970	4	1	18	11	143	214	22	20	54	66	3	557
1975	38	11	52	56	416	828	55	50	223	172	12	1,912
1980	68	7	72	53	749	1,074	90	96	675	354	18	3,254
1985	81	9	91	84	1,483	1,454	130	145	503	361	26	4,366
1988	107	10	143	87	1,486	2,140	169	182	626	452	40	5,441
1990	119	18	204	102	2,293	2,809	265	225	661	706	55	7,456

Table C.3e: Federal Government Expenditure on the Environment (Millions of Dollars)

	Nfld	PEI	NS	NB	Que	Ont	Man	Sask	Alta	BC	Terr	Cda
Gross expenditure	0	0	0	0	0	0	0	0	0	0	0	0
Transfer to provincial government	0	0	0	0	0	0	0	0	0	0	0	0
Transfer to municipal government	0	0	0	0	0	0	0	0	0	0	0	0
Net expenditure 1970	0	0	0	0	0	0	0	0	0	0	0	0
Gross expenditure	6	1	10	9	76	110	13	10	22	32	1	290
Transfer to provincial government	0	0	0	0	0	0	0	0	0	0	0	0
Transfer to municipal government	1	0	2	2	12	25	2	0	4	6	0	54
Net expenditure 1975	6	1	9	7	64	85	11	9	19	25	1	236
Gross expenditure	8	1	12	9	97	122	15	12	32	33	1	343
Transfer to provincial government	0	0	0	0	14	2	2	0	0	0	0	18
Transfer to municipal government	2	0	3	1	13	25	2	1	8	3	0	58
Net expenditure 1980	6	1	9	8	71	95	11	11	24	30	1	267
Gross expenditure	11	2	14	12	109	151	17	19	38	47	1	422

Table C.3e: Federal Government Expenditure on the Environment (Millions of Dollars)

	Nfld	PEI	NS	NB	Que	Ont	Man	Sask	Alta	BC	Terr	Cda
Transfer to provincial government	0	0	0	0	1	5	0	3	0	0	0	9
Transfer to municipal government	1	0	0	0	2	0	0	0	0	0	0	3
Net expenditure 1985	9	2	14	12	106	147	17	16	38	47	1	410
Gross expenditure	12	3	18	14	136	194	22	21	48	60	2	530
Transfer to provincial government	0	0	0	0	1	4	0	1	0	0	0	6
Transfer to municipal government	1	0	0	0	1	0	0	0	0	0	0	2
Net expenditure 1988	11	3	18	14	134	190	22	20	48	60	2	522
Gross expenditure	16	3	23	19	180	260	29	27	65	82	2	707
Transfer to provincial government	0	0	0	0	1	4	0	1	0	0	0	7
Transfer to municipal government	1	0	0	0	1	0	0	0	0	0	0	2
Net expenditure 1990	15	3	23	19	178	256	29	26	65	82	2	698

Table C.3f: Provincial Government Expenditure on the Environment (Millions of Dollars)

	Nfld	PEI	NS	NB	Que	Ont	Man	Sask	Alta	BC	Terr	Cda
Gross expenditure	2	1	1	0	7	20	1	0	0	1	1	34
Transfer to municipal government	2	0	0	0	7	4	0	0	0	0	0	14
Net expenditure 1970	0	1	1	0	0	16	1	0	0	1	1	20
Gross expenditure	17	3	7	3	47	263	5	4	59	12	5	425
Transfer to municipal government	7	1	2	1	36	44	0	1	3	8	0	103
Net expenditure 1975	10	2	5	2	11	219	5	3	56	4	5	322
Gross expenditure	26	1	9	18	127	304	8	16	305	87	2	903
Transfer to municipal government	17	0	0	13	82	67	0	3	92	40	0	315
Net expenditure 1980	9	1	9	5	45	237	8	13	212	47	2	588
Gross expenditure	40	2	9	28	658	332	15	29	186	133	2	1,432
Transfer to municipal government	23	0	0	23	120	117	0	10	59	104	0	456
Net expenditure 1985	17	2	9	5	537	215	14	19	127	29	2	976

Table C.3f: Provincial Government Expenditure on the Environment (Millions of Dollars)

	Nfld	PEI	NS	NB	Que	Ont	Man	Sask	Alta	BC	Terr	Cda
Gross expenditure	46	5	25	28	528	547	11	37	300	171	4	1,702
Transfer to municipal government	27	1	0	22	272	184	0	12	91	125	1	735
Net expenditure 1988	20	4	25	6	256	363	11	24	210	46	3	967
Gross expenditure	61	12	29	39	462	582	22	43	273	231	13	1,765
Transfer to municipal government	35	3	0	31	238	196	0	14	82	168	3	772
Net expenditure 1990	26	10	29	8	224	386	21	28	190	63	9	993

Table C.3g: Municipal Government Expenditure on the Environment (Millions of Dollars)

Year	Nfld	PEI	NS	NB	Que	Ont	Man	Sask	Alta	BC	Terr	Cda
1970	3.99	0.73	17.45	10.73	143.17	197.71	21.76	20.30	53.60	65.29	1.63	536.36
1975	22.74	7.11	38.86	47.29	341.42	523.87	38.64	37.35	147.67	142.30	6.39	1,353.65
1980	52.45	3.84	53.43	40.20	633.47	741.58	70.40	72.66	438.92	277.37	14.78	2,399.09
1985	54.26	4.59	67.85	67.17	839.39	1,091.78	98.08	110.25	338.54	285.44	23.06	2,980.41
1988	75.64	3.96	100.02	66.70	1,096.35	1,587.54	136.45	137.01	368.13	345.75	34.79	3,952.33
1990	78.50	4.57	151.71	75.15	1,891.21	2,166.93	215.74	170.62	405.30	561.32	43.66	5,764.70

Table C.4a: Federal Funding of Spendng on Foreign Affairs and International Assistance (Millions of Dollars)

Year	Nfld	PEI	NS	NB	Que	Ont	Man	Sask	Alta	BC	Terr	Cda
1970	7	1	11	9	82	102	13	13	22	29	1	289
1975	18	4	27	22	204	269	33	30	59	80	2	748
1980	25	5	38	31	286	384	46	43	96	119	3	1,076
1985	47	10	71	58	531	734	87	82	191	234	6	2,050
1988	80	18	124	100	931	1,322	152	142	335	418	11	3,632
1990	75	17	118	95	889	1,281	143	131	325	411	10	3,495

Table C.4b: Provincial Funding of Spendng on Foreign Affairs and International Assistance (Millions of Dollars)

Year	Nfld	PEI	NS	NB	Que	Ont	Man	Sask	Alta	BC	Terr	Cda
1970	0	0	0	0	0	0	0	0	0	0	0	0
1975	0	0	0	0	0	0	0	0	0	0	0	0
1980	0	0	0	0	0	0	0	0	0	0	0	0
1985	0	0	0	0	0	0	0	0	0	0	0	0
1988	0	0	0	0	0	0	0	0	0	0	0	0
1990	0	0	0	0	0	0	0	0	0	0	0	0

Table C.4c: Municipal Funding of Spendng on Foreign Affairs and International Assistance (Millions of Dollars)

Year	Nfld	PEI	NS	NB	Que	Ont	Man	Sask	Alta	BC	Terr	Cda
1970	0	0	0	0	0	0	0	0	0	0	0	0
1975	0	0	0	0	0	0	0	0	0	0	0	0
1980	0	0	0	0	0	0	0	0	0	0	0	0
1985	0	0	0	0	0	0	0	0	0	0	0	0
1988	0	0	0	0	0	0	0	0	0	0	0	0
1990	0	0	0	0	0	0	0	0	0	0	0	0

Table C.4d: Total Funding of Spendng on Foreign Affairs and International Assistance (Millions of Dollars)

Year	Nfld	PEI	NS	NB	Que	Ont	Man	Sask	Alta	BC	Terr	Cda
1970	7	1	11	9	82	102	13	13	22	29	1	289
1975	18	4	27	22	204	269	33	30	59	80	2	748
1980	25	5	38	31	286	384	46	43	96	119	3	1,076
1985	47	10	71	58	531	734	87	82	191	234	6	2,050
1988	80	18	124	100	931	1,322	152	142	335	418	11	3,632
1990	75	17	118	95	889	1,281	143	131	325	411	10	3,495

Table C.4e: Federal Government Expenditure on Foreign Affairs and International Assistance (Millions of Dollars)

	Nfld	PEI	NS	NB	Que	Ont	Man	Sask	Alta	BC	Terr	Cda
Gross expenditure	7	1	11	9	82	102	13	13	22	29	1	289
Transfer to provincial government	0	0	0	0	0	0	0	0	0	0	0	0
Transfer to municipal government	0	0	0	0	0	0	0	0	0	0	0	0
Net expenditure 1970	7	1	11	9	82	102	13	13	22	29	1	289
Gross expenditure	18	4	27	22	204	269	33	30	59	80	2	748
Transfer to provincial government	0	0	0	0	0	0	0	0	0	0	0	0
Transfer to municipal government	0	0	0	0	0	0	0	0	0	0	0	0
Net expenditure 1975	18	4	27	22	204	269	33	30	59	80	2	748
Gross expenditure	25	5	38	31	286	384	46	43	96	119	3	1,076
Transfer to provincial government	0	0	0	0	0	0	0	0	0	0	0	0
Transfer to municipal government	0	0	0	0	0	0	0	0	0	0	0	0
Net expenditure 1980	25	5	38	31	286	384	46	43	96	119	3	1,076

Table C.4e: Federal Government Expenditure on Foreign Affairs and International Assistance (Millions of Dollars)

	Nfld	PEI	NS	NB	Que	Ont	Man	Sask	Alta	BC	Terr	Cda
Gross expenditure	47	10	71	58	531	734	87	82	191	234	6	2,050
Transfer to provincial government	0	0	0	0	0	0	0	0	0	0	0	0
Transfer to municipal government	0	0	0	0	0	0	0	0	0	0	0	0
Net expenditure 1985	47	10	71	58	531	734	87	82	191	234	6	2,050
Gross expenditure	80	18	124	100	931	1,322	152	142	335	418	11	3,632
Transfer to provincial government	0	0	0	0	0	0	0	0	0	0	0	0
Transfer to municipal government	0	0	0	0	0	0	0	0	0	0	0	0
Net expenditure 1988	80	18	124	100	931	1,322	152	142	335	418	11	3,632
Gross expenditure	75	17	118	95	889	1,281	143	131	325	411	10	3,495
Transfer to provincial government	0	0	0	0	0	0	0	0	0	0	0	0
Transfer to municipal government	0	0	0	0	0	0	0	0	0	0	0	0
Net expenditure 1990	75	17	118	95	889	1,281	143	131	325	411	10	3,495

Table C.5a: Federal Funding of Spending on General Services (Millions of Dollars)

Year	Nfld	PEI	NS	NB	Que	Ont	Man	Sask	Alta	BC	Terr	Cda
1970	25	7	65	34	226	477	44	32	58	89	19	1,076
1975	58	16	169	76	458	1,238	119	85	155	236	69	2,679
1980	86	30	286	126	827	1,368	166	108	228	327	94	3,646
1985	141	54	432	206	1,166	2,084	259	145	354	504	157	5,503
1988	196	70	543	268	1,412	2,457	329	191	426	615	211	6,719
1990	218	77	644	308	1,704	3,066	372	240	519	751	68	7,966

Table C.5b: Provincial Funding of Spending on General Services (Millions of Dollars)

Year	Nfld	PEI	NS	NB	Que	Ont	Man	Sask	Alta	BC	Terr	Cda
1970	13	3	18	19	180	250	22	13	47	62	18	646
1975	31	10	30	27	355	580	65	78	233	252	20	1,680
1980	52	16	55	56	1,455	770	68	141	465	477	34	3,586
1985	77	17	87	109	1,866	1,420	201	314	534	565	77	5,266
1988	115	26	117	156	2,063	2,020	251	229	718	682	94	6,470
1990	127	36	126	177	2,741	1,918	210	373	693	908	261	7,569

Table C.5c: Municipal Funding of Spending on General Services (Millions of Dollars)

Year	Nfld	PEI	NS	NB	Que	Ont	Man	Sask	Alta	BC	Terr	Cda
1970	3	0	9	3	116	96	17	13	21	27	1	306
1975	6	2	17	7	207	227	25	28	55	63	5	641
1980	14	1	20	9	555	370	39	42	198	101	8	1,358
1985	25	3	39	14	708	615	71	68	224	159	18	1,944
1988	36	4	47	17	902	837	92	87	240	185	20	2,467
1990	40	3	52	18	971	1,115	112	86	279	205	21	2,903

Table C.5d: Total Funding of Spending on General Services (Millions of Dollars)

Year	Nfld	PEI	NS	NB	Que	Ont	Man	Sask	Alta	BC	Terr	Cda
1970	41	10	92	56	522	823	83	59	126	178	38	2,028
1975	94	28	217	109	1,019	2,045	209	191	443	551	94	5,000
1980	151	48	360	191	2,837	2,509	272	291	891	904	136	8,589
1985	243	73	558	329	3,740	4,119	530	526	1,113	1,228	251	12,712
1988	347	99	707	440	4,376	5,314	673	508	1,384	1,483	324	15,655
1990	384	117	822	503	5,416	6,099	694	699	1,490	1,864	350	18,438

Table C.5e: Federal Government Expenditure on General Services (Millions of Dollars)

	Nfld	PEI	NS	NB	Que	Ont	Man	Sask	Alta	BC	Terr	Cda
Gross expenditure	18	4	59	28	183	473	41	31	57	88	8	991
Transfer to provincial government	0	0	1	4	30	12	1	1	1	1	0	50
Transfer to municipal government	0	0	0	0	0	0	0	0	0	0	0	0
Net expenditure 1970	18	4	58	25	153	461	41	30	56	87	8	941
Gross expenditure	47	11	154	65	406	1,223	107	80	149	232	27	2,503
Transfer to provincial government	0	0	0	0	0	0	0	0	0	0	6	6
Transfer to municipal government	0	0	0	0	0	0	0	0	0	0	0	0
Net expenditure 1975	47	11	154	65	406	1,223	107	80	149	232	22	2,497
Gross expenditure	64	21	263	106	632	1,357	149	103	223	325	29	3,273
Transfer to provincial government	0	0	0	0	0	0	0	0	0	0	0	0
Transfer to municipal government	0	0	0	0	0	0	0	0	0	0	0	0
Net expenditure 1980	64	21	263	106	632	1,357	149	103	223	325	29	3,272

Table C.5e: Federal Government Expenditure on General Services (Millions of Dollars)

	Nfld	PEI	NS	NB	Que	Ont	Man	Sask	Alta	BC	Terr	Cda
Gross expenditure	102	44	407	164	925	2,069	233	144	343	501	47	4,979
Transfer to provincial government	0	0	0	0	0	0	0	0	0	0	0	0
Transfer to municipal government	0	0	0	0	0	0	0	0	0	0	0	0
Net expenditure 1985	102	44	407	164	925	2,069	233	144	343	501	47	4,979
Gross expenditure	134	55	505	210	1,143	2,437	280	172	412	610	53	6,012
Transfer to provincial government	0	0	0	0	0	0	0	0	0	0	0	0
Transfer to municipal government	0	0	0	0	0	0	0	0	0	0	0	0
Net expenditure 1988	134	55	505	210	1,143	2,437	280	172	412	610	53	6,012
Gross expenditure	174	64	612	261	1,436	3,045	343	211	510	747	67	7,469
Transfer to provincial government	0	0	0	0	0	0	0	0	0	0	0	0
Transfer to municipal government	0	0	0	0	0	0	0	0	0	0	0	0
Net expenditure 1990	174	64	612	261	1,436	3,045	343	211	510	747	67	7,469

Table C.5f: Provincial Government Expenditure on General Services (Millions of Dollars)

	Nfld	PEI	NS	NB	Que	Ont	Man	Sask	Alta	BC	Terr	Cda
Gross expenditure	20	5	24	27	237	262	25	15	47	61	29	752
Transfer to municipal government	0	0	0	0	0	0	0	0	0	0	0	0
Net expenditure 1970	20	5	24	27	237	262	25	15	47	61	29	752
Gross expenditure	41	14	43	36	372	571	75	83	236	252	67	1,789
Transfer to municipal government	0	0	0	0	1	0	0	0	0	0	0	1
Net expenditure 1975	41	14	43	35	372	570	75	83	236	252	67	1,788
Gross expenditure	71	25	71	71	1,616	751	80	141	461	471	98	3,855
Transfer to municipal government	0	0	0	0	0	0	0	0	0	0	0	1
Net expenditure 1980	71	25	70	71	1,615	750	79	141	461	471	98	3,853
Gross expenditure	110	26	106	143	2,062	1,374	218	306	525	560	186	5,616
Transfer to municipal government	0	0	0	0	21	0	16	0	0	0	0	36
Net expenditure 1985	110	26	106	143	2,041	1,374	203	306	525	560	186	5,579

Table C.5f: Provincial Government Expenditure on General Services (Millions of Dollars)

	Nfld	PEI	NS	NB	Que	Ont	Man	Sask	Alta	BC	Terr	Cda
Gross expenditure	169	40	150	201	2,278	1,935	288	237	710	678	245	6,932
Transfer to municipal government	0	0	0	0	0	0	1	0	0	0	0	1
Net expenditure 1988	169	40	150	201	2,278	1,935	287	237	710	678	245	6,931
Gross expenditure	162	49	153	211	2,956	1,851	227	391	683	901	255	7,839
Transfer to municipal government	0	0	0	0	0	0	0	0	0	0	0	0
Net expenditure 1990	162	49	153	211	2,956	1,851	227	391	683	901	255	7,839

Table C.5g: Municipal Government Expenditure on General Services (Millions of Dollars)

Year	Nfld	PEI	NS	NB	Que	Ont	Man	Sask	Alta	BC	Terr	Cda
1970	4.20	0.40	9.52	4.16	132.10	100.37	17.54	13.14	22.66	30.10	0.68	334.87
1975	6.84	1.93	18.98	8.52	241.84	251.78	25.99	28.58	57.51	67.58	5.03	714.56
1980	17.28	1.69	26.86	13.23	589.35	401.28	43.79	47.27	206.92	107.77	8.41	1,463.86
1985	31.29	3.22	45.47	22.04	773.42	676.55	95.13	76.12	244.13	167.19	19.16	2,153.72
1988	43.55	4.37	52.12	28.86	955.93	941.73	105.31	98.33	261.54	194.23	25.72	2,711.69
1990	48.41	4.12	57.14	31.36	1,023.18	1,203.21	123.85	97.23	297.38	215.60	28.27	3,129.74

Table C.6a: Federal Funding of Spending on Health (Millions of Dollars)

Year	Nfld	PEI	NS	NB	Que	Ont	Man	Sask	Alta	BC	Terr	Cda
1970	53	10	82	48	294	614	95	83	144	163	9	1,597
1975	108	22	180	127	603	1,255	193	142	294	370	28	3,320
1980	178	40	286	210	1,303	1,686	330	221	379	498	50	5,182
1985	293	65	432	350	2,087	2,572	469	370	688	881	105	8,314
1988	330	73	495	393	2,600	2,779	542	396	750	899	166	9,423
1990	317	68	489	375	2,471	2,718	525	398	723	887	68	9,040

Table C.6b: Provincial Funding of Spending on Health (Millions of Dollars)

Year	Nfld	PEI	NS	NB	Que	Ont	Man	Sask	Alta	BC	Terr	Cda
1970	24	5	55	42	781	996	101	76	208	232	3	2,522
1975	84	13	116	81	1,854	1,976	194	156	468	607	4	5,553
1980	128	24	222	177	2,885	3,447	361	382	1,275	1,542	8	10,451
1985	212	43	480	314	4,265	7,268	736	752	2,478	2,331	23	18,902
1988	288	60	648	472	5,282	10,629	864	908	2,780	3,162	58	25,151
1990	450	87	845	634	6,659	13,450	1,194	1,202	3,243	4,235	202	32,200

Table C.6c: Municipal Funding of Spending on Health (Millions of Dollars)											
Year	Nfld	PEI	NS	NB	Que	Ont	Man	Sask	Alta	BC	Terr	Cda
1970	0	0	31	0	10	174	24	50	124	5	0	419
1975	0	0	45	0	4	229	52	92	196	9	0	628
1980	0	0	50	1	0	355	81	121	326	120	0	1,054
1985	0	0	7	2	6	78	13	34	0	69	1	209
1988	0	0	0	2	7	112	12	18	0	100	0	251
1990	0	0	0	2	10	62	25	44	0	109	1	253

Table C.6d: Total Funding of Spending on Health (Millions of Dollars)												
Year	Nfld	PEI	NS	NB	Que	Ont	Man	Sask	Alta	BC	Terr	Cda
1970	76	15	168	90	1,086	1,784	221	210	476	400	12	4,537
1975	191	35	341	209	2,461	3,460	439	390	958	986	31	9,501
1980	306	64	558	388	4,188	5,489	772	723	1,980	2,160	59	16,687
1985	505	107	919	666	6,357	9,918	1,218	1,157	3,166	3,280	129	27,424
1988	618	133	1,143	867	7,889	13,520	1,418	1,322	3,530	4,160	225	34,825
1990	767	156	1,333	1,012	9,140	16,229	1,745	1,643	3,966	5,231	271	41,492

Table C.6e: Federal Government Expenditure on Health (Millions of Dollars)

	Nfld	PEI	NS	NB	Que	Ont	Man	Sask	Alta	BC	Terr	Cda
Gross expenditure	38	6	64	35	95	602	82	75	140	163	7	1,308
Transfer to provincial government	37	6	57	32	67	569	72	70	127	151	2	1,190
Transfer to municipal government	0	0	0	0	0	0	0	0	0	0	0	0
Net expenditure 1970	1	0	8	2	28	33	10	5	13	12	5	118
Gross expenditure	77	15	122	94	313	1,209	159	132	281	361	20	2,782
Transfer to provincial government	75	14	108	89	260	1,147	140	122	257	339	11	2,563
Transfer to municipal government	0	0	0	0	0	0	0	0	0	0	0	0
Net expenditure 1975	2	1	14	5	52	62	18	10	24	22	9	219
Gross expenditure	120	26	189	143	919	1,652	241	207	366	494	35	4,391
Transfer to provincial government	113	25	171	135	837	1,538	203	188	327	455	20	4,012
Transfer to municipal government	0	0	0	0	0	0	0	0	0	0	0	0
Net expenditure 1980	6	1	18	8	81	115	37	19	39	39	15	379

Table C.6e: Federal Government Expenditure on Health (Millions of Dollars)

	Nfld	PEI	NS	NB	Que	Ont	Man	Sask	Alta	BC	Terr	Cda
Gross expenditure	179	39	292	220	1,540	2,533	373	370	641	873	72	7,134
Transfer to provincial government	167	37	252	203	1,404	2,307	308	324	577	792	39	6,409
Transfer to municipal government	0	0	0	0	0	0	0	0	0	0	0	0
Net expenditure 1985	12	3	40	17	136	227	65	46	64	81	33	725
Gross expenditure	168	38	284	209	1,917	2,728	370	320	705	885	62	7,685
Transfer to provincial government	151	34	230	186	1,740	2,436	280	261	622	780	20	6,739
Transfer to municipal government	0	0	0	0	0	0	0	0	0	0	0	0
Net expenditure 1988	17	4	54	23	177	292	90	58	83	105	42	946
Gross expenditure	158	36	276	198	1,829	2,656	358	301	688	876	68	7,444
Transfer to provincial government	138	31	213	171	1,624	2,320	255	234	592	755	19	6,353
Transfer to municipal government	0	0	0	0	0	0	0	0	0	0	0	0
Net expenditure 1990	20	5	63	27	204	336	103	67	96	121	49	1,091

Table C.6f: Provincial Government Expenditure on Health (Millions of Dollars)

	Nfld	PEI	NS	NB	Que	Ont	Man	Sask	Alta	BC	Terr	Cda
Gross expenditure	75	14	128	88	1,046	1,570	185	154	329	383	7	3,979
Transfer to municipal government	0	0	1	0	0	20	0	2	2	1	0	25
Net expenditure 1970	75	14	127	87	1,046	1,551	185	152	327	382	7	3,953
Gross expenditure	189	35	278	203	2,405	3,144	366	286	727	955	22	8,608
Transfer to municipal government	0	0	0	0	0	50	0	3	17	5	0	76
Net expenditure 1975	189	35	277	203	2,404	3,095	366	282	710	950	22	8,532
Gross expenditure	300	63	473	379	4,106	4,990	645	569	1,601	1,993	43	15,160
Transfer to municipal government	0	0	0	0	8	109	0	4	150	4	0	274
Net expenditure 1980	300	63	473	379	4,099	4,881	645	565	1,451	1,989	43	14,886
Gross expenditure	493	105	871	646	6,215	9,606	1,139	1,073	3,102	3,127	94	26,471
Transfer to municipal government	0	0	90	0	0	804	110	199	994	9	0	2,205
Net expenditure 1985	493	105	782	646	6,215	8,802	1,029	874	2,107	3,118	94	24,265

Table C.6f: Provincial Government Expenditure on Health (Millions of Dollars)

	Nfld	PEI	NS	NB	Que	Ont	Man	Sask	Alta	BC	Terr	Cda
Gross expenditure	601	129	1,088	841	7,705	13,102	1,315	1,243	3,447	3,950	182	33,603
Transfer to municipal government	0	0	117	0	0	1,072	129	254	1,152	16	0	2,739
Net expenditure 1988	601	129	971	841	7,705	12,030	1,186	989	2,295	3,935	182	30,864
Gross expenditure	748	151	1,271	981	8,925	15,826	1,613	1,527	3,870	4,995	221	40,128
Transfer to municipal government	0	0	137	0	0	1,280	154	303	1,293	19	0	3,187
Net expenditure 1990	748	151	1,133	981	8,925	14,546	1,459	1,224	2,577	4,977	221	36,941

Table C.6g: Municipal Government Expenditure on Health (Millions of Dollars)

Year	Nfld	PEI	NS	NB	Que	Ont	Man	Sask	Alta	BC	Terr	Cda
1970	0.01	0.00	33.79	0.24	11.25	200.03	25.88	52.63	136.30	6.04	0.03	466.20
1975	0.06	0.01	49.60	0.94	4.94	303.98	54.19	98.24	223.83	14.30	0.13	750.22
1980	0.14	0.02	66.68	1.90	7.64	493.13	89.57	139.06	490.10	132.59	0.47	1,421.30
1985	0.02	0.02	97.19	2.72	6.76	889.62	124.26	237.05	994.41	80.97	0.71	2,433.73
1988	0.04	0.01	116.92	3.26	7.79	1,197.83	142.67	274.30	1,151.75	120.24	0.65	3,015.44
1990	0.03	0.01	137.41	3.91	10.73	1,346.76	182.06	352.28	1,293.36	133.32	0.77	3,460.65

Table C.7a: Federal Funding of Spending on Housing (Millions of Dollars)

Year	Nfld	PEI	NS	NB	Que	Ont	Man	Sask	Alta	BC	Terr	Cda
1970	4	1	2	3	14	20	2	2	1	2	2	51
1975	9	3	20	10	75	162	21	19	13	21	6	360
1980	19	6	44	36	309	333	65	66	57	93	11	1,040
1985	48	9	56	73	413	433	83	180	135	88	35	1,553
1988	38	13	56	55	354	431	108	222	277	87	27	1,668
1990	69	21	83	78	457	626	107	198	250	139	35	2,066

Table C.7b: Provincial Funding of Spending on Housing (Millions of Dollars)

Year	Nfld	PEI	NS	NB	Que	Ont	Man	Sask	Alta	BC	Terr	Cda
1970	3	1	1	0	18	12	0	10	0	6	2	53
1975	2	3	9	0	36	177	0	39	2	23	2	291
1980	0	0	15	0	216	37	0	1	157	76	0	501
1985	1	0	21	0	384	241	15	1	59	55	0	778
1988	1	0	21	1	416	113	21	0	46	19	1	640
1990	1	0	22	0	639	386	13	34	158	38	2	1,293

Table C.7c: Municipal Funding of Spending on Housing (Millions of Dollars)												
Year	Nfld	PEI	NS	NB	Que	Ont	Man	Sask	Alta	BC	Terr	Cda
1970	0	0	0	0	1	0	0	0	0	0	0	1
1975	0	0	0	0	0	0	0	0	0	0	0	0
1980	0	0	0	0	0	0	0	0	0	0	0	0
1985	5	0	3	1	0	100	0	11	20	23	1	164
1988	1	0	4	2	0	123	4	1	22	19	2	177
1990	1	0	4	0	0	122	3	1	25	20	6	182

Table C.7d: Total Funding of Spending on Housing (Millions of Dollars)												
Year	Nfld	PEI	NS	NB	Que	Ont	Man	Sask	Alta	BC	Terr	Cda
1970	7	2	2	3	33	32	2	12	1	8	4	106
1975	10	5	29	10	111	339	21	58	15	44	8	651
1980	19	6	59	36	525	370	65	67	214	169	11	1,541
1985	53	10	80	74	797	774	98	192	213	167	37	2,495
1988	40	13	81	58	770	667	133	222	346	124	30	2,485
1990	72	21	109	79	1,096	1,134	123	233	433	197	43	3,540

Table C.7e: Federal Government Expenditure on Housing (Millions of Dollars)

	Nfld	PEI	NS	NB	Que	Ont	Man	Sask	Alta	BC	Terr	Cda
Gross expenditure	2	0	1	3	9	20	2	0	1	2	0	41
Transfer to provincial government	1	0	0	0	0	0	0	0	0	0	0	1
Transfer to municipal government	0	0	0	0	0	2	0	0	0	0	0	3
Net expenditure 1970	2	0	1	3	9	18	2	0	0	2	0	37
Gross expenditure	8	1	16	10	70	158	21	17	13	21	3	338
Transfer to provincial government	0	0	0	0	0	0	0	0	0	0	0	0
Transfer to municipal government	0	0	0	0	6	1	0	0	0	1	0	8
Net expenditure 1975	8	1	16	10	64	157	21	17	13	20	3	329
Gross expenditure	19	6	38	36	280	333	65	66	55	93	11	1,002
Transfer to provincial government	0	0	0	0	0	0	0	0	0	0	0	0
Transfer to municipal government	0	0	1	0	7	10	0	0	0	4	0	22
Net expenditure 1980	18	6	37	36	273	323	65	66	55	90	11	980

Table C.7e: Federal Government Expenditure on Housing (Millions of Dollars)

	Nfld	PEI	NS	NB	Que	Ont	Man	Sask	Alta	BC	Terr	Cda
Gross expenditure	48	9	50	73	364	431	81	179	133	88	35	1,491
Transfer to provincial government	0	0	0	0	0	0	0	0	0	0	0	0
Transfer to municipal government	0	0	0	0	0	0	0	0	0	0	0	0
Net expenditure 1985	48	9	50	73	364	431	81	179	133	88	34	1,490
Gross expenditure	38	13	49	55	300	428	104	222	276	86	26	1,598
Transfer to provincial government	0	0	0	0	0	0	0	0	0	0	0	0
Transfer to municipal government	0	0	0	0	0	0	0	0	0	0	0	0
Net expenditure 1988	38	13	49	55	300	428	104	222	276	86	26	1,598
Gross expenditure	69	21	77	78	395	623	106	196	248	139	35	1,988
Transfer to provincial government	0	0	0	0	0	0	0	0	0	0	0	0
Transfer to municipal government	0	0	0	0	0	0	0	0	0	0	0	0
Net expenditure 1990	69	21	77	78	395	623	106	196	248	139	35	1,988

Table C.7f: Provincial Government Expenditure on Housing (Millions of Dollars)

	Nfld	PEI	NS	NB	Que	Ont	Man	Sask	Alta	BC	Terr	Cda
Gross expenditure	5	2	1	0	22	12	0	12	0	6	4	64
Transfer to municipal government	0	0	0	0	0	0	0	0	0	0	0	0
Net expenditure 1970	5	2	1	0	22	12	0	11	0	6	4	64
Gross expenditure	2	4	14	0	42	181	1	42	2	23	5	314
Transfer to municipal government	0	0	0	0	5	0	0	0	0	0	0	5
Net expenditure 1975	2	4	14	0	36	181	1	42	2	23	5	308
Gross expenditure	0	0	21	0	245	37	0	1	159	76	0	539
Transfer to municipal government	0	0	0	0	5	13	0	0	4	9	0	31
Net expenditure 1980	0	0	21	0	240	24	0	1	155	67	0	508
Gross expenditure	0	0	27	0	433	234	17	0	58	55	1	824
Transfer to municipal government	0	0	0	0	32	11	0	0	0	2	0	45
Net expenditure 1985	0	0	27	0	401	222	17	0	58	52	1	779

Table C.7f: Provincial Government Expenditure on Housing (Millions of Dollars)

	Nfld	PEI	NS	NB	Que	Ont	Man	Sask	Alta	BC	Terr	Cda
Gross expenditure	1	0	28	0	470	100	25	0	45	18	2	688
Transfer to municipal government	0	0	0	0	26	21	0	0	0	0	0	46
Net expenditure 1988	1	0	28	0	444	79	25	0	45	18	2	642
Gross expenditure	2	0	27	0	701	379	14	37	158	37	0	1,355
Transfer to municipal government	0	0	0	0	31	40	0	0	0	0	0	71
Net expenditure 1990	2	0	27	0	670	339	14	37	158	37	0	1,284

Table C.7g: Municipal Government Expenditure on Housing (Millions of Dollars)

Year	Nfld	PEI	NS	NB	Que	Ont	Man	Sask	Alta	BC	Terr	Cda
1970	0.00	0.00	0.14	0.11	1.13	2.03	0.02	0.05	0.70	0.06	0.03	4
1975	0.08	0.00	0.10	0.23	10.93	0.90	0.11	0.02	0.49	0.85	0.06	14
1980	0.18	0.10	0.66	0.24	11.43	23.32	0.24	0.20	3.91	12.56	0.13	53
1985	5.59	0.08	3.50	1.16	31.83	121.03	0.34	12.64	22.11	26.88	0.89	226
1988	1.28	0.07	4.22	2.72	25.57	159.49	4.55	0.61	23.85	19.75	2.60	245
1990	1.53	0.08	4.63	0.50	31.10	171.17	3.05	0.70	27.15	20.52	7.96	268

Table C.8a: Federal Funding of Spending on Interest Payments (Millions of Dollars)

Year	Nfld	PEI	NS	NB	Que	Ont	Man	Sask	Alta	BC	Terr	Cda
1970	22	8	67	35	498	935	65	48	73	124	6	1,881
1975	53	19	162	76	857	2,212	151	100	196	324	16	4,167
1980	151	35	362	172	2,375	6,145	386	197	607	777	39	11,245
1985	328	80	869	422	5,449	14,549	853	415	1,301	2,046	101	26,413
1988	457	117	1,102	578	6,471	19,488	1,106	659	1,658	2,716	161	34,513
1990	470	129	1,136	642	8,000	26,193	1,089	692	1,924	3,306	194	43,774

Table C.8b: Provincial Funding of Spending on Interest Payments (Millions of Dollars)

Year	Nfld	PEI	NS	NB	Que	Ont	Man	Sask	Alta	BC	Terr	Cda
1970	24	4	45	24	186	518	43	38	71	30	2	984
1975	79	9	64	40	450	1,136	83	60	130	64	1	2,114
1980	187	19	143	114	1,265	2,102	231	232	270	221	1	4,785
1985	301	36	441	302	3,280	4,309	706	857	644	992	0	11,869
1988	336	47	476	355	3,852	5,123	957	1,069	1,056	1,507	1	14,779
1990	372	63	567	448	4,449	5,197	1,148	882	1,817	1,741	7	16,691

Table C.8c: Municipal Funding of Spending on Interest Payments (Millions of Dollars)

Year	Nfld	PEI	NS	NB	Que	Ont	Man	Sask	Alta	BC	Terr	Cda
1970	4	1	11	3	192	204	21	17	46	47	0	547
1975	8	2	19	8	282	267	42	18	94	108	1	849
1980	34	4	33	17	796	393	80	30	224	238	3	1,853
1985	38	5	46	26	1,082	529	112	54	641	486	4	3,022
1988	46	6	47	24	1,209	479	102	62	640	512	3	3,131
1990	49	7	50	23	1,335	577	125	62	662	557	4	3,450

Table C.8d: Total Funding of Spending on Interest Payments (Millions of Dollars)

Year	Nfld	PEI	NS	NB	Que	Ont	Man	Sask	Alta	BC	Terr	Cda
1970	50	14	123	62	876	1,657	129	103	190	200	8	3,412
1975	139	30	244	124	1,588	3,615	276	178	421	497	17	7,130
1980	372	58	538	303	4,436	8,640	697	459	1,101	1,235	43	17,883
1985	668	121	1,356	751	9,811	19,387	1,671	1,325	2,586	3,524	105	41,304
1988	840	171	1,625	958	11,532	25,090	2,165	1,791	3,353	4,735	165	52,423
1990	890	199	1,753	1,113	13,784	31,966	2,362	1,636	4,403	5,604	205	63,915

Table C.8e: Federal Government Expenditure on Interest Payments

	Nfld	PEI	NS	NB	Que	Ont	Man	Sask	Alta	BC	Terr	Cda
Gross expenditure	8	5	53	28	455	927	59	44	72	123	5	1,778
Transfer to provincial government	0	0	0	0	0	0	0	0	0	0	0	0
Transfer to municipal government	0	0	0	0	0	0	0	0	0	0	0	0
Net expenditure 1970	8	5	53	28	455	927	59	44	72	123	5	1,778
Gross expenditure	25	15	130	61	791	2,185	136	96	193	322	14	3,968
Transfer to provincial government	0	0	0	0	0	0	0	0	0	0	0	0
Transfer to municipal government	0	0	0	0	0	0	0	0	0	0	0	0
Net expenditure 1975	25	15	130	61	791	2,185	136	96	193	322	14	3,968
Gross expenditure	69	24	300	132	2,204	6,123	329	189	604	775	37	10,784
Transfer to provincial government	0	0	0	0	0	0	0	0	0	0	0	0
Transfer to municipal government	0	0	0	0	0	0	0	0	0	0	0	0
Net expenditure 1980	69	24	300	132	2,204	6,123	329	189	604	775	37	10,784

Table C.8e: Federal Government Expenditure on Interest Payments

	Nfld	PEI	NS	NB	Que	Ont	Man	Sask	Alta	BC	Terr	Cda
Gross expenditure	170	59	740	302	5,027	14,520	760	414	1,286	2,038	100	25,417
Transfer to provincial government	0	0	0	0	0	0	0	0	0	0	0	0
Transfer to municipal government	0	0	0	0	0	0	0	0	0	0	0	0
Net expenditure 1985	170	59	740	302	5,027	14,520	760	414	1,286	2,038	100	25,417
Gross expenditure	271	90	947	445	5,969	19,458	915	569	1,637	2,705	161	33,167
Transfer to provincial government	0	0	0	0	0	0	0	0	0	0	0	0
Transfer to municipal government	0	0	0	0	0	0	0	0	0	0	0	0
Net expenditure 1988	271	90	947	445	5,969	19,458	915	569	1,637	2,705	161	33,167
Gross expenditure	340	106	993	519	7,567	26,163	929	621	1,902	3,297	194	42,630
Transfer to provincial government	0	0	0	0	0	0	0	0	0	0	0	0
Transfer to municipal government	0	0	0	0	0	0	0	0	0	0	0	0
Net expenditure 1990	340	106	993	519	7,567	26,163	929	621	1,902	3,297	194	42,630

Table C.8f: Provincial Government Expenditure on Interest Payments

	Nfld	PEI	NS	NB	Que	Ont	Man	Sask	Alta	BC	Terr	Cda
Gross expenditure	38	8	58	29	202	518	48	42	68	25	3	1,039
Transfer to municipal government	0	0	0	0	0	0	0	0	0	0	0	0
Net expenditure 1970	38	8	58	29	202	518	48	42	68	25	3	1,039
Gross expenditure	106	13	94	53	469	1,134	96	63	128	58	2	2,226
Transfer to municipal government	0	0	0	0	0	0	0	0	0	0	0	0
Net expenditure 1975	106	13	94	53	469	1,134	96	63	128	58	2	2,226
Gross expenditure	262	29	194	145	1,386	2,092	279	237	264	205	4	5,097
Transfer to municipal government	0	0	0	0	0	0	0	0	0	0	0	0
Net expenditure 1980	262	29	194	145	1,386	2,092	279	237	264	205	4	5,097
Gross expenditure	451	56	563	407	3,634	4,286	785	851	601	975	1	12,608
Transfer to municipal government	0	0	0	0	0	0	0	0	0	0	0	0
Net expenditure 1985	451	56	563	407	3,634	4,286	785	851	601	975	1	12,608

Table C.8f: Provincial Government Expenditure on Interest Payments

	Nfld	PEI	NS	NB	Que	Ont	Man	Sask	Alta	BC	Terr	Cda
Gross expenditure	513	73	626	471	4,281	5,093	1,134	1,151	1,021	1,492	0	15,921
Transfer to municipal government	0	0	0	0	0	0	0	0	0	0	0	0
Net expenditure 1988	513	73	626	471	4,281	5,093	1,134	1,151	1,021	1,492	0	15,921
Gross expenditure	491	85	705	555	4,811	5,181	1,295	944	1,794	1,721	6	17,589
Transfer to municipal government	0	0	0	0	0	0	0	0	0	0	0	0
Net expenditure 1990	491	85	705	555	4,811	5,181	1,295	944	1,794	1,721	6	17,589

Table C.8g: Municipal Government Expenditure on Interest Payments (Millions of Dollars)

Year	Nfld	PEI	NS	NB	Que	Ont	Man	Sask	Alta	BC	Terr	Cda
1970	4.99	1.59	11.96	4.57	218.96	212.15	22.50	17.28	49.92	51.25	0.15	595.31
1975	8.92	2.54	20.77	10.40	328.39	295.86	43.20	18.79	99.46	116.06	0.97	945.36
1980	41.92	4.73	44.90	26.13	845.71	425.27	88.75	33.82	233.80	254.78	2.65	2,002.46
1985	46.60	6.00	52.67	41.00	1,150.43	581.61	126.09	60.62	698.52	511.47	3.89	3,278.92
1988	56.10	7.60	51.85	41.43	1,281.30	539.36	115.98	70.03	695.78	538.55	3.40	3,401.39
1990	59.41	8.16	55.32	38.86	1,405.99	622.34	137.45	70.34	706.68	586.19	4.95	3,695.69

Table C.9a: Federal Funding of Spending on Labour, Employment, and Immigration (Millions of Dollars)

Year	Nfld	PEI	NS	NB	Que	Ont	Man	Sask	Alta	BC	Terr	Cda
1970	8	2	13	9	67	117	12	9	18	27	2	285
1975	16	4	37	20	167	300	31	30	50	81	6	742
1980	24	7	70	34	266	457	54	39	94	126	10	1,182
1985	40	15	119	55	427	718	86	56	145	194	14	1,869
1988	55	19	159	78	544	962	110	73	183	258	18	2,459
1990	60	20	186	86	615	1,112	121	77	208	294	18	2,798

Table C.9b: Provincial Funding of Spending on Labour, Employment, and Immigration (Millions of Dollars)

Year	Nfld	PEI	NS	NB	Que	Ont	Man	Sask	Alta	BC	Terr	Cda
1970	5	1	3	8	44	54	0	1	5	1	0	123
1975	5	1	8	0	94	74	4	0	14	3	1	204
1980	6	1	7	3	170	159	8	15	30	40	2	440
1985	9	3	13	4	349	370	44	39	208	40	2	1,081
1988	13	3	17	13	492	473	31	28	205	40	1	1,315
1990	16	4	67	19	626	338	38	24	169	31	20	1,353

Table C.9c: Municipal Funding of Spending on Labour, Employment, and Immigration (Millions of Dollars)

Year	Nfld	PEI	NS	NB	Que	Ont	Man	Sask	Alta	BC	Terr	Cda
1970	0	0	0	0	0	0	0	0	0	0	0	0
1975	0	0	0	0	0	0	0	0	0	0	0	0
1980	0	0	0	0	0	0	0	0	0	0	0	0
1985	0	0	0	0	0	0	0	0	0	0	0	0
1988	0	0	0	0	0	0	0	0	0	0	0	0
1990	0	0	0	0	0	0	0	0	0	0	0	0

Table C.9d: Total Funding of Spending on Labour, Employment, and Immigration (Millions of Dollars)

Year	Nfld	PEI	NS	NB	Que	Ont	Man	Sask	Alta	BC	Terr	Cda
1970	13	3	17	17	111	172	12	10	23	28	2	408
1975	21	5	44	20	261	374	35	30	64	84	7	946
1980	30	8	77	37	436	616	62	54	124	166	12	1,622
1985	49	18	132	59	776	1,088	130	95	353	234	16	2,950
1988	68	22	175	91	1,036	1,435	141	100	389	298	18	3,774
1990	76	24	253	106	1,242	1,449	159	102	377	325	39	4,151

Table C.9e: Federal Government Expenditure on Labour, Employment, and Immigration (Millions of Dollars)

	Nfld	PEI	NS	NB	Que	Ont	Man	Sask	Alta	BC	Terr	Cda
Gross expenditure	5	1	12	7	56	117	12	9	18	27	1	265
Transfer to provincial government	0	0	0	0	0	1	0	0	0	0	0	3
Transfer to municipal government	0	0	0	0	0	0	0	0	0	0	0	0
Net expenditure 1970	5	1	12	7	55	116	12	9	18	27	1	263
Gross expenditure	14	3	33	20	152	298	31	30	50	81	4	716
Transfer to provincial government	1	0	2	3	17	11	2	4	4	12	0	57
Transfer to municipal government	0	0	0	0	0	0	0	0	0	0	0	0
Net expenditure 1975	13	3	31	17	136	287	28	26	46	68	4	659
Gross expenditure	22	6	66	33	244	456	52	38	94	126	7	1,144
Transfer to provincial government	0	0	0	0	1	2	0	0	1	0	0	4
Transfer to municipal government	0	0	0	0	0	0	0	0	0	0	0	0
Net expenditure 1980	22	6	66	33	242	454	52	38	93	126	7	1,139

Table C.9e: Federal Government Expenditure on Labour, Employment, and Immigration (Millions of Dollars)

	Nfld	PEI	NS	NB	Que	Ont	Man	Sask	Alta	BC	Terr	Cda
Gross expenditure	35	13	115	53	382	716	80	56	141	194	12	1,798
Transfer to provincial government	0	0	4	1	18	4	1	0	1	3	0	33
Transfer to municipal government	0	0	0	0	0	0	0	0	0	0	0	0
Net expenditure 1985	35	13	110	52	365	712	79	56	139	190	12	1,765
Gross expenditure	48	18	154	73	481	959	104	70	180	258	16	2,360
Transfer to provincial government	0	0	0	1	6	4	1	1	3	5	0	21
Transfer to municipal government	0	0	0	0	0	0	0	0	0	0	0	0
Net expenditure 1988	48	17	153	71	475	955	103	70	177	254	16	2,339
Gross expenditure	55	19	169	81	555	1,110	116	76	206	294	18	2,698
Transfer to provincial government	0	1	0	2	8	6	1	1	4	6	0	29
Transfer to municipal government	0	0	0	0	0	0	0	0	0	0	0	0
Net expenditure 1990	55	18	168	79	547	1,104	115	75	202	288	18	2,669

Table C.9f: Provincial Government Expenditure on Labour, Employment, & Immigration (Millions of Dollars)

	Nfld	PEI	NS	NB	Que	Ont	Man	Sask	Alta	BC	Terr	Cda
Gross expenditure	8	2	5	10	55	56	1	1	5	2	1	145
Transfer to municipal government	0	0	0	0	0	0	0	0	0	0	0	0
Net expenditure 1970	8	2	5	10	55	56	1	1	5	2	1	145
Gross expenditure	8	2	14	3	126	86	7	4	18	16	4	287
Transfer to municipal government	0	0	0	0	0	0	0	0	0	0	0	0
Net expenditure 1975	8	2	14	3	126	86	7	4	18	16	4	287
Gross expenditure	8	1	10	4	194	162	10	16	31	40	5	483
Transfer to municipal government	0	0	0	0	0	0	0	0	0	0	0	0
Net expenditure 1980	8	1	10	4	194	162	10	16	31	40	5	483
Gross expenditure	14	5	22	7	411	376	51	39	213	44	4	1,185
Transfer to municipal government	0	0	0	0	0	0	0	0	0	0	0	0
Net expenditure 1985	14	5	22	7	411	376	51	39	213	44	4	1,185

Table C.9f: Provincial Government Expenditure on Labour, Employment, & Immigration (Millions of Dollars)

	Nfld	PEI	NS	NB	Que	Ont	Man	Sask	Alta	BC	Terr	Cda
Gross expenditure	20	5	22	20	561	480	38	31	211	45	3	1,435
Transfer to municipal government	0	0	0	0	0	0	0	0	0	0	0	0
Net expenditure 1988	20	5	22	20	561	480	38	30	211	45	3	1,435
Gross expenditure	21	5	85	27	695	345	44	27	175	38	21	1,482
Transfer to municipal government	0	0	0	0	0	0	0	0	0	0	0	0
Net expenditure 1990	21	5	85	27	695	345	44	27	175	38	21	1,482

Table C.9g: Municipal Government Expenditure on Labour, Employment, and Immigration (millions of dollars)

Year	Nfld	PEI	NS	NB	Que	Ont	Man	Sask	Alta	BC	Terr	Cda
1970	0.0	0.0	0.0	0.0	0.0	0.0	0.0	0.0	0.0	0.0	0.0	0.0
1975	0.0	0.0	0.0	0.0	0.0	0.0	0.0	0.0	0.0	0.0	0.0	0.0
1980	0.0	0.0	0.0	0.0	0.0	0.0	0.0	0.0	0.0	0.0	0.0	0.0
1985	0.0	0.0	0.0	0.0	0.0	0.0	0.0	0.0	0.0	0.0	0.0	0.0
1988	0.0	0.0	0.0	0.0	0.0	0.0	0.0	0.0	0.0	0.0	0.0	0.0
1990	0.0	0.0	0.0	0.0	0.0	0.0	0.0	0.0	0.0	0.0	0.0	0.0

Table C.10a: Federal Funding of Spending on Other (Millions of Dollars)

Year	Nfld	PEI	NS	NB	Que	Ont	Man	Sask	Alta	BC	Terr	Cda
1970	4	3	32	19	95	86	15	7	16	22	3	305
1975	29	6	52	33	167	148	21	18	26	62	6	568
1980	60	7	83	90	327	442	98	140	95	154	23	1,519
1985	597	7	320	156	600	492	91	197	87	103	789	3,438
1988	126	19	112	92	507	423	55	170	601	94	132	2,332
1990	89	27	162	142	829	798	84	73	207	212	26	2,647

Table C.10b: Provincial Funding of Spending on Other (Millions of Dollars)

Year	Nfld	PEI	NS	NB	Que	Ont	Man	Sask	Alta	BC	Terr	Cda
1970	0	0	3	6	0	1	0	0	1	0	0	12
1975	45	7	14	2	19	14	16	19	15	232	3	386
1980	21	2	33	15	179	172	36	28	48	153	11	698
1985	38	2	16	19	206	340	98	38	211	131	27	1,128
1988	32	3	63	22	352	434	29	84	219	236	44	1,518
1990	25	3	12	26	245	1,129	30	69	235	252	83	2,109

Table C.10c: Municipal Funding of Spending on Other (Millions of Dollars)

Year	Nfld	PEI	NS	NB	Que	Ont	Man	Sask	Alta	BC	Terr	Cda
1970	1	0	2	0	0	30	6	1	4	2	0	45
1975	1	0	2	0	64	94	7	2	14	14	0	199
1980	2	0	3	2	139	212	20	8	21	33	0	440
1985	3	0	6	2	394	501	29	14	101	19	1	1,069
1988	4	0	8	3	430	474	40	10	149	34	1	1,152
1990	4	0	10	3	437	598	34	21	149	53	1	1,310

Table C.10d: Total Funding of Spending on Other (Millions of Dollars)

Year	Nfld	PEI	NS	NB	Que	Ont	Man	Sask	Alta	BC	Terr	Cda
1970	5	4	37	25	95	117	21	9	21	24	3	361
1975	75	13	68	35	250	256	44	39	55	307	9	1,152
1980	83	9	120	106	645	826	154	176	165	339	34	2,657
1985	637	9	342	178	1,200	1,333	217	249	399	253	817	5,634
1988	162	23	182	117	1,290	1,331	124	265	969	364	176	5,003
1990	118	31	183	170	1,511	2,525	148	163	591	517	110	6,067

Table C.10e: Federal Government Expenditure on Other (Millions of Dollars)

	Nfld	PEI	NS	NB	Que	Ont	Man	Sask	Alta	BC	Terr	Cda
Gross expenditure	4	3	32	17	95	86	15	7	16	22	3	301
Transfer to provincial government	0	0	0	0	0	0	0	0	0	0	0	0
Transfer to municipal government	0	0	0	0	0	0	0	0	0	0	0	0
Net expenditure 1970	4	3	32	17	95	86	15	7	16	22	3	301
Gross expenditure	13	2	45	33	165	147	18	16	25	58	0	522
Transfer to provincial government	0	0	0	0	0	0	0	0	0	0	0	0
Transfer to municipal government	0	0	0	0	0	0	0	0	0	0	0	0
Net expenditure 1975	13	2	45	33	165	147	18	16	25	58	0	522
Gross expenditure	50	6	69	85	303	438	89	139	95	153	2	1,428
Transfer to provincial government	0	0	0	0	0	0	0	0	0	0	0	0
Transfer to municipal government	0	0	0	0	0	0	0	0	0	0	0	0
Net expenditure 1980	50	6	69	85	303	438	89	139	95	153	2	1,428

Table C.10e: Federal Government Expenditure on Other (Millions of Dollars)

	Nfld	PEI	NS	NB	Que	Ont	Man	Sask	Alta	BC	Terr	Cda
Gross expenditure	577	6	315	149	573	484	78	196	82	102	750	3,312
Transfer to provincial government	0	0	0	0	0	0	0	0	0	0	0	0
Transfer to municipal government	0	0	0	0	0	0	0	0	0	0	0	0
Net expenditure 1985	577	6	315	149	573	484	78	196	82	102	750	3,312
Gross expenditure	108	17	91	84	460	415	50	163	597	93	54	2,133
Transfer to provincial government	0	0	0	0	0	0	0	0	0	0	0	0
Transfer to municipal government	0	0	0	0	0	0	0	0	0	0	0	0
Net expenditure 1988	108	17	91	84	460	415	50	163	597	93	54	2,133
Gross expenditure	80	26	159	135	804	786	80	68	203	211	26	2,577
Transfer to provincial government	0	0	0	0	0	0	0	0	0	0	0	0
Transfer to municipal government	0	0	0	0	0	0	0	0	0	0	0	0
Net expenditure 1990	80	26	159	135	804	786	80	68	203	211	26	2,577

Table C.10f: Provincial Government Expenditure on Other (Millions of Dollars)

	Nfld	PEI	NS	NB	Que	Ont	Man	Sask	Alta	BC	Terr	Cda
Gross expenditure	0	1	3	8	0	0	0	0	1	0	0	13
Transfer to municipal government	0	0	0	0	0	0	0	0	0	0	0	0
Net expenditure 1970	0	1	3	8	0	0	0	0	1	0	0	13
Gross expenditure	61	11	21	2	11	5	19	20	15	234	9	408
Transfer to municipal government	0	0	0	0	0	0	0	0	0	0	0	0
Net expenditure 1975	61	11	21	2	11	5	19	20	15	234	9	408
Gross expenditure	30	2	47	19	195	159	43	28	48	151	32	753
Transfer to municipal government	0	0	0	0	0	0	0	0	0	0	0	0
Net expenditure 1980	30	2	47	19	195	159	43	28	48	151	32	753
Gross expenditure	57	4	20	26	208	298	107	37	207	131	66	1,160
Transfer to municipal government	0	0	0	0	0	0	0	0	0	0	0	0
Net expenditure 1985	57	4	20	26	208	298	107	37	207	131	66	1,160

Table C.10f: Provincial Government Expenditure on Other (Millions of Dollars)

	Nfld	PEI	NS	NB	Que	Ont	Man	Sask	Alta	BC	Terr	Cda
Gross expenditure	49	5	83	28	374	383	29	90	210	235	122	1,607
Transfer to municipal government	0	0	0	0	0	0	0	0	0	0	0	0
Net expenditure 1988	49	5	83	28	374	383	29	90	210	235	122	1,607
Gross expenditure	33	4	14	31	246	1,094	31	71	228	251	83	2,086
Transfer to municipal government	0	0	0	0	0	0	0	0	0	0	0	0
Net expenditure 1990	33	4	14	31	246	1,094	31	71	228	251	83	2,086

Table C.10g: Municipal Government Expenditure on Other (Millions of Dollars)

Year	Nfld	PEI	NS	NB	Que	Ont	Man	Sask	Alta	BC	Terr	Cda
1970	0.65	0.00	1.69	0.20	0.35	30.70	5.94	1.29	4.53	1.96	0.01	47.34
1975	1.15	0.00	1.76	0.40	74.67	104.71	7.37	2.39	14.83	14.70	0.01	221.98
1980	2.43	0.07	4.46	2.60	147.23	229.08	22.71	8.51	22.18	35.37	0.36	475.00
1985	3.17	0.01	6.89	3.78	418.70	550.68	32.28	16.04	110.24	19.64	0.91	1,162.32
1988	4.37	0.26	8.46	4.78	456.05	533.34	45.14	11.78	162.19	35.68	0.79	1,262.81
1990	5.18	0.28	10.52	5.05	460.85	645.03	37.12	24.04	158.89	55.88	1.97	1,404.81

Table C.11a: Federal Funding of Spending on Protection of Persons and Property (Millions of Dollars)

Year	Nfld	PEI	NS	NB	Que	Ont	Man	Sask	Alta	BC	Terr	Cda
1970	26	21	243	90	403	772	103	48	169	202	8	2,086
1975	47	34	397	146	664	1,329	174	83	279	339	18	3,510
1980	103	55	749	264	1,303	2,397	339	155	495	638	49	6,547
1985	211	107	1,261	494	2,253	4,581	578	295	998	1,259	97	12,133
1988	266	100	1,221	1,022	2,698	5,235	662	253	1,014	1,228	105	13,804
1990	291	106	1,349	1,128	2,987	5,853	724	279	1,125	1,368	55	15,266

Table C.11b: Provincial Funding of Spending on Protection of Persons and Property (Millions of Dollars)

Year	Nfld	PEI	NS	NB	Que	Ont	Man	Sask	Alta	BC	Terr	Cda
1970	6	1	10	9	131	214	17	16	51	43	3	502
1975	19	3	28	19	342	452	42	47	116	133	2	1,204
1980	41	5	47	42	519	661	73	91	262	251	8	2,000
1985	61	8	69	71	678	1,095	140	144	434	344	26	3,070
1988	78	16	106	94	844	1,560	148	131	446	385	34	3,841
1990	113	18	130	118	970	2,197	158	161	506	544	91	5,006

Table C.11c: Municipal Funding of Spending on Protection of Persons and Property (Millions of Dollars)

Year	Nfld	PEI	NS	NB	Que	Ont	Man	Sask	Alta	BC	Terr	Cda
1970	1	1	10	6	145	229	20	15	39	56	0	523
1975	2	1	26	17	291	437	42	30	84	129	2	1,061
1980	4	2	39	28	497	781	75	65	197	234	3	1,925
1985	9	4	79	45	767	1,253	118	96	287	395	5	3,057
1988	20	5	89	53	938	1,525	138	109	347	471	6	3,699
1990	20	5	97	58	1,052	1,903	165	126	391	546	7	4,371

Table C.11d: Total Funding of Spending on Protection of Persons and Property (Millions of Dollars)

Year	Nfld	PEI	NS	NB	Que	Ont	Man	Sask	Alta	BC	Terr	Cda
1970	33	23	263	106	679	1,216	140	80	259	301	11	3,110
1975	68	38	451	181	1,297	2,218	258	160	479	601	22	5,775
1980	148	62	834	335	2,320	3,839	488	310	954	1,122	61	10,473
1985	281	118	1,409	610	3,698	6,930	836	535	1,718	1,998	128	18,261
1988	363	120	1,416	1,168	4,480	8,320	947	493	1,808	2,083	145	21,345
1990	424	130	1,576	1,305	5,009	9,954	1,047	566	2,022	2,459	153	24,643

Table C.11e: Federal Government Expenditure on Protection of Persons and Property (Millions of Dollars)

	Nfld	PEI	NS	NB	Que	Ont	Man	Sask	Alta	BC	Terr	Cda
Gross expenditure	23	20	239	88	373	767	101	47	168	201	7	2,034
Transfer to provincial government	0	0	0	2	1	1	0	0	0	0	0	5
Transfer to municipal government	0	0	0	0	0	0	0	0	0	0	0	0
Net expenditure 1970	22	20	239	87	372	766	101	46	168	201	7	2,030
Gross expenditure	40	32	383	140	615	1,315	167	80	276	337	13	3,398
Transfer to provincial government	0	0	0	0	4	5	1	1	1	2	0	15
Transfer to municipal government	0	0	0	0	0	0	0	0	0	0	0	0
Net expenditure 1975	40	32	383	140	612	1,310	166	79	275	335	13	3,383
Gross expenditure	84	52	732	253	1,233	2,382	322	151	492	636	33	6,372
Transfer to provincial government	0	0	1	1	8	10	15	1	3	4	1	43
Transfer to municipal government	0	0	0	0	0	0	0	0	0	0	0	0
Net expenditure 1980	84	52	731	252	1,226	2,371	307	150	489	633	33	6,328

Table C.11e: Federal Government Expenditure on Protection of Persons and Property (Millions of Dollars)

	Nfld	PEI	NS	NB	Que	Ont	Man	Sask	Alta	BC	Terr	Cda
Gross expenditure	180	102	1,241	474	2,164	4,560	559	294	989	1,254	59	11,876
Transfer to provincial government	5	0	6	6	11	61	4	9	21	19	3	145
Transfer to municipal government	0	0	0	0	0	1	0	0	0	0	0	1
Net expenditure 1985	175	102	1,235	468	2,153	4,498	555	285	967	1,235	57	11,730
Gross expenditure	224	90	1,187	996	2,587	5,208	633	242	1,005	1,221	48	13,440
Transfer to provincial government	11	1	9	8	22	93	14	13	33	35	4	244
Transfer to municipal government	0	0	0	0	0	1	0	0	1	0	0	4
Net expenditure 1988	212	89	1,177	987	2,565	5,114	619	228	971	1,186	43	13,192
Gross expenditure	252	100	1,316	1,102	2,890	5,822	702	267	1,118	1,362	54	14,985
Transfer to provincial government	11	1	9	8	22	92	14	13	32	34	4	242
Transfer to municipal government	0	0	0	0	0	1	0	0	1	0	0	3
Net expenditure 1990	241	99	1,306	1,094	2,869	5,729	688	253	1,084	1,328	50	14,740

Table C.11f: Provincial Government Expenditure on Protection of Persons and Property (Millions of Dollars)

	Nfld	PEI	NS	NB	Que	Ont	Man	Sask	Alta	BC	Terr	Cda
Gross expenditure	10	2	13	10	142	211	18	18	49	39	4	514
Transfer to municipal government	0	0	2	0	2	1	0	0	0	1	0	6
Net expenditure 1970	10	2	11	10	140	210	18	18	49	38	4	508
Gross expenditure	26	4	40	20	346	424	48	50	116	129	8	1,222
Transfer to municipal government	0	0	1	0	3	2	1	3	14	2	0	27
Net expenditure 1975	25	4	39	20	342	422	47	47	103	127	7	1,196
Gross expenditure	58	7	51	40	567	623	97	88	259	239	25	2,054
Transfer to municipal government	1	0	1	0	5	1	2	0	27	0	0	37
Net expenditure 1980	58	7	50	40	561	621	95	88	232	239	25	2,017
Gross expenditure	95	12	84	70	729	1,053	148	142	438	347	66	3,184
Transfer to municipal government	9	0	0	0	13	4	0	0	32	1	0	60
Net expenditure 1985	86	12	84	70	715	1,048	148	142	406	346	66	3,124

Table C.11f: Provincial Government Expenditure on Protection of Persons and Property (Millions of Dollars)

	Nfld	PEI	NS	NB	Que	Ont	Man	Sask	Alta	BC	Terr	Cda
Gross expenditure	127	25	141	92	921	1,489	172	142	458	402	94	4,063
Transfer to municipal government	1	0	0	1	7	29	1	0	36	1	0	75
Net expenditure 1988	126	25	141	90	915	1,461	171	142	422	401	94	3,988
Gross expenditure	159	25	162	112	1,032	2,169	177	171	520	556	93	5,176
Transfer to municipal government	1	0	0	2	7	42	1	0	41	1	0	95
Net expenditure 1990	158	25	162	110	1,025	2,128	176	170	479	555	93	5,081

Table C.11g: Municipal Government Expenditure on Protection of Persons and Property (Millions of Dollars)

Year	Nfld	PEI	NS	NB	Que	Ont	Man	Sask	Alta	BC	Terr	Cda
1970	0.86	0.82	12.40	9.61	167.35	239.68	20.74	15.45	42.67	62.52	0.38	572.47
1975	3.17	1.64	30.00	21.40	343.17	486.34	44.96	33.86	102.12	139.77	1.71	1,208.14
1980	5.97	2.80	53.82	42.68	533.06	845.64	85.32	72.29	232.34	250.62	3.37	2,127.91
1985	19.45	4.64	90.84	71.39	829.47	1,382.89	132.68	108.63	344.98	416.28	5.65	3,406.89
1988	24.89	5.72	98.50	90.92	1,000.34	1,745.19	157.47	123.32	414.97	495.70	8.07	4,165.08
1990	25.59	6.46	107.09	100.51	1,115.32	2,096.70	183.28	142.63	459.39	575.63	9.73	4,822.31

Table C.12a: Federal Funding of Spending on Regional Planning and Development (Millions of Dollars)

Year	Nfld	PEI	NS	NB	Que	Ont	Man	Sask	Alta	BC	Terr	Cda
1970	6	0	3	2	27	31	2	1	2	4	2	81
1975	6	1	14	9	63	69	11	3	6	11	11	204
1980	6	2	13	6	47	60	28	27	11	11	24	234
1985	9	1	12	12	83	146	24	4	17	23	42	373
1988	15	2	23	12	125	216	34	13	26	38	33	537
1990	12	3	22	16	137	250	27	10	32	44	1	554

Table C.12b: Provincial Funding of Spending on Regional Planning and Development (Millions of Dollars)

Year	Nfld	PEI	NS	NB	Que	Ont	Man	Sask	Alta	BC	Terr	Cda
1970	9	0	7	3	41	42	4	2	8	1	4	121
1975	2	1	14	14	141	248	35	31	15	34	6	542
1980	11	3	24	11	113	207	28	22	28	51	12	509
1985	15	1	27	8	107	134	126	57	56	45	29	606
1988	14	0	29	10	114	277	91	51	77	58	18	739
1990	12	1	36	21	114	271	82	15	54	92	78	776

Table C.12c: Municipal Funding of Spending on Regional Planning and Development (Millions of Dollars)

Year	Nfld	PEI	NS	NB	Que	Ont	Man	Sask	Alta	BC	Terr	Cda
1970	0	0	0	0	0	4	0	1	13	2	0	21
1975	1	0	0	0	0	0	0	0	34	0	0	35
1980	0	0	0	0	0	54	10	0	72	4	0	141
1985	1	0	0	0	52	75	14	0	45	34	0	222
1988	0	0	0	2	78	70	0	0	43	29	0	222
1990	1	0	0	0	86	92	10	8	105	40	0	342

Table C.12d: Total Funding of Spending on Regional Planning and Development (Millions of Dollars)

Year	Nfld	PEI	NS	NB	Que	Ont	Man	Sask	Alta	BC	Terr	Cda
1970	15	1	10	5	68	78	6	4	22	8	6	223
1975	8	2	28	23	204	318	46	34	55	46	17	781
1980	17	4	37	16	160	322	66	49	111	66	36	884
1985	25	2	39	21	241	355	163	62	118	102	72	1,201
1988	29	3	52	24	317	563	125	64	146	125	51	1,499
1990	25	4	58	37	338	613	119	32	191	176	79	1,672

Table C.12e: Federal Government Expenditure on Regional Planning and Development (Millions of Dollars)

	Nfld	PEI	NS	NB	Que	Ont	Man	Sask	Alta	BC	Terr	Cda
Gross expenditure	0	0	1	1	16	31	1	1	2	4	0	58
Transfer to provincial government	0	0	0	0	0	0	0	0	0	0	0	0
Transfer to municipal government	0	0	0	0	0	0	0	0	0	0	0	0
Net expenditure 1970	0	0	1	1	16	31	1	1	2	4	0	58
Gross expenditure	5	0	7	3	41	64	5	1	5	11	0	142
Transfer to provincial government	4	0	4	1	7	0	1	0	0	0	0	19
Transfer to municipal government	0	0	0	0	0	0	0	0	0	0	0	0
Net expenditure 1975	1	0	2	2	33	64	3	1	5	11	0	123
Gross expenditure	1	0	2	2	32	57	21	26	10	11	0	163
Transfer to provincial government	0	0	0	0	0	0	18	25	5	0	0	48
Transfer to municipal government	0	0	0	0	0	0	0	0	0	0	0	0
Net expenditure 1980	1	0	2	2	32	57	3	1	6	11	0	115

Table C.12e: Federal Government Expenditure on Regional Planning and Development (Millions of Dollars)

	Nfld	PEI	NS	NB	Que	Ont	Man	Sask	Alta	BC	Terr	Cda
Gross expenditure	2	0	5	8	69	144	7	4	15	23	0	277
Transfer to provincial government	0	0	0	4	0	0	0	0	0	0	0	4
Transfer to municipal government	0	0	0	0	0	0	0	0	0	2	0	2
Net expenditure 1985	2	0	4	4	69	144	7	4	15	21	0	271
Gross expenditure	8	2	14	8	110	214	15	9	24	37	1	443
Transfer to provincial government	4	2	7	1	2	1	4	1	1	1	1	25
Transfer to municipal government	0	0	0	0	0	0	0	0	0	0	0	0
Net expenditure 1988	3	1	7	7	108	213	11	9	23	36	1	418
Gross expenditure	8	2	13	10	126	248	16	9	31	43	1	507
Transfer to provincial government	3	1	6	1	2	1	3	1	1	1	1	20
Transfer to municipal government	0	0	0	0	0	0	0	0	0	0	0	0
Net expenditure 1990	4	1	8	9	124	247	12	8	30	43	1	487

Table C.12f: Provincial Government Expenditure on Regional Planning & Development (Millions of Dollars)

	Nfld	PEI	NS	NB	Que	Ont	Man	Sask	Alta	BC	Terr	Cda
Gross expenditure	15	1	9	4	52	43	4	2	7	1	6	142
Transfer to municipal government	0	0	3	0	8	8	1	0	1	0	0	21
Net expenditure 1970	14	1	6	4	44	34	4	2	6	1	6	121
Gross expenditure	7	2	26	21	171	254	42	33	14	35	17	622
Transfer to municipal government	2	1	12	3	36	107	11	4	0	24	5	205
Net expenditure 1975	5	1	14	18	135	147	31	28	14	11	12	417
Gross expenditure	16	4	35	15	128	205	51	47	30	51	36	619
Transfer to municipal government	1	1	6	4	61	60	6	8	6	18	2	172
Net expenditure 1980	15	4	29	11	67	145	46	39	24	32	34	446
Gross expenditure	22	2	35	16	117	128	141	58	54	44	72	687
Transfer to municipal government	1	0	13	3	45	33	7	7	0	5	1	116
Net expenditure 1985	21	2	22	13	73	95	134	50	54	38	71	572

Table C.12f: Provincial Government Expenditure on Regional Planning & Development (Millions of Dollars)

	Nfld	PEI	NS	NB	Que	Ont	Man	Sask	Alta	BC	Terr	Cda
Gross expenditure	26	2	46	13	126	272	114	56	75	58	50	838
Transfer to municipal government	1	0	11	3	53	68	15	10	0	7	1	172
Net expenditure 1988	24	2	34	10	73	204	99	45	75	51	49	667
Gross expenditure	20	3	50	28	123	267	96	16	49	91	78	820
Transfer to municipal government	1	0	13	6	52	67	13	3	0	11	1	167
Net expenditure 1990	19	3	37	22	71	200	83	12	49	80	77	653

Table C.12g: Municipal Government Expenditure on Regional Planning & Development (Millions of Dollars)

Year	Nfld	PEI	NS	NB	Que	Ont	Man	Sask	Alta	BC	Terr	Cda
1970	0.15	0.04	2.60	0.65	7.91	12.87	0.62	1.85	14.22	2.58	0.14	43.63
1975	2.78	0.56	11.98	3.15	36.04	107.28	10.93	4.04	36.35	23.90	4.51	241.52
1980	0.72	0.58	5.82	3.70	60.77	118.92	17.26	8.49	81.19	23.21	1.62	322.28
1985	1.59	0.16	13.29	3.89	99.88	116.14	22.12	7.48	49.57	43.30	0.68	358.10
1988	1.63	0.19	11.43	6.28	135.86	146.78	15.50	10.33	47.13	37.45	1.49	414.07
1990	2.11	0.23	12.81	5.88	142.75	166.16	24.24	11.76	111.78	53.01	1.31	532.04

Table C.13a: Federal Funding of Spending on Resource Conservation and Industrial Development (Millions of Dollars)

Year	Nfld	PEI	NS	NB	Que	Ont	Man	Sask	Alta	BC	Terr	Cda
1970	52	15	35	56	219	286	77	172	144	59	24	1,138
1975	155	42	386	295	1,339	517	198	540	409	128	13	4,022
1980	243	46	982	1,001	2,091	1,138	323	595	666	365	36	7,485
1985	478	63	512	172	1,112	1,269	450	1,388	2,022	374	606	8,446
1988	155	70	270	162	1,043	1,484	628	1,704	1,925	449	141	8,032
1990	157	67	246	161	886	1,337	425	1,034	1,189	379	80	5,960

Table C.13b: Provincial Funding of Spending on Resource Conservation and Industrial Development (Millions of Dollars)

Year	Nfld	PEI	NS	NB	Que	Ont	Man	Sask	Alta	BC	Terr	Cda
1970	0	0	8	0	108	151	29	22	58	78	0	453
1975	13	0	40	22	331	267	60	76	230	201	3	1,243
1980	89	5	78	27	624	556	113	306	839	419	6	3,064
1985	61	19	98	93	1,059	915	160	592	2,777	812	27	6,612
1988	80	35	138	108	1,203	1,228	220	611	2,053	771	24	6,470
1990	97	40	134	125	1,297	1,361	199	568	1,986	749	144	6,700

Table C.13c: Municipal Funding of Spending on Resource Conservation and Industrial Development (Millions of Dollars)

Year	Nfld	PEI	NS	NB	Que	Ont	Man	Sask	Alta	BC	Terr	Cda
1970	0	0	2	0	0	15	0	1	0	1	0	18
1975	0	0	2	0	0	55	2	1	8	8	0	77
1980	0	0	1	1	42	106	8	1	60	11	0	231
1985	0	0	12	7	54	110	8	6	23	18	0	240
1988	3	0	13	4	73	165	14	20	25	53	0	369
1990	0	0	0	5	72	40	12	0	0	43	0	172

Table C.13d: Total Funding of Spending on Resource Conservation and Industrial Development (Millions of Dollars)

Year	Nfld	PEI	NS	NB	Que	Ont	Man	Sask	Alta	BC	Terr	Cda
1970	52	15	45	56	326	452	105	195	202	137	24	1,609
1975	168	42	428	317	1,671	839	260	617	647	336	16	5,341
1980	332	51	1,062	1,030	2,758	1,800	444	902	1,566	795	43	10,780
1985	539	82	621	272	2,224	2,294	618	1,986	4,822	1,205	633	15,298
1988	238	106	421	273	2,319	2,877	862	2,335	4,003	1,273	165	14,871
1990	254	106	380	291	2,255	2,738	636	1,602	3,175	1,171	224	12,832

Table C.13e: Federal Government Expenditure on Resource Conservation and Industrial Development (Millions of Dollars)

	Nfld	PEI	NS	NB	Que	Ont	Man	Sask	Alta	BC	Terr	Cda
Gross expenditure	52	15	32	56	191	285	73	170	143	59	24	1,099
Transfer to provincial government	28	6	12	33	39	6	8	3	6	3	5	149
Transfer to municipal government	0	0	0	0	0	4	0	0	0	0	0	5
Net expenditure 1970	24	9	20	23	152	274	64	166	137	55	20	945
Gross expenditure	151	42	365	286	1,288	510	188	535	403	125	7	3,899
Transfer to provincial government	49	19	22	42	59	32	23	56	21	11	0	336
Transfer to municipal government	0	0	0	0	0	0	0	0	0	0	0	0
Net expenditure 1975	101	23	344	243	1,228	478	165	479	381	114	7	3,563
Gross expenditure	202	43	946	991	2,008	1,132	294	584	658	364	24	7,246
Transfer to provincial government	43	31	44	52	100	42	34	64	60	42	3	514
Transfer to municipal government	0	0	0	0	0	0	0	0	0	0	0	0
Net expenditure 1980	159	12	902	939	1,909	1,090	260	520	598	322	20	6,731

Table C.13e: Federal Government Expenditure on Resource Conservation and Industrial Development (Millions of Dollars)

	Nfld	PEI	NS	NB	Que	Ont	Man	Sask	Alta	BC	Terr	Cda
Gross expenditure	446	52	483	135	976	1,263	429	1,388	1,970	371	568	8,080
Transfer to provincial government	27	26	102	16	41	43	44	202	172	25	18	715
Transfer to municipal government	0	0	0	0	0	5	0	0	0	5	0	11
Net expenditure 1985	419	26	381	119	935	1,214	385	1,186	1,798	341	550	7,354
Gross expenditure	110	50	226	120	888	1,476	584	1,653	1,892	445	99	7,542
Transfer to provincial government	41	21	73	16	57	62	53	131	157	34	15	660
Transfer to municipal government	0	0	0	0	0	5	1	0	0	3	0	10
Net expenditure 1988	69	29	153	104	830	1,409	530	1,522	1,735	408	83	6,872
Gross expenditure	123	52	213	127	760	1,330	397	988	1,168	377	80	5,614
Transfer to provincial government	50	25	70	20	61	62	52	101	117	36	17	611
Transfer to municipal government	0	0	0	0	0	7	1	0	0	4	0	14
Net expenditure 1990	72	27	143	106	700	1,261	343	886	1,051	337	63	4,989

Table C.13f: Provincial Government Expenditure on Resource Conservation and Industrial Development (Millions of Dollars)

	Nfld	PEI	NS	NB	Que	Ont	Man	Sask	Alta	BC	Terr	Cda
Gross expenditure	28	6	23	33	175	158	41	28	64	81	5	641
Transfer to municipal government	0	0	0	0	1	2	0	0	0	0	0	4
Net expenditure 1970	28	6	23	32	174	156	41	28	64	81	5	637
Gross expenditure	67	19	82	73	442	300	93	137	257	214	9	1,694
Transfer to municipal government	0	0	2	1	5	5	0	0	3	0	1	17
Net expenditure 1975	67	19	80	72	437	295	93	137	254	214	9	1,677
Gross expenditure	173	38	158	88	805	595	175	381	905	461	22	3,802
Transfer to municipal government	0	0	0	0	1	48	0	1	26	0	0	76
Net expenditure 1980	173	38	158	88	803	548	175	380	879	461	22	3,725
Gross expenditure	120	56	226	142	1,232	953	225	793	3,000	839	83	7,667
Transfer to municipal government	0	0	1	0	1	51	0	4	107	0	0	163
Net expenditure 1985	120	56	225	142	1,231	902	225	789	2,892	839	83	7,504

Table C.13f: Provincial Government Expenditure on Resource Conservation and Industrial Development (Millions of Dollars)

	Nfld	PEI	NS	NB	Que	Ont	Man	Sask	Alta	BC	Terr	Cda
Gross expenditure	166	76	254	163	1,412	1,277	315	790	2,241	806	82	7,581
Transfer to municipal government	0	0	1	0	7	73	0	5	118	0	0	204
Net expenditure 1988	166	76	253	163	1,404	1,204	315	785	2,123	806	82	7,377
Gross expenditure	182	80	237	176	1,479	1,426	278	715	2,125	785	161	7,643
Transfer to municipal government	4	0	10	0	13	213	5	32	137	0	1	414
Net expenditure 1990	178	79	227	176	1,466	1,214	273	683	1,987	785	160	7,229

Table C.13g: Municipal Government Expenditure on Resource Conservation and Industrial Development (Millions of Dollars)

Year	Nfld	PEI	NS	NB	Que	Ont	Man	Sask	Alta	BC	Terr	Cda
1970	0.03	0.00	2.46	0.14	0.54	21.24	0.13	1.00	0.66	0.99	0.01	27.19
1975	0.00	0.00	4.81	1.12	4.62	66.51	2.24	1.51	11.80	8.26	0.52	101.38
1980	0.15	0.01	1.15	1.99	45.72	162.24	9.17	2.71	88.81	11.94	0.10	323.99
1985	0.31	0.32	14.56	11.77	58.63	177.50	9.34	10.84	131.89	24.43	0.42	440.01
1988	3.32	0.22	15.04	6.11	84.70	263.59	17.18	27.59	144.55	58.86	0.41	621.57
1990	3.80	0.15	10.15	8.05	89.37	263.27	20.26	31.87	137.14	49.15	0.68	613.89

Table C.14a: Federal Funding of Spending on Research Establishments (Millions of Dollars)

Year	Nfld	PEI	NS	NB	Que	Ont	Man	Sask	Alta	BC	Terr	Cda
1970	8	2	14	11	102	142	17	16	31	40	1	384
1975	12	2	19	14	131	189	22	19	42	55	1	505
1980	25	5	40	30	274	395	45	43	96	122	3	1,076
1985	23	4	39	30	273	405	44	42	101	124	2	1,086
1988	20	3	37	29	272	409	40	40	99	128	2	1,080
1990	27	4	48	36	350	535	51	51	129	170	2	1,403

Table C.14b: Provincial Funding of Spending on Research Establishments (Millions of Dollars)

Year	Nfld	PEI	NS	NB	Que	Ont	Man	Sask	Alta	BC	Terr	Cda
1970	0	0	1	1	0	4	0	2	4	0	0	11
1975	0	0	1	1	0	9	0	3	7	0	0	22
1980	0	0	3	2	0	15	1	7	22	10	0	61
1985	0	0	5	5	68	27	1	15	92	12	0	225
1988	0	0	5	5	102	30	1	15	98	12	0	269
1990	0	0	6	6	137	69	1	15	83	59	1	378

Table C.14c: Municipal Funding of Spendng on Research Establishments (Millions of Dollars)

Year	Nfld	PEI	NS	NB	Que	Ont	Man	Sask	Alta	BC	Terr	Cda
1970	0	0	0	0	0	0	0	0	0	0	0	0
1975	0	0	0	0	0	0	0	0	0	0	0	0
1980	0	0	0	0	0	0	0	0	0	0	0	0
1985	0	0	0	0	0	0	0	0	0	0	0	0
1988	0	0	0	0	0	0	0	0	0	0	0	0
1990	0	0	0	0	0	0	0	0	0	0	0	0

Table C.14d: Total Funding of Spendng on Research Establishments (Millions of Dollars)

Year	Nfld	PEI	NS	NB	Que	Ont	Man	Sask	Alta	BC	Terr	Cda
1970	8	2	15	12	102	146	17	18	34	40	1	395
1975	12	2	20	15	131	197	22	22	49	55	2	527
1980	25	5	42	32	274	410	47	50	119	132	3	1,137
1985	23	4	45	35	341	432	45	57	193	136	2	1,311
1988	20	3	43	34	374	438	41	55	198	140	2	1,349
1990	27	4	54	42	487	605	52	66	212	229	4	1,782

Table C.14e: Federal Government Expenditure on Research Establishments (Millions of Dollars)

	Nfld	PEI	NS	NB	Que	Ont	Man	Sask	Alta	BC	Terr	Cda
Gross expenditure	8	2	14	11	102	142	17	16	31	40	1	384
Transfer to provincial government	0	0	0	0	0	0	0	0	0	0	0	0
Transfer to municipal government	0	0	0	0	0	0	0	0	0	0	0	0
Net expenditure 1970	8	2	14	11	102	142	17	16	31	40	1	384
Gross expenditure	12	2	18	14	131	189	22	19	41	55	1	503
Transfer to provincial government	0	0	0	0	0	0	0	0	0	0	0	0
Transfer to municipal government	0	0	0	0	0	0	0	0	0	0	0	0
Net expenditure 1975	12	2	18	14	131	189	22	19	41	55	1	503
Gross expenditure	25	5	38	29	274	394	45	43	96	122	3	1,073
Transfer to provincial government	0	0	0	0	0	0	0	0	0	0	0	0
Transfer to municipal government	0	0	0	0	0	0	0	0	0	0	0	0
Net expenditure 1980	25	5	38	29	274	394	45	43	96	122	3	1,073

Table C.14e: Federal Government Expenditure on Research Establishments (Millions of Dollars)

	Nfld	PEI	NS	NB	Que	Ont	Man	Sask	Alta	BC	Terr	Cda
Gross expenditure	23	4	38	28	264	405	43	42	99	124	2	1,072
Transfer to provincial government	0	0	0	0	0	0	0	0	0	0	0	0
Transfer to municipal government	0	0	0	0	0	0	0	0	0	0	0	0
Net expenditure 1985	23	4	38	28	264	405	43	42	99	124	2	1,072
Gross expenditure	20	3	36	27	259	408	40	39	98	128	2	1,059
Transfer to provincial government	0	0	0	0	0	0	0	0	0	0	0	0
Transfer to municipal government	0	0	0	0	0	0	0	0	0	0	0	0
Net expenditure 1988	20	3	36	27	259	408	40	39	98	128	2	1,059
Gross expenditure	27	4	47	34	336	535	51	50	128	169	2	1,384
Transfer to provincial government	0	0	0	0	0	0	0	0	0	0	0	0
Transfer to municipal government	0	0	0	0	0	0	0	0	0	0	0	0
Net expenditure 1990	27	4	47	34	336	535	51	50	128	169	2	1,384

Table C.14f: Provincial Government Expenditure on Research Establishments (Millions of Dollars)

	Nfld	PEI	NS	NB	Que	Ont	Man	Sask	Alta	BC	Terr	Cda
Gross expenditure	0	0	1	1	0	4	0	2	4	0	0	12
Transfer to municipal government	0	0	0	0	0	0	0	0	0	0	0	0
Net expenditure 1970	0	0	1	1	0	4	0	2	4	0	0	12
Gross expenditure	0	0	2	1	0	9	0	4	7	0	0	24
Transfer to municipal government	0	0	0	0	0	0	0	0	0	0	0	0
Net expenditure 1975	0	0	2	1	0	9	0	4	7	0	0	24
Gross expenditure	0	0	4	3	0	16	2	8	23	10	0	64
Transfer to municipal government	0	0	0	0	0	0	0	0	0	0	0	0
Net expenditure 1980	0	0	4	3	0	16	2	8	23	10	0	64
Gross expenditure	0	0	7	7	77	27	1	15	94	12	0	239
Transfer to municipal government	0	0	0	0	0	0	0	0	0	0	0	0
Net expenditure 1985	0	0	7	7	77	27	1	15	94	12	0	239

Table C.14f: Provincial Government Expenditure on Research Establishments (Millions of Dollars)

	Nfld	PEI	NS	NB	Que	Ont	Man	Sask	Alta	BC	Terr	Cda
Gross expenditure	0	0	7	8	115	30	1	16	100	12	1	290
Transfer to municipal government	0	0	0	0	0	0	0	0	0	0	0	0
Net expenditure 1988	0	0	7	8	115	30	1	16	100	12	1	290
Gross expenditure	0	0	8	8	151	69	1	16	84	59	1	398
Transfer to municipal government	0	0	0	0	0	0	0	0	0	0	0	0
Net expenditure 1990	0	0	8	8	151	69	1	16	84	59	1	398

Table C.14g: Municipal Government Expenditure on Research Establishments (Millions of Dollars)

Year	Nfld	PEI	NS	NB	Que	Ont	Man	Sask	Alta	BC	Terr	Cda
1970	0	0	0	0	0	0	0	0	0	0	0	0
1975	0	0	0	0	0	0	0	0	0	0	0	0
1980	0	0	0	0	0	0	0	0	0	0	0	0
1985	0	0	0	0	0	0	0	0	0	0	0	0
1988	0	0	0	0	0	0	0	0	0	0	0	0
1990	0	0	0	0	0	0	0	0	0	0	0	0

Table C.15a: Federal Funding of Spending on Social Services (Millions of Dollars)

Year	Nfld	PEI	NS	NB	Que	Ont	Man	Sask	Alta	BC	Terr	Cda
1970	148	39	215	169	1,109	1,612	235	212	305	539	8	4,592
1975	425	98	555	502	3,232	4,113	527	448	727	1,456	37	12,121
1980	686	162	913	815	5,427	5,933	832	710	1,139	2,102	60	18,778
1985	1,218	287	1,515	1,413	9,446	10,134	1,441	1,265	2,628	4,278	114	33,739
1988	1,520	340	1,741	1,630	10,817	11,292	1,708	1,496	2,995	4,941	151	38,631
1990	1,763	381	2,011	1,825	12,936	14,024	1,888	1,641	3,390	5,613	120	45,593

Table C.15b: Provincial Funding of Spending on Social Services (Millions of Dollars)

Year	Nfld	PEI	NS	NB	Que	Ont	Man	Sask	Alta	BC	Terr	Cda
1970	16	3	17	17	494	401	32	27	85	165	2	1,258
1975	39	8	37	58	982	1,103	120	112	191	493	3	3,147
1980	67	15	112	101	1,914	2,329	230	305	478	840	9	6,401
1985	130	24	184	188	3,680	3,685	401	336	990	1,239	17	10,875
1988	135	32	203	227	4,595	5,194	497	290	1,227	1,328	28	13,757
1990	210	44	273	269	4,886	7,611	636	289	1,423	1,784	84	17,510

Table C.15c: Municipal Funding of Spending on Social Services (Millions of Dollars)

Year	Nfld	PEI	NS	NB	Que	Ont	Man	Sask	Alta	BC	Terr	Cda
1970	0	0	7	0	5	81	0	3	3	23	0	122
1975	0	0	18	0	0	222	0	5	7	11	0	264
1980	0	0	31	0	0	206	4	7	17	29	0	294
1985	0	0	52	0	17	265	6	11	27	2	2	380
1988	0	0	113	0	23	541	11	8	45	3	2	745
1990	0	0	119	0	0	409	9	16	0	0	0	553

Table C.15d: Total Funding of Spending on Social Services (Millions of Dollars)

Year	Nfld	PEI	NS	NB	Que	Ont	Man	Sask	Alta	BC	Terr	Cda
1970	164	42	239	186	1,608	2,094	267	242	392	728	11	5,972
1975	463	106	611	560	4,214	5,438	647	565	926	1,960	40	15,531
1980	753	177	1,055	916	7,342	8,469	1,066	1,023	1,633	2,972	68	25,474
1985	1,348	311	1,751	1,602	13,143	14,084	1,848	1,612	3,645	5,519	133	44,995
1988	1,654	372	2,058	1,858	15,435	17,028	2,216	1,794	4,267	6,271	181	53,133
1990	1,972	425	2,403	2,095	17,822	22,044	2,533	1,946	4,813	7,397	205	63,655

Table C.15e: Federal Government Expenditure on Social Services (Millions of Dollars)

	Nfld	PEI	NS	NB	Que	Ont	Man	Sask	Alta	BC	Terr	Cda
Gross expenditure	138	36	209	164	983	1,608	231	209	303	539	7	4,427
Transfer to provincial government	23	4	18	17	0	183	30	22	41	70	1	409
Transfer to municipal government	0	0	0	0	0	0	0	0	0	0	0	0
Net expenditure 1970	115	33	191	147	982	1,425	201	187	262	469	6	4,018
Gross expenditure	411	94	537	478	3,078	4,086	507	441	723	1,449	31	11,833
Transfer to provincial government	37	9	46	54	177	451	76	49	109	186	6	1,200
Transfer to municipal government	0	0	0	0	13	6	0	0	0	3	0	23
Net expenditure 1975	374	85	490	424	2,888	3,629	430	392	614	1,260	25	10,610
Gross expenditure	656	153	865	776	5,172	5,911	774	700	1,134	2,100	42	18,283
Transfer to provincial government	57	13	65	81	646	565	73	76	162	315	8	2,061
Transfer to municipal government	0	0	2	0	5	0	0	0	0	0	0	8
Net expenditure 1980	598	140	798	695	4,521	5,345	701	624	972	1,785	34	16,214

Table C.15e: Federal Government Expenditure on Social Services (Millions of Dollars)

	Nfld	PEI	NS	NB	Que	Ont	Man	Sask	Alta	BC	Terr	Cda
Gross expenditure	1,148	273	1,461	1,335	8,974	10,112	1,388	1,265	2,609	4,274	89	32,928
Transfer to provincial government	85	21	113	142	1,213	1,087	162	153	411	621	18	4,027
Transfer to municipal government	0	0	2	0	9	6	3	0	2	4	0	26
Net expenditure 1985	1,063	252	1,346	1,193	7,752	9,019	1,223	1,112	2,196	3,649	71	28,876
Gross expenditure	1,444	322	1,675	1,542	10,223	11,261	1,609	1,472	2,974	4,935	101	37,557
Transfer to provincial government	106	24	150	171	1,370	1,317	206	187	507	751	21	4,810
Transfer to municipal government	0	0	1	0	6	10	3	0	1	4	0	26
Net expenditure 1988	1,337	297	1,523	1,371	8,847	9,935	1,400	1,285	2,466	4,181	80	32,721
Gross expenditure	1,688	364	1,942	1,750	12,465	13,984	1,799	1,618	3,375	5,609	120	44,715
Transfer to provincial government	127	29	179	204	1,633	1,570	245	223	605	895	25	5,735
Transfer to municipal government	0	0	2	0	8	12	4	0	1	5	0	40
Net expenditure 1990	1,556	336	1,761	1,543	10,824	12,403	1,549	1,395	2,769	4,709	96	38,940

Table C.15f: Provincial Government Expenditure on Social Services (Millions of Dollars)

	Nfld	PEI	NS	NB	Que	Ont	Man	Sask	Alta	BC	Terr	Cda
Gross expenditure	49	9	40	39	619	586	66	52	127	233	5	1,825
Transfer to municipal government	0	0	9	0	0	91	7	0	8	55	0	169
Net expenditure 1970	49	9	31	39	619	495	60	52	119	178	5	1,656
Gross expenditure	90	21	100	137	1,313	1,556	217	169	304	686	15	4,608
Transfer to municipal government	0	0	15	0	0	133	6	0	12	41	0	207
Net expenditure 1975	90	21	86	137	1,313	1,423	211	169	292	645	15	4,400
Gross expenditure	154	37	214	220	2,815	2,901	361	391	643	1,155	34	8,926
Transfer to municipal government	0	0	49	0	13	424	8	0	20	0	0	514
Net expenditure 1980	154	37	165	220	2,802	2,477	353	391	623	1,155	34	8,412
Gross expenditure	284	60	343	409	5,364	4,768	615	488	1,418	1,864	61	15,673
Transfer to municipal government	0	0	88	0	0	894	37	4	23	0	0	1,047
Net expenditure 1985	284	60	255	409	5,364	3,874	578	484	1,395	1,864	61	14,626

Table C.15f: Provincial Government Expenditure on Social Services (Millions of Dollars)

	Nfld	PEI	NS	NB	Que	Ont	Man	Sask	Alta	BC	Terr	Cda
Gross expenditure	317	75	409	487	6,557	6,474	801	500	1,751	2,084	98	19,552
Transfer to municipal government	0	0	101	0	0	1,091	39	8	22	0	0	1,261
Net expenditure 1988	317	75	308	487	6,557	5,384	761	492	1,729	2,084	98	18,292
Gross expenditure	411	89	510	549	6,991	9,188	970	533	2,043	2,683	109	24,075
Transfer to municipal government	0	0	149	0	35	1,719	47	0	70	3	3	2,025
Net expenditure 1990	411	89	361	549	6,956	7,469	923	533	1,973	2,680	106	22,050

Table C.15g: Municipal Government Expenditure on Social Services (Millions of Dollars)

Year	Nfld	PEI	NS	NB	Que	Ont	Man	Sask	Alta	BC	Terr	Cda
1970	0.00	0.04	15.66	0.03	6.14	174.59	6.56	2.88	10.71	81.33	0.00	297.93
1975	0.00	0.01	34.70	0.00	12.89	385.11	5.87	5.18	20.70	56.36	0.00	520.82
1980	0.00	0.01	92.09	0.00	17.98	647.21	12.41	8.51	37.72	31.91	0.02	847.85
1985	0.05	0.00	150.65	0.00	27.04	1,191.62	46.79	15.90	53.56	5.82	1.63	1,493.06
1988	0.05	0.01	227.25	0.00	30.79	1,709.23	54.73	17.02	71.98	6.84	2.32	2,120.22
1990	0.06	0.01	281.30	0.00	42.90	2,171.55	61.10	18.47	71.00	7.64	2.63	2,656.64

Table C.16a: Federal Funding of Spending on Transportation & Communications (Millions of Dollars)

Year	Nfld	PEI	NS	NB	Que	Ont	Man	Sask	Alta	BC	Terr	Cda
1970	38	8	47	35	203	268	30	30	34	48	8	751
1975	61	15	122	80	406	675	94	100	111	132	26	1,822
1980	92	34	243	142	637	1,028	142	120	176	247	55	2,915
1985	154	58	290	215	874	1,308	187	153	267	334	72	3,913
1988	181	56	319	217	916	1,391	224	217	290	350	105	4,267
1990	178	54	301	229	847	1,344	199	172	351	347	46	4,068

Table C.16b: Provincial Funding of Spending on Transportation & Communications (Millions of Dollars)

Year	Nfld	PEI	NS	NB	Que	Ont	Man	Sask	Alta	BC	Terr	Cda
1970	27	7	49	56	354	505	46	73	97	138	5	1,358
1975	84	14	78	91	808	762	75	121	283	391	6	2,712
1980	80	28	137	134	965	1,245	124	176	638	660	10	4,198
1985	113	32	167	173	1,283	1,626	174	237	907	992	26	5,730
1988	121	38	184	183	1,346	1,920	173	228	808	551	40	5,592
1990	156	48	197	253	1,537	2,438	223	232	915	889	114	7,001

Table C.16c: Municipal Funding of Spending on Transportation & Communications (Millions of Dollars)

Year	Nfld	PEI	NS	NB	Que	Ont	Man	Sask	Alta	BC	Terr	Cda
1970	3	1	10	9	200	267	27	33	79	63	1	693
1975	17	2	27	30	402	387	61	74	176	128	5	1,308
1980	24	3	31	32	534	490	87	142	464	213	8	2,027
1985	37	4	43	47	912	616	154	179	516	294	20	2,822
1988	51	7	46	47	1,176	824	173	191	538	336	23	3,412
1990	54	6	62	51	1,726	876	196	207	629	441	23	4,271

Table C.16d: Total Funding of Spending on Transportation & Communications (Millions of Dollars)

Year	Nfld	PEI	NS	NB	Que	Ont	Man	Sask	Alta	BC	Terr	Cda
1970	68	16	107	99	757	1,041	103	136	211	250	14	2,802
1975	162	30	226	200	1,615	1,824	229	296	570	651	37	5,842
1980	196	65	410	308	2,136	2,763	353	437	1,278	1,120	73	9,140
1985	304	94	500	435	3,070	3,550	516	570	1,690	1,620	118	12,466
1988	353	101	550	446	3,438	4,136	570	635	1,637	1,238	167	13,272
1990	388	108	560	532	4,111	4,657	618	610	1,895	1,677	182	15,340

Table C.16e: Federal Government Expenditure on Transportation and Communications (Millions of Dollars)

	Nfld	PEI	NS	NB	Que	Ont	Man	Sask	Alta	BC	Terr	Cda
Gross expenditure	22	2	32	18	117	260	24	22	33	48	5	583
Transfer to provincial government	10	0	1	4	16	7	1	1	1	3	0	45
Transfer to municipal government	0	0	0	0	2	6	1	0	1	1	0	11
Net expenditure 1970	12	2	30	14	99	248	23	20	30	44	5	527
Gross expenditure	31	8	83	46	286	655	80	92	103	125	13	1,524
Transfer to provincial government	1	0	0	3	14	14	11	9	12	4	0	68
Transfer to municipal government	0	0	0	0	1	10	1	3	1	1	0	19
Net expenditure 1975	30	8	83	43	270	631	68	80	91	120	13	1,437
Gross expenditure	57	18	183	97	507	1,011	112	113	169	245	35	2,546
Transfer to provincial government	6	1	5	13	16	2	2	10	4	12	12	83
Transfer to municipal government	0	0	0	1	3	22	1	0	2	1	3	33
Net expenditure 1980	51	17	178	82	489	987	108	103	164	232	21	2,430

Table C.16e: Federal Government Expenditure on Transportation and Communications (Millions of Dollars)

	Nfld	PEI	NS	NB	Que	Ont	Man	Sask	Alta	BC	Terr	Cda
Gross expenditure	98	39	241	153	708	1,292	164	152	248	328	35	3,457
Transfer to provincial government	20	10	10	44	16	1	1	0	0	15	6	123
Transfer to municipal government	10	0	0	1	2	13	2	0	1	4	1	34
Net expenditure 1985	68	29	231	108	690	1,278	162	152	246	310	28	3,300
Gross expenditure	117	34	259	155	738	1,372	191	198	274	344	44	3,727
Transfer to provincial government	27	5	9	33	22	1	2	0	0	17	7	122
Transfer to municipal government	10	0	0	2	5	18	3	1	1	4	1	44
Net expenditure 1988	81	29	250	120	712	1,352	186	198	273	323	37	3,561
Gross expenditure	125	36	251	164	694	1,323	168	153	338	341	45	3,640
Transfer to provincial government	28	5	9	35	23	1	2	0	0	18	7	127
Transfer to municipal government	10	0	0	2	5	19	3	1	1	4	1	46
Net expenditure 1990	88	31	242	128	666	1,303	163	153	337	319	37	3,467

Table C.16f: Provincial Government Expenditure on Transportation & Communications (Millions of Dollars)

	Nfld	PEI	NS	NB	Que	Ont	Man	Sask	Alta	BC	Terr	Cda
Gross expenditure	52	13	66	73	427	510	51	83	94	135	8	1,511
Transfer to municipal government	2	0	0	1	10	162	12	13	18	0	0	218
Net expenditure 1970	50	13	65	72	417	347	39	69	76	135	8	1,293
Gross expenditure	113	21	114	119	875	754	97	136	293	392	19	2,929
Transfer to municipal government	4	0	0	1	38	303	27	24	57	0	1	457
Net expenditure 1975	109	21	114	118	836	451	69	111	235	392	18	2,472
Gross expenditure	116	45	191	177	1,077	1,223	147	176	629	659	42	4,482
Transfer to municipal government	3	0	16	4	213	551	39	13	160	16	0	1,015
Net expenditure 1980	112	45	175	173	864	673	108	163	469	643	41	3,467
Gross expenditure	181	60	219	251	1,408	1,582	178	216	881	997	68	6,041
Transfer to municipal government	5	0	14	1	87	872	2	9	163	16	0	1,169
Net expenditure 1985	176	60	206	250	1,321	710	176	207	718	981	68	4,873

Table C.16f: Provincial Government Expenditure on Transportation & Communications (Millions of Dollars)

	Nfld	PEI	NS	NB	Que	Ont	Man	Sask	Alta	BC	Terr	Cda
Gross expenditure	201	63	248	246	1,475	1,838	185	223	778	557	100	5,913
Transfer to municipal government	8	0	16	2	81	999	8	10	186	12	0	1,321
Net expenditure 1988	193	63	232	244	1,394	839	177	213	592	545	99	4,592
Gross expenditure	224	70	250	316	1,621	2,390	236	223	886	890	115	7,220
Transfer to municipal government	9	0	16	2	89	1,299	10	10	212	19	1	1,666
Net expenditure 1990	215	70	234	314	1,532	1,091	225	214	674	871	114	5,554

Table C.16g: Municipal Government Expenditure on Transportation & Communications (Millions of Dollars)

Year	Nfld	PEI	NS	NB	Que	Ont	Man	Sask	Alta	BC	Terr	Cda
1970	5.49	1.13	10.87	13.69	241.11	446.13	40.92	46.64	104.50	70.62	0.91	982.02
1975	22.80	1.87	29.21	40.01	508.90	742.23	91.71	104.85	243.67	138.87	6.03	1,930.14
1980	33.08	3.23	57.00	52.51	782.82	1,102.96	136.46	171.92	646.15	245.46	11.11	3,242.71
1985	60.56	4.43	63.84	76.72	1,059.61	1,562.06	177.89	211.09	725.59	328.99	21.69	4,292.47
1988	79.48	8.76	67.37	82.39	1,331.94	1,944.44	207.07	224.52	771.87	369.50	31.56	5,118.91
1990	85.16	6.79	84.86	90.04	1,912.18	2,263.04	229.79	243.91	883.93	487.17	31.26	6,318.12

Table C.17a: Federal Funding of Total Spending (Millions of Dollars)

Year	Nfld	PEI	NS	NB	Que	Ont	Man	Sask	Alta	BC	Terr	Cda
1970	454	139	883	583	3,814	5,725	797	736	1,101	1,416	109	15,757
1975	1,090	290	2,289	1,528	9,171	13,087	1,724	1,699	2,512	3,424	282	37,095
1980	1,885	481	4,367	3,169	16,775	22,907	3,100	2,631	4,392	5,927	531	66,163
1985	3,874	828	6,297	3,988	26,571	41,127	5,042	4,865	9,408	11,032	2,258	115,289
1988	3,804	977	6,651	5,003	30,589	49,825	6,186	5,930	11,219	12,936	1,442	134,562
1990	4,054	1,049	7,215	5,474	34,884	61,013	6,234	5,375	10,990	14,632	756	151,675

Table C.17b: Provincial Funding of Total Spending (Millions of Dollars)

Year	Nfld	PEI	NS	NB	Que	Ont	Man	Sask	Alta	BC	Terr	Cda
1970	177	28	308	287	3,130	4,573	425	384	1,073	1,056	54	11,495
1975	603	106	607	568	7,492	9,686	971	997	2,544	3,167	67	26,808
1980	953	168	1,188	986	14,661	15,466	1,581	2,103	6,299	5,799	134	49,338
1985	1,380	249	2,186	1,726	23,430	28,739	3,548	4,084	11,976	9,552	325	87,194
1988	1,666	344	2,665	2,209	27,703	37,010	4,114	4,315	12,629	10,942	431	104,028
1990	2,187	464	3,152	2,809	32,418	45,020	4,959	4,766	14,214	15,211	1,383	126,584

Table C.17c: Municipal Funding of Total Spending (Millions of Dollars)

Year	Nfld	PEI	NS	NB	Que	Ont	Man	Sask	Alta	BC	Terr	Cda
1970	15	10	149	32	1,166	2,243	228	241	540	509	3	5,137
1975	62	14	259	110	2,042	3,606	482	420	1,081	1,099	21	9,194
1980	126	16	377	122	3,837	6,012	741	712	2,638	2,128	47	16,756
1985	179	30	450	199	5,558	9,034	825	943	3,014	2,357	93	22,683
1988	254	30	724	206	6,523	11,772	1,031	1,065	3,173	2,831	98	27,707
1990	261	30	767	217	7,955	14,049	1,273	1,141	3,568	3,594	109	32,964

Table C.17d: Total Spending (Millions of Dollars)

Year	Nfld	PEI	NS	NB	Que	Ont	Man	Sask	Alta	BC	Terr	Cda
1970	645	178	1,340	902	8,111	12,541	1,450	1,361	2,715	2,981	166	32,390
1975	1,754	410	3,154	2,205	18,705	26,378	3,177	3,116	6,137	7,690	370	73,097
1980	2,964	665	5,933	4,276	35,273	44,384	5,421	5,446	13,329	13,854	711	132,257
1985	5,434	1,107	8,932	5,913	55,560	78,899	9,414	9,892	24,398	22,941	2,676	225,165
1988	5,723	1,351	10,040	7,418	64,816	98,607	11,331	11,310	27,022	26,709	1,970	266,298
1990	6,502	1,543	11,134	8,500	75,257	120,083	12,465	11,282	28,772	33,438	2,248	311,223

Table C.17e: Total Federal Government Expenditure (Millions of Dollars)

	Nfld	PEI	NS	NB	Que	Ont	Man	Sask	Alta	BC	Terr	Cda
Gross expenditure	444	137	873	572	3,723	5,622	790	729	1,080	1,387	110	15,466
Transfer to provincial government	218	55	197	196	1,100	975	214	173	248	268	44	3,689
Transfer to municipal government	0	0	5	1	13	40	5	3	6	5	1	79
Net expenditure 1970	225	81	672	376	2,609	4,607	571	552	826	1,114	65	11,698
Gross expenditure	1,070	285	2,261	1,506	8,954	12,816	1,706	1,673	2,453	3,344	287	36,356
Transfer to provincial government	387	98	509	426	1,960	2,073	457	323	513	619	171	7,535
Transfer to municipal government	2	0	8	2	48	77	10	6	11	19	1	185
Net expenditure 1975	682	187	1,744	1,078	6,946	10,665	1,240	1,344	1,929	2,707	115	28,636
Gross expenditure	1,857	475	4,329	3,137	16,468	22,522	3,090	2,593	4,296	5,807	544	65,118
Transfer to provincial government	686	175	853	701	3,961	2,953	852	520	736	1,039	322	12,797
Transfer to municipal government	4	0	16	4	66	132	15	8	18	20	4	289
Net expenditure 1980	1,168	299	3,460	2,432	12,440	19,436	2,224	2,065	3,542	4,748	218	52,032

Table C.17e: Total Federal Government Expenditure (Millions of Dollars)

	Nfld	PEI	NS	NB	Que	Ont	Man	Sask	Alta	BC	Terr	Cda
Gross expenditure	3,823	815	6,225	3,930	25,998	40,391	4,995	4,783	9,213	10,798	2,374	113,347
Transfer to provincial government	1,083	255	1,204	1,191	6,257	4,550	1,134	818	1,614	1,838	677	20,622
Transfer to municipal government	14	0	19	5	64	142	20	7	21	40	4	336
Net expenditure 1985	2,726	560	5,002	2,733	19,677	35,700	3,841	3,958	7,578	8,920	1,693	92,390
Gross expenditure	3,717	957	6,527	4,898	29,598	48,501	6,121	5,823	10,881	12,519	1,563	131,103
Transfer to provincial government	1,320	296	1,439	1,313	7,158	5,045	1,584	1,109	1,860	2,074	950	24,148
Transfer to municipal government	16	2	24	14	74	195	24	11	25	45	5	434
Net expenditure 1988	2,381	659	5,064	3,572	22,366	43,261	4,513	4,703	8,995	10,400	608	106,522
Gross expenditure	3,973	1,030	7,085	5,375	33,942	59,731	6,169	5,268	10,663	14,221	745	148,203
Transfer to provincial government	1,178	276	1,356	1,269	6,808	5,036	1,454	1,089	1,805	2,148	90	22,510
Transfer to municipal government	16	1	20	15	73	200	26	10	21	45	5	441
Net expenditure 1990	2,773	752	5,709	4,088	27,061	54,495	4,689	4,169	8,838	12,028	650	125,252

Table C.17f: Total Provincial Government Expenditure (Millions of Dollars)

	Nfld	PEI	NS	NB	Que	Ont	Man	Sask	Alta	BC	Terr	Cda
Gross expenditure	398	85	504	485	4,241	5,549	633	551	1,321	1,324	96	15,188
Transfer to municipal government	7	12	83	16	943	1,239	123	97	267	275	2	3,064
Net expenditure 1970	391	73	421	469	3,298	4,310	510	455	1,054	1,049	95	12,124
Gross expenditure	991	205	1,117	994	9,466	11,760	1,413	1,315	3,057	3,785	231	34,354
Transfer to municipal government	21	33	201	39	1,919	2,591	203	202	558	610	10	6,387
Net expenditure 1975	970	172	916	955	7,547	9,169	1,209	1,113	2,499	3,176	221	27,967
Gross expenditure	1,641	344	2,042	1,687	18,644	18,420	2,396	2,618	7,035	6,838	439	62,104
Transfer to municipal government	49	55	443	82	3,805	3,904	354	374	1,249	707	5	11,027
Net expenditure 1980	1,592	289	1,599	1,606	14,839	14,517	2,041	2,245	5,786	6,131	434	51,078
Gross expenditure	2,467	506	3,391	2,918	29,730	33,290	4,642	4,902	13,593	11,390	880	107,707
Transfer to municipal government	76	79	757	141	4,835	6,976	840	754	2,927	1,460	15	18,860
Net expenditure 1985	2,391	427	2,633	2,777	24,895	26,314	3,802	4,148	10,666	9,930	864	88,847

Table C.17f: Total Provincial Government Expenditure (Millions of Dollars)

	Nfld	PEI	NS	NB	Que	Ont	Man	Sask	Alta	BC	Terr	Cda
Gross expenditure	2,992	642	4,104	3,527	34,922	42,057	5,612	5,389	14,493	13,015	1,249	128,068
Transfer to municipal government	85	93	882	161	5,601	9,007	968	864	3,265	1,654	54	22,634
Net expenditure 1988	2,907	550	3,223	3,366	29,321	33,050	4,643	4,525	11,228	11,362	1,194	105,435
Gross expenditure	3,371	742	4,521	4,082	39,279	50,058	6,334	5,831	16,020	17,360	1,473	149,072
Transfer to municipal government	101	104	1,060	180	6,312	10,666	1,106	1,022	3,670	2,010	61	26,292
Net expenditure 1990	3,270	638	3,461	3,902	32,967	39,392	5,228	4,809	12,350	15,350	1,413	122,780

Table C.17g: Total Municipal Government Expenditure (Millions of Dollars)

Year	Nfld	PEI	NS	NB	Que	Ont	Man	Sask	Alta	BC	Terr	Cda
1970	22	22	237	49	2,122	3,522	356	341	813	790	6	8,279
1975	84	47	467	151	4,009	6,274	695	628	1,650	1,727	32	15,766
1980	179	71	836	208	7,708	10,048	1,110	1,093	3,906	2,856	56	28,071
1985	270	110	1,226	344	10,457	16,151	1,685	1,704	5,962	3,857	112	41,878
1988	355	124	1,629	380	12,198	20,975	2,023	1,940	6,464	4,529	157	50,775
1990	379	135	1,846	412	14,341	24,915	2,405	2,173	7,259	5,648	175	59,688

Table C.18a: Federal Government Expenditure: General Purpose Transfers (Millions of Dollars)

	Nfld	PEI	NS	NB	Que	Ont	Man	Sask	Alta	BC	Terr	Cda
Gross expenditure	105	23	102	86	761	70	63	49	19	6	35	1,319
Transfer to provincial government	105	23	97	85	751	44	60	48	16	2	35	1,265
Transfer to municipal government	0	0	4	1	11	26	3	1	3	4	1	54
Net expenditure 1970	0	0	0	0	0	0	0	0	0	0	0	0
Gross expenditure	214	53	304	219	1,125	245	187	71	68	55	147	2,688
Transfer to provincial government	213	53	298	219	1,110	209	181	69	64	47	146	2,609
Transfer to municipal government	1	0	5	0	15	36	6	2	5	8	1	78
Net expenditure 1975	0	0	0	0	0	0	0	0	0	0	0	0
Gross expenditure	421	95	506	353	1,940	204	423	81	66	25	274	4,387
Transfer to provincial government	419	95	495	351	1,904	129	416	77	58	13	273	4,230
Transfer to municipal government	2	0	10	2	35	75	8	4	8	12	1	158
Net expenditure 1980	0	0	0	0	0	0	0	0	0	0	0	0

Table C.18a: Federal Government Expenditure: General Purpose Transfers (Millions of Dollars)

	Nfld	PEI	NS	NB	Que	Ont	Man	Sask	Alta	BC	Terr	Cda
Gross expenditure	717	146	638	673	2,971	261	508	8	235	52	589	6,799
Transfer to provincial government	714	146	621	669	2,922	144	494	2	220	27	586	6,545
Transfer to municipal government	3	0	17	3	50	117	14	6	15	25	3	254
Net expenditure 1985	0	0	0	0	0	0	0	0	0	0	0	0
Gross expenditure	912	195	870	817	3,539	321	902	395	222	76	856	9,104
Transfer to provincial government	907	193	849	805	3,477	164	886	386	200	44	852	8,763
Transfer to municipal government	5	2	21	11	62	157	16	9	22	32	4	341
Net expenditure 1988	0	0	0	0	0	0	0	0	0	0	0	0
Gross expenditure	759	170	783	757	3,099	359	771	404	167	66	5	7,340
Transfer to provincial government	754	168	766	744	3,040	199	754	396	150	35	1	7,007
Transfer to municipal government	5	1	17	12	59	160	17	8	17	31	4	333
Net expenditure 1990	0	0	0	0	0	0	0	0	0	0	0	0

Table C.18b: Provincial Government Expenditure: General Purpose Transfers (Millions of Dollars)

	Nfld	PEI	NS	NB	Que	Ont	Man	Sask	Alta	BC	Terr	Cda
Gross expenditure	3	1	3	15	157	64	11	0	41	48	0	342
Transfer to municipal government	3	1	3	15	157	64	11	0	41	48	0	342
Net expenditure 1970	0	0	0	0	0	0	0	0	0	0	0	0
Gross expenditure	7	2	19	32	324	355	13	12	52	73	0	891
Transfer to municipal government	7	2	19	32	324	355	13	12	52	73	0	891
Net expenditure 1975	0	0	0	0	0	0	0	0	0	0	0	0
Gross expenditure	28	3	119	61	202	417	75	81	105	141	0	1,231
Transfer to municipal government	28	3	119	61	202	417	75	81	105	141	0	1,231
Net expenditure 1980	0	0	0	0	0	0	0	0	0	0	0	0

Table C.18b: Provincial Government Expenditure: General Purpose Transfers (Millions of Dollars)

	Nfld	PEI	NS	NB	Que	Ont	Man	Sask	Alta	BC	Terr	Cda
Gross expenditure	39	4	53	113	304	784	91	112	253	99	2	1,854
Transfer to municipal government	39	4	53	113	304	784	91	112	253	99	2	1,854
Net expenditure 1985	0	0	0	0	0	0	0	0	0	0	0	0
Gross expenditure	48	4	55	132	330	1,318	121	123	257	114	28	2,528
Transfer to municipal government	48	4	55	132	330	1,318	121	123	257	114	28	2,528
Net expenditure 1988	0	0	0	0	0	0	0	0	0	0	0	0
Gross expenditure	51	5	57	140	367	956	113	140	224	155	31	2,238
Transfer to municipal government	51	5	57	140	367	956	113	140	224	155	31	2,238
Net expenditure 1990	0	0	0	0	0	0	0	0	0	0	0	0

Appendix D: Funding of Each Dollar Spent by Government by Function

Funding of Each Dollar Spent by Government on Culture and Recreation

Table D.1a: Federal (Dollar)

Year	Nfld	PEI	NS	NB	Que	Ont	Man	Sask	Alta	BC	Terr	Cda
1970	0.58	0.47	0.55	0.34	0.22	0.20	0.34	0.21	0.15	0.17	0.53	0.22
1975	0.31	0.45	0.59	0.34	0.21	0.24	0.20	0.22	0.14	0.16	0.58	0.22
1980	0.41	0.47	0.54	0.38	0.20	0.21	0.27	0.16	0.08	0.16	0.60	0.20
1985	0.40	0.51	0.51	0.37	0.21	0.21	0.25	0.15	0.11	0.15	0.41	0.21
1988	0.40	0.52	0.49	0.41	0.22	0.21	0.27	0.17	0.12	0.19	0.59	0.22
1990	0.38	0.42	0.45	0.38	0.20	0.20	0.18	0.15	0.12	0.16	0.20	0.20

Table D.1b: Provincial (Dollar)

Year	Nfld	PEI	NS	NB	Que	Ont	Man	Sask	Alta	BC	Terr	Cda
1970	0.29	0.32	0.19	0.41	0.30	0.23	0.29	0.28	0.22	0.23	0.38	0.26
1975	0.44	0.36	0.24	0.28	0.39	0.24	0.29	0.23	0.33	0.29	0.13	0.30
1980	0.38	0.34	0.28	0.36	0.31	0.26	0.26	0.31	0.36	0.24	0.23	0.29
1985	0.31	0.26	0.20	0.34	0.34	0.25	0.32	0.35	0.47	0.34	0.18	0.32
1988	0.28	0.23	0.22	0.31	0.31	0.28	0.29	0.32	0.37	0.23	0.15	0.29
1990	0.31	0.34	0.23	0.37	0.30	0.24	0.27	0.36	0.31	0.27	0.61	0.28

Funding of Each Dollar Spent by Government on Culture and Recreation

Table D.1c: Municipal (Dollar)

Year	Nfld	PEI	NS	NB	Que	Ont	Man	Sask	Alta	BC	Terr	Cda
1970	0.13	0.21	0.26	0.25	0.48	0.56	0.37	0.51	0.63	0.59	0.09	0.52
1975	0.25	0.19	0.18	0.38	0.40	0.52	0.51	0.55	0.53	0.54	0.29	0.48
1980	0.22	0.19	0.18	0.26	0.48	0.53	0.47	0.53	0.56	0.60	0.17	0.51
1985	0.29	0.23	0.29	0.29	0.45	0.53	0.43	0.49	0.42	0.51	0.41	0.47
1988	0.32	0.25	0.29	0.28	0.48	0.51	0.44	0.51	0.51	0.59	0.26	0.49
1990	0.31	0.24	0.32	0.25	0.50	0.57	0.55	0.49	0.58	0.57	0.19	0.53

Note: Figures may not add up due to rounding.

Funding of Each Dollar Spent by Government on Education

Table D.2a: Federal (Dollar)

Year	Nfld	PEI	NS	NB	Que	Ont	Man	Sask	Alta	BC	Terr	Cda
1970	0.49	0.72	0.26	0.38	0.30	0.09	0.27	0.25	0.12	0.11	0.50	0.18
1975	0.29	0.37	0.34	0.33	0.22	0.09	0.19	0.15	0.10	0.06	0.70	0.15
1980	0.39	0.47	0.34	0.40	0.19	0.13	0.29	0.21	0.09	0.14	0.64	0.18
1985	0.42	0.47	0.32	0.43	0.20	0.11	0.29	0.20	0.12	0.18	0.61	0.18
1988	0.42	0.45	0.29	0.38	0.18	0.11	0.29	0.25	0.15	0.18	0.66	0.17
1990	0.32	0.35	0.26	0.31	0.15	0.08	0.26	0.23	0.13	0.11	0.05	0.14

Table D.2b: Provincial (Dollar)

Year	Nfld	PEI	NS	NB	Que	Ont	Man	Sask	Alta	BC	Terr	Cda
1970	0.50	0.07	0.49	0.62	0.49	0.57	0.44	0.42	0.67	0.53	0.50	0.54
1975	0.70	0.63	0.46	0.67	0.65	0.66	0.48	0.59	0.72	0.59	0.30	0.64
1980	0.58	0.53	0.46	0.60	0.73	0.54	0.39	0.52	0.68	0.47	0.30	0.60
1985	0.55	0.49	0.61	0.57	0.74	0.60	0.59	0.54	0.68	0.67	0.38	0.64
1988	0.55	0.55	0.52	0.62	0.78	0.55	0.54	0.47	0.69	0.64	0.34	0.62
1990	0.65	0.65	0.59	0.69	0.85	0.55	0.61	0.56	0.70	0.73	0.95	0.67

Funding of Each Dollar Spent by Government on Education

Table D.2c: Municipal (Dollar)

Year	Nfld	PEI	NS	NB	Que	Ont	Man	Sask	Alta	BC	Terr	Cda
1970	0.01	0.21	0.26	0.00	0.21	0.34	0.30	0.33	0.21	0.36	0.00	0.28
1975	0.01	0.00	0.19	0.00	0.13	0.25	0.33	0.26	0.19	0.36	0.00	0.21
1980	0.03	0.00	0.20	0.00	0.08	0.32	0.32	0.27	0.23	0.39	0.06	0.22
1985	0.03	0.05	0.07	0.00	0.06	0.29	0.12	0.26	0.20	0.15	0.00	0.18
1988	0.03	0.00	0.19	0.00	0.04	0.35	0.17	0.28	0.16	0.18	0.01	0.20
1990	0.03	0.00	0.15	0.00	0.00	0.37	0.13	0.22	0.17	0.16	0.00	0.19

Note: Figures may not add up due to rounding.

Funding of Each Dollar Spent by Government on the Environment

Table D.3a: Federal (Dollar)

Year	Nfld	PEI	NS	NB	Que	Ont	Man	Sask	Alta	BC	Terr	Cda
1970	0.22	0.38	0.04	0.01	0.02	0.01	0.02	0.01	0.00	0.01	0.33	0.02
1975	0.29	0.23	0.26	0.17	0.20	0.14	0.26	0.20	0.11	0.19	0.35	0.17
1980	0.24	0.30	0.22	0.27	0.15	0.12	0.19	0.13	0.05	0.10	0.15	0.12
1985	0.31	0.35	0.20	0.24	0.13	0.11	0.16	0.14	0.09	0.14	0.11	0.13
1988	0.28	0.44	0.19	0.27	0.14	0.10	0.15	0.14	0.09	0.14	0.13	0.12
1990	0.27	0.39	0.16	0.28	0.10	0.10	0.13	0.14	0.10	0.12	0.06	0.11

Table D.3b: Provincial (Dollar)

Year	Nfld	PEI	NS	NB	Que	Ont	Man	Sask	Alta	BC	Terr	Cda
1970	0.41	0.45	0.06	0.32	0.15	0.12	0.07	0.01	0.07	0.10	0.21	0.12
1975	0.37	0.25	0.14	0.22	0.19	0.36	0.10	0.09	0.29	0.12	0.14	0.27
1980	0.35	0.22	0.25	0.41	0.17	0.32	0.13	0.23	0.47	0.28	0.04	0.30
1985	0.39	0.23	0.15	0.42	0.42	0.28	0.17	0.25	0.40	0.39	0.04	0.35
1988	0.35	0.34	0.18	0.42	0.34	0.32	0.14	0.25	0.50	0.40	0.22	0.34
1990	0.43	0.53	0.16	0.46	0.21	0.25	0.14	0.25	0.44	0.35	0.39	0.27

Funding of Each Dollar Spent by Government on the Environment

Table D.3c: Municipal (Dollar)

Year	Nfld	PEI	NS	NB	Que	Ont	Man	Sask	Alta	BC	Terr	Cda
1970	0.37	0.17	0.90	0.67	0.83	0.87	0.92	0.98	0.92	0.90	0.46	0.86
1975	0.34	0.52	0.61	0.61	0.60	0.50	0.64	0.70	0.60	0.69	0.51	0.56
1980	0.41	0.48	0.52	0.32	0.68	0.56	0.68	0.64	0.48	0.62	0.81	0.58
1985	0.30	0.43	0.65	0.34	0.45	0.61	0.67	0.61	0.51	0.48	0.85	0.53
1988	0.37	0.22	0.63	0.30	0.52	0.58	0.71	0.61	0.41	0.47	0.64	0.53
1990	0.29	0.08	0.68	0.26	0.68	0.65	0.74	0.61	0.46	0.53	0.55	0.62

Note: Figures may not add up due to rounding.

Funding of Each Dollar Spent by Government on Foreign Affairs and International Assistance

Table D.4a: Federal (Dollar)

Year	Nfld	PEI	NS	NB	Que	Ont	Man	Sask	Alta	BC	Terr	Cda
1970	1.00	1.00	1.00	1.00	1.00	1.00	1.00	1.00	1.00	1.00	1.00	1.00
1975	1.00	1.00	1.00	1.00	1.00	1.00	1.00	1.00	1.00	1.00	1.00	1.00
1980	1.00	1.00	1.00	1.00	1.00	1.00	1.00	1.00	1.00	1.00	1.00	1.00
1985	1.00	1.00	1.00	1.00	1.00	1.00	1.00	1.00	1.00	1.00	1.00	1.00
1988	1.00	1.00	1.00	1.00	1.00	1.00	1.00	1.00	1.00	1.00	1.00	1.00
1990	1.00	1.00	1.00	1.00	1.00	1.00	1.00	1.00	1.00	1.00	1.00	1.00

Table D.4b: Provincial (Dollar)

Year	Nfld	PEI	NS	NB	Que	Ont	Man	Sask	Alta	BC	Terr	Cda
1970	0.00	0.00	0.00	0.00	0.00	0.00	0.00	0.00	0.00	0.00	0.00	0.00
1975	0.00	0.00	0.00	0.00	0.00	0.00	0.00	0.00	0.00	0.00	0.00	0.00
1980	0.00	0.00	0.00	0.00	0.00	0.00	0.00	0.00	0.00	0.00	0.00	0.00
1985	0.00	0.00	0.00	0.00	0.00	0.00	0.00	0.00	0.00	0.00	0.00	0.00
1988	0.00	0.00	0.00	0.00	0.00	0.00	0.00	0.00	0.00	0.00	0.00	0.00
1990	0.00	0.00	0.00	0.00	0.00	0.00	0.00	0.00	0.00	0.00	0.00	0.00

Funding of Each Dollar Spent by Government on Foreign Affairs and International Assistance

Table D.4c: Municipal (Dollar)

Year	Nfld	PEI	NS	NB	Que	Ont	Man	Sask	Alta	BC	Terr	Cda
1970	0.00	0.00	0.00	0.00	0.00	0.00	0.00	0.00	0.00	0.00	0.00	0.00
1975	0.00	0.00	0.00	0.00	0.00	0.00	0.00	0.00	0.00	0.00	0.00	0.00
1980	0.00	0.00	0.00	0.00	0.00	0.00	0.00	0.00	0.00	0.00	0.00	0.00
1985	0.00	0.00	0.00	0.00	0.00	0.00	0.00	0.00	0.00	0.00	0.00	0.00
1988	0.00	0.00	0.00	0.00	0.00	0.00	0.00	0.00	0.00	0.00	0.00	0.00
1990	0.00	0.00	0.00	0.00	0.00	0.00	0.00	0.00	0.00	0.00	0.00	0.00

Note: Figures may not add up due to rounding.

Funding of Each Dollar Spent by Government on General Services

Table D.5a: Federal (Dollar)

Year	Nfld	PEI	NS	NB	Que	Ont	Man	Sask	Alta	BC	Terr	Cda
1970	0.61	0.68	0.71	0.61	0.43	0.58	0.54	0.55	0.46	0.50	0.51	0.53
1975	0.61	0.59	0.78	0.69	0.45	0.61	0.57	0.44	0.35	0.43	0.74	0.54
1980	0.57	0.63	0.79	0.66	0.29	0.55	0.61	0.37	0.26	0.36	0.69	0.42
1985	0.58	0.73	0.77	0.63	0.31	0.51	0.49	0.27	0.32	0.41	0.62	0.43
1988	0.57	0.70	0.77	0.61	0.32	0.46	0.49	0.38	0.31	0.42	0.65	0.43
1990	0.57	0.66	0.78	0.61	0.31	0.50	0.54	0.34	0.35	0.40	0.19	0.43

Table D.5b: Provincial (Dollar)

Year	Nfld	PEI	NS	NB	Que	Ont	Man	Sask	Alta	BC	Terr	Cda
1970	0.31	0.28	0.20	0.34	0.35	0.30	0.26	0.23	0.37	0.35	0.47	0.32
1975	0.32	0.35	0.14	0.25	0.35	0.28	0.31	0.41	0.53	0.46	0.21	0.34
1980	0.34	0.34	0.15	0.29	0.51	0.31	0.25	0.48	0.52	0.53	0.25	0.42
1985	0.32	0.23	0.16	0.33	0.50	0.34	0.38	0.60	0.48	0.46	0.30	0.41
1988	0.33	0.26	0.17	0.35	0.47	0.38	0.37	0.45	0.52	0.46	0.29	0.41
1990	0.33	0.31	0.15	0.35	0.51	0.31	0.30	0.53	0.47	0.49	0.75	0.41

Funding of Each Dollar Spent by Government on General Services

Table D.5c: Municipal (Dollar)

Year	Nfld	PEI	NS	NB	Que	Ont	Man	Sask	Alta	BC	Terr	Cda
1970	0.08	0.04	0.10	0.05	0.22	0.12	0.20	0.22	0.17	0.15	0.01	0.15
1975	0.06	0.06	0.08	0.06	0.20	0.11	0.12	0.14	0.12	0.11	0.05	0.13
1980	0.09	0.03	0.06	0.04	0.20	0.15	0.14	0.15	0.22	0.11	0.06	0.16
1985	0.10	0.04	0.07	0.04	0.19	0.15	0.13	0.13	0.20	0.13	0.07	0.15
1988	0.10	0.04	0.07	0.04	0.21	0.16	0.14	0.17	0.17	0.12	0.06	0.16
1990	0.10	0.03	0.06	0.04	0.18	0.18	0.16	0.12	0.19	0.11	0.06	0.16

Note: Figures may not add up due to rounding.

Funding of Each Dollar Spent by Government on Health

Table D.6a: Federal (Dollar)

Year	Nfld	PEI	NS	NB	Que	Ont	Man	Sask	Alta	BC	Terr	Cda
1970	0.69	0.69	0.49	0.53	0.27	0.34	0.43	0.40	0.30	0.41	0.77	0.35
1975	0.56	0.62	0.53	0.61	0.25	0.36	0.44	0.36	0.31	0.38	0.88	0.35
1980	0.58	0.63	0.51	0.54	0.31	0.31	0.43	0.31	0.19	0.23	0.86	0.31
1985	0.58	0.60	0.47	0.53	0.33	0.26	0.39	0.32	0.22	0.27	0.82	0.30
1988	0.53	0.55	0.43	0.45	0.33	0.21	0.38	0.30	0.21	0.22	0.74	0.27
1990	0.41	0.44	0.37	0.37	0.27	0.17	0.30	0.24	0.18	0.17	0.25	0.22

Table D.6b: Provincial (Dollar)

Year	Nfld	PEI	NS	NB	Que	Ont	Man	Sask	Alta	BC	Terr	Cda
1970	0.31	0.31	0.32	0.46	0.72	0.56	0.46	0.36	0.44	0.58	0.23	0.56
1975	0.44	0.38	0.34	0.39	0.75	0.57	0.44	0.40	0.49	0.62	0.11	0.58
1980	0.42	0.37	0.40	0.46	0.69	0.63	0.47	0.53	0.64	0.71	0.14	0.63
1985	0.42	0.40	0.52	0.47	0.67	0.73	0.60	0.65	0.78	0.71	0.18	0.69
1988	0.47	0.45	0.57	0.54	0.67	0.79	0.61	0.69	0.79	0.76	0.26	0.72
1990	0.59	0.56	0.63	0.63	0.73	0.83	0.68	0.73	0.82	0.81	0.75	0.78

Funding of Each Dollar Spent by Government on Health

Table D.6c: Municipal (Dollar)

Year	Nfld	PEI	NS	NB	Que	Ont	Man	Sask	Alta	BC	Terr	Cda
1970	0.00	0.00	0.19	0.00	0.01	0.10	0.11	0.24	0.26	0.01	0.00	0.09
1975	0.00	0.00	0.13	0.00	0.00	0.07	0.12	0.24	0.20	0.01	0.00	0.07
1980	0.00	0.00	0.09	0.00	0.00	0.06	0.10	0.17	0.16	0.06	0.01	0.06
1985	0.00	0.00	0.01	0.00	0.00	0.01	0.01	0.03	0.00	0.02	0.01	0.01
1988	0.00	0.00	0.00	0.00	0.00	0.01	0.01	0.01	0.00	0.02	0.00	0.01
1990	0.00	0.00	0.00	0.00	0.00	0.00	0.01	0.03	0.00	0.02	0.00	0.01

Note: Figures may not add up due to rounding.

Funding of Each Dollar Spent by Government on Housing

Table D.7a: Federal (Dollar)

Year	Nfld	PEI	NS	NB	Que	Ont	Man	Sask	Alta	BC	Terr	Cda
1970	0.60	0.48	0.63	1.00	0.43	0.63	0.87	0.13	0.79	0.25	0.40	0.48
1975	0.85	0.52	0.70	1.00	0.68	0.48	0.98	0.33	0.89	0.48	0.79	0.55
1980	1.00	1.00	0.75	1.00	0.59	0.90	1.00	0.99	0.27	0.55	0.98	0.67
1985	0.90	0.99	0.70	0.99	0.52	0.56	0.84	0.93	0.63	0.53	0.96	0.62
1988	0.96	0.99	0.69	0.95	0.46	0.65	0.81	1.00	0.80	0.70	0.90	0.67
1990	0.96	1.00	0.76	0.99	0.42	0.55	0.87	0.85	0.58	0.71	0.82	0.58

Table D.7b: Provincial (Dollar)

Year	Nfld	PEI	NS	NB	Que	Ont	Man	Sask	Alta	BC	Terr	Cda
1970	0.40	0.52	0.37	0.00	0.54	0.37	0.13	0.87	0.01	0.75	0.60	0.50
1975	0.15	0.48	0.30	0.00	0.32	0.52	0.02	0.67	0.11	0.52	0.20	0.45
1980	0.00	0.00	0.25	0.00	0.41	0.10	0.00	0.01	0.73	0.45	0.01	0.33
1985	0.02	0.00	0.26	0.01	0.48	0.31	0.15	0.01	0.27	0.33	0.01	0.31
1988	0.01	0.00	0.26	0.02	0.54	0.17	0.16	0.00	0.13	0.15	0.03	0.26
1990	0.02	0.00	0.20	0.00	0.58	0.34	0.10	0.15	0.36	0.19	0.04	0.37

Funding of Each Dollar Spent by Government on Housing

Table D.7c: Municipal (Dollar)

Year	Nfld	PEI	NS	NB	Que	Ont	Man	Sask	Alta	BC	Terr	Cda
1970	0.00	0.00	0.00	0.00	0.03	0.00	0.00	0.00	0.20	0.00	0.01	0.01
1975	0.01	0.00	0.00	0.00	0.00	0.00	0.00	0.00	0.00	0.00	0.01	0.00
1980	0.00	0.00	0.00	0.00	0.00	0.00	0.00	0.00	0.00	0.00	0.01	0.00
1985	0.09	0.01	0.04	0.01	0.00	0.13	0.00	0.06	0.09	0.14	0.02	0.07
1988	0.03	0.00	0.05	0.03	0.00	0.18	0.03	0.00	0.06	0.15	0.07	0.07
1990	0.02	0.00	0.04	0.00	0.00	0.11	0.02	0.00	0.06	0.10	0.14	0.05

Note: Figures may not add up due to rounding.

Funding of Each Dollar Spent by Government on Interest Payments

Table D.8a: Federal (Dollar)

Year	Nfld	PEI	NS	NB	Que	Ont	Man	Sask	Alta	BC	Terr	Cda
1970	0.44	0.60	0.54	0.57	0.57	0.56	0.50	0.47	0.38	0.62	0.77	0.55
1975	0.38	0.64	0.66	0.61	0.54	0.61	0.55	0.56	0.47	0.65	0.90	0.58
1980	0.41	0.60	0.67	0.57	0.54	0.71	0.55	0.43	0.55	0.63	0.91	0.63
1985	0.49	0.66	0.64	0.56	0.56	0.75	0.51	0.31	0.50	0.58	0.96	0.64
1988	0.54	0.69	0.68	0.60	0.56	0.78	0.51	0.37	0.49	0.57	0.98	0.66
1990	0.53	0.65	0.65	0.58	0.58	0.82	0.46	0.42	0.44	0.59	0.95	0.68

Table D.8b: Provincial (Dollar)

Year	Nfld	PEI	NS	NB	Que	Ont	Man	Sask	Alta	BC	Terr	Cda
1970	0.48	0.30	0.36	0.38	0.21	0.31	0.33	0.37	0.37	0.15	0.21	0.29
1975	0.56	0.29	0.26	0.32	0.28	0.31	0.30	0.33	0.31	0.13	0.04	0.30
1980	0.50	0.33	0.27	0.38	0.29	0.24	0.33	0.51	0.25	0.18	0.03	0.27
1985	0.45	0.30	0.33	0.40	0.33	0.22	0.42	0.65	0.25	0.28	0.00	0.29
1988	0.40	0.28	0.29	0.37	0.33	0.20	0.44	0.60	0.31	0.32	0.00	0.28
1990	0.42	0.32	0.32	0.40	0.32	0.16	0.49	0.54	0.41	0.31	0.03	0.26

Funding of Each Dollar Spent by Government on Interest Payments

Table D.8c: Municipal (Dollar)

Year	Nfld	PEI	NS	NB	Que	Ont	Man	Sask	Alta	BC	Terr	Cda
1970	0.08	0.11	0.09	0.05	0.22	0.12	0.16	0.17	0.24	0.23	0.02	0.16
1975	0.06	0.08	0.08	0.06	0.18	0.07	0.15	0.10	0.22	0.22	0.05	0.12
1980	0.09	0.07	0.06	0.06	0.18	0.05	0.11	0.07	0.20	0.19	0.06	0.10
1985	0.06	0.04	0.03	0.03	0.11	0.03	0.07	0.04	0.25	0.14	0.04	0.07
1988	0.06	0.04	0.03	0.03	0.10	0.02	0.05	0.03	0.19	0.11	0.02	0.06
1990	0.05	0.03	0.03	0.02	0.10	0.02	0.05	0.04	0.15	0.10	0.02	0.05

Note: Figures may not add up due to rounding.

Funding of Each Dollar Spent by Government on Labour, Employment, and Immigration

Table D.9a: Federal (Dollar)

Year	Nfld	PEI	NS	NB	Que	Ont	Man	Sask	Alta	BC	Terr	Cda
1970	0.63	0.65	0.79	0.54	0.61	0.68	0.96	0.89	0.79	0.96	0.81	0.70
1975	0.75	0.77	0.83	0.99	0.64	0.80	0.90	1.00	0.79	0.96	0.84	0.78
1980	0.81	0.88	0.91	0.92	0.61	0.74	0.88	0.72	0.76	0.76	0.85	0.73
1985	0.81	0.83	0.90	0.93	0.55	0.66	0.66	0.59	0.41	0.83	0.90	0.63
1988	0.81	0.87	0.91	0.85	0.53	0.67	0.78	0.72	0.47	0.87	0.95	0.65
1990	0.79	0.85	0.73	0.82	0.50	0.77	0.76	0.76	0.55	0.90	0.47	0.67

Table D.9b: Provincial (Dollar)

Year	Nfld	PEI	NS	NB	Que	Ont	Man	Sask	Alta	BC	Terr	Cda
1970	0.37	0.35	0.21	0.46	0.39	0.32	0.04	0.11	0.21	0.04	0.19	0.30
1975	0.25	0.23	0.17	0.01	0.36	0.20	0.10	0.00	0.21	0.04	0.16	0.22
1980	0.19	0.12	0.09	0.08	0.39	0.26	0.12	0.28	0.24	0.24	0.15	0.27
1985	0.19	0.17	0.10	0.07	0.45	0.34	0.34	0.41	0.59	0.17	0.10	0.37
1988	0.19	0.13	0.09	0.15	0.47	0.33	0.22	0.28	0.53	0.13	0.05	0.35
1990	0.21	0.15	0.27	0.18	0.50	0.23	0.24	0.24	0.45	0.10	0.53	0.33

Funding of Each Dollar Spent by Government on Labour, Employment, and Immigration

Table D.9c: Municipal (Dollar)

Year	Nfld	PEI	NS	NB	Que	Ont	Man	Sask	Alta	BC	Terr	Cda
1970	0.00	0.00	0.00	0.00	0.00	0.00	0.00	0.00	0.00	0.00	0.00	0.00
1975	0.00	0.00	0.00	0.00	0.00	0.00	0.00	0.00	0.00	0.00	0.00	0.00
1980	0.00	0.00	0.00	0.00	0.00	0.00	0.00	0.00	0.00	0.00	0.00	0.00
1985	0.00	0.00	0.00	0.00	0.00	0.00	0.00	0.00	0.00	0.00	0.00	0.00
1988	0.00	0.00	0.00	0.00	0.00	0.00	0.00	0.00	0.00	0.00	0.00	0.00
1990	0.00	0.00	0.00	0.00	0.00	0.00	0.00	0.00	0.00	0.00	0.00	0.00

Note: Figures may not add up due to rounding.

Funding of Each Dollar Spent by Government on Other

Table 10a: Federal (Dollar)

Year	Nfld	PEI	NS	NB	Que	Ont	Man	Sask	Alta	BC	Terr	Cda
1970	0.83	0.90	0.88	0.76	1.00	0.74	0.73	0.85	0.75	0.92	1.00	0.84
1975	0.39	0.43	0.77	0.94	0.67	0.58	0.47	0.45	0.47	0.20	0.67	0.49
1980	0.72	0.81	0.70	0.85	0.51	0.54	0.63	0.80	0.58	0.45	0.67	0.57
1985	0.94	0.76	0.94	0.88	0.50	0.37	0.42	0.79	0.22	0.41	0.97	0.61
1988	0.78	0.85	0.61	0.79	0.39	0.32	0.45	0.64	0.62	0.26	0.75	0.47
1990	0.75	0.90	0.88	0.83	0.55	0.32	0.57	0.45	0.35	0.41	0.23	0.44

Table 10b: Provincial (Dollar)

Year	Nfld	PEI	NS	NB	Que	Ont	Man	Sask	Alta	BC	Terr	Cda
1970	0.06	0.10	0.07	0.23	0.00	0.01	0.01	0.00	0.06	0.01	0.00	0.03
1975	0.60	0.57	0.21	0.05	0.08	0.05	0.37	0.49	0.28	0.75	0.32	0.34
1980	0.26	0.18	0.28	0.14	0.28	0.21	0.23	0.16	0.29	0.45	0.32	0.26
1985	0.06	0.24	0.05	0.11	0.17	0.25	0.45	0.15	0.53	0.52	0.03	0.20
1988	0.20	0.14	0.35	0.19	0.27	0.33	0.23	0.32	0.23	0.65	0.25	0.30
1990	0.21	0.09	0.07	0.15	0.16	0.45	0.21	0.42	0.40	0.49	0.75	0.35

Funding of Each Dollar Spent by Government on Other

Table 10c: Municipal (Dollar)

Year	Nfld	PEI	NS	NB	Que	Ont	Man	Sask	Alta	BC	Terr	Cda
1970	0.11	0.00	0.04	0.01	0.00	0.25	0.26	0.15	0.20	0.07	0.00	0.12
1975	0.01	0.00	0.02	0.01	0.26	0.37	0.16	0.06	0.25	0.04	0.00	0.17
1980	0.02	0.01	0.03	0.02	0.21	0.26	0.13	0.04	0.13	0.10	0.01	0.17
1985	0.00	0.00	0.02	0.01	0.33	0.38	0.13	0.06	0.25	0.07	0.00	0.19
1988	0.02	0.01	0.04	0.02	0.33	0.36	0.32	0.04	0.15	0.09	0.00	0.23
1990	0.04	0.01	0.05	0.02	0.29	0.24	0.23	0.13	0.25	0.10	0.01	0.22

Note: Figures may not add up due to rounding.

Funding of Each Dollar Spent by Government on Protection of Persons and Property

Table D.11a: Federal (Dollar)

Year	Nfld	PEI	NS	NB	Que	Ont	Man	Sask	Alta	BC	Terr	Cda
1970	0.80	0.93	0.92	0.85	0.59	0.63	0.74	0.61	0.65	0.67	0.74	0.67
1975	0.68	0.88	0.88	0.80	0.51	0.60	0.67	0.52	0.58	0.56	0.82	0.61
1980	0.69	0.88	0.90	0.79	0.56	0.62	0.70	0.50	0.52	0.57	0.81	0.63
1985	0.75	0.90	0.89	0.81	0.61	0.66	0.69	0.55	0.58	0.63	0.75	0.66
1988	0.73	0.83	0.86	0.87	0.60	0.63	0.70	0.51	0.56	0.59	0.72	0.65
1990	0.69	0.82	0.86	0.86	0.60	0.59	0.69	0.49	0.56	0.56	0.36	0.62

Table D.11b: Provincial (Dollar)

Year	Nfld	PEI	NS	NB	Que	Ont	Man	Sask	Alta	BC	Terr	Cda
1970	0.18	0.04	0.04	0.09	0.19	0.18	0.12	0.20	0.20	0.14	0.24	0.16
1975	0.28	0.08	0.06	0.10	0.26	0.20	0.16	0.30	0.24	0.22	0.11	0.21
1980	0.28	0.08	0.06	0.13	0.22	0.17	0.15	0.29	0.27	0.22	0.14	0.19
1985	0.22	0.07	0.05	0.12	0.18	0.16	0.17	0.27	0.25	0.17	0.20	0.17
1988	0.21	0.13	0.07	0.08	0.19	0.19	0.16	0.27	0.25	0.18	0.23	0.18
1990	0.27	0.14	0.08	0.09	0.19	0.22	0.15	0.28	0.25	0.22	0.59	0.20

Funding of Each Dollar Spent by Government on Protection of Persons and Property

Table D.11c: Municipal (Dollar)

Year	Nfld	PEI	NS	NB	Que	Ont	Man	Sask	Alta	BC	Terr	Cda
1970	0.02	0.03	0.04	0.06	0.21	0.19	0.14	0.19	0.15	0.19	0.03	0.17
1975	0.04	0.04	0.06	0.09	0.22	0.20	0.16	0.19	0.18	0.21	0.08	0.18
1980	0.03	0.04	0.05	0.08	0.21	0.20	0.15	0.21	0.21	0.21	0.05	0.18
1985	0.03	0.03	0.06	0.07	0.21	0.18	0.14	0.18	0.17	0.20	0.04	0.17
1988	0.05	0.04	0.06	0.05	0.21	0.18	0.15	0.22	0.19	0.23	0.04	0.17
1990	0.05	0.04	0.06	0.04	0.21	0.19	0.16	0.22	0.19	0.22	0.05	0.18

Note: Figures may not add up due to rounding.

Funding of Each Dollar Spent by Government on Regional Planning and Development

Table D.12a: Federal (Dollar)

Year	Nfld	PEI	NS	NB	Que	Ont	Man	Sask	Alta	BC	Terr	Cda
1970	0.40	0.48	0.31	0.33	0.40	0.40	0.33	0.19	0.09	0.54	0.38	0.36
1975	0.70	0.38	0.50	0.39	0.31	0.22	0.23	0.10	0.11	0.25	0.67	0.26
1980	0.35	0.39	0.36	0.36	0.29	0.19	0.42	0.55	0.10	0.17	0.66	0.26
1985	0.38	0.48	0.32	0.57	0.34	0.41	0.15	0.07	0.14	0.23	0.59	0.31
1988	0.52	0.93	0.44	0.50	0.39	0.38	0.27	0.21	0.18	0.30	0.65	0.36
1990	0.47	0.69	0.39	0.43	0.41	0.41	0.23	0.30	0.17	0.25	0.02	0.33

Table D.12b: Provincial (Dollar)

Year	Nfld	PEI	NS	NB	Que	Ont	Man	Sask	Alta	BC	Terr	Cda
1970	0.60	0.48	0.69	0.59	0.60	0.54	0.67	0.46	0.34	0.17	0.62	0.54
1975	0.24	0.62	0.50	0.61	0.69	0.78	0.76	0.90	0.28	0.75	0.33	0.69
1980	0.65	0.61	0.64	0.64	0.71	0.64	0.42	0.45	0.25	0.76	0.34	0.58
1985	0.59	0.52	0.68	0.41	0.44	0.38	0.77	0.93	0.48	0.44	0.41	0.50
1988	0.47	0.07	0.56	0.42	0.36	0.49	0.73	0.79	0.53	0.47	0.35	0.49
1990	0.49	0.31	0.61	0.57	0.34	0.44	0.69	0.46	0.28	0.52	0.98	0.46

Funding of Each Dollar Spent by Government on Regional Planning and Development

Table D.12c: Municipal (Dollar)

Year	Nfld	PEI	NS	NB	Que	Ont	Man	Sask	Alta	BC	Terr	Cda
1970	0.00	0.04	0.00	0.08	0.00	0.06	0.00	0.35	0.57	0.28	0.00	0.10
1975	0.06	0.00	0.00	0.00	0.00	0.00	0.01	0.00	0.62	0.00	0.00	0.04
1980	0.00	0.00	0.00	0.00	0.00	0.17	0.16	0.00	0.65	0.07	0.00	0.16
1985	0.02	0.00	0.00	0.02	0.22	0.21	0.08	0.00	0.38	0.33	0.00	0.18
1988	0.01	0.00	0.00	0.08	0.25	0.12	0.00	0.00	0.30	0.23	0.00	0.15
1990	0.04	0.00	0.00	0.00	0.26	0.15	0.09	0.24	0.55	0.23	0.00	0.20

Note: Figures may not add up due to rounding.

Funding of Each Dollar Spent by Government on Resource Conservation and Industrial Development

Table D.13a: Federal (Dollar)

Year	Nfld	PEI	NS	NB	Que	Ont	Man	Sask	Alta	BC	Terr	Cda
1970	1.00	1.00	0.77	1.00	0.67	0.63	0.73	0.88	0.71	0.43	1.00	0.71
1975	0.92	1.00	0.90	0.93	0.80	0.62	0.76	0.88	0.63	0.38	0.81	0.75
1980	0.73	0.91	0.93	0.97	0.76	0.63	0.73	0.66	0.43	0.46	0.85	0.69
1985	0.89	0.77	0.82	0.63	0.50	0.55	0.73	0.70	0.42	0.31	0.96	0.55
1988	0.65	0.67	0.64	0.59	0.45	0.52	0.73	0.73	0.48	0.35	0.86	0.54
1990	0.62	0.63	0.65	0.55	0.39	0.49	0.67	0.65	0.37	0.32	0.36	0.46

Table D.13b: Provincial (Dollar)

Year	Nfld	PEI	NS	NB	Que	Ont	Man	Sask	Alta	BC	Terr	Cda
1970	0.00	0.00	0.19	0.00	0.33	0.33	0.27	0.11	0.29	0.57	0.00	0.28
1975	0.08	0.00	0.09	0.07	0.20	0.32	0.23	0.12	0.36	0.60	0.19	0.23
1980	0.27	0.09	0.07	0.03	0.23	0.31	0.26	0.34	0.54	0.53	0.15	0.28
1985	0.11	0.23	0.16	0.34	0.48	0.40	0.26	0.30	0.58	0.67	0.04	0.43
1988	0.34	0.33	0.33	0.39	0.52	0.43	0.25	0.26	0.51	0.61	0.14	0.44
1990	0.38	0.37	0.35	0.43	0.58	0.50	0.31	0.35	0.63	0.64	0.64	0.52

Funding of Each Dollar Spent by Government on Resource Conservation and Industrial Development

Table D.13c: Municipal (Dollar)

Year	Nfld	PEI	NS	NB	Que	Ont	Man	Sask	Alta	BC	Terr	Cda
1970	0.00	0.00	0.04	0.00	0.00	0.03	0.00	0.00	0.00	0.01	0.00	0.01
1975	0.00	0.00	0.01	0.00	0.00	0.07	0.01	0.00	0.01	0.02	0.00	0.01
1980	0.00	0.00	0.00	0.00	0.02	0.06	0.02	0.00	0.04	0.01	0.00	0.02
1985	0.00	0.00	0.02	0.03	0.02	0.05	0.01	0.00	0.00	0.02	0.00	0.02
1988	0.01	0.00	0.03	0.01	0.03	0.06	0.02	0.01	0.01	0.04	0.00	0.02
1990	0.00	0.00	0.00	0.02	0.03	0.01	0.02	0.00	0.00	0.04	0.00	0.01

Note: Figures may not add up due to rounding.

Funding of Each Dollar Spent by Government on Research Establishments

Table D.14a: Federal (Dollar)

Year	Nfld	PEI	NS	NB	Que	Ont	Man	Sask	Alta	BC	Terr	Cda
1970	1.00	1.00	0.95	0.94	1.00	0.97	1.00	0.91	0.89	1.00	1.00	0.97
1975	1.00	1.00	0.93	0.94	1.00	0.96	1.00	0.85	0.85	1.00	0.90	0.96
1980	1.00	1.00	0.94	0.94	1.00	0.96	0.97	0.86	0.81	0.92	1.00	0.95
1985	1.00	1.00	0.88	0.87	0.80	0.94	0.98	0.74	0.52	0.91	1.00	0.83
1988	1.00	1.00	0.88	0.84	0.73	0.93	0.98	0.73	0.50	0.91	0.92	0.80
1990	1.00	1.00	0.89	0.85	0.72	0.89	0.98	0.77	0.61	0.74	0.63	0.79

Table D.14b: Provincial (Dollar)

Year	Nfld	PEI	NS	NB	Que	Ont	Man	Sask	Alta	BC	Terr	Cda
1970	0.00	0.00	0.05	0.06	0.00	0.03	0.00	0.09	0.11	0.00	0.00	0.03
1975	0.00	0.00	0.07	0.06	0.00	0.04	0.00	0.15	0.15	0.00	0.10	0.04
1980	0.00	0.00	0.06	0.06	0.00	0.04	0.03	0.14	0.19	0.08	0.00	0.05
1985	0.00	0.00	0.12	0.13	0.20	0.06	0.02	0.26	0.48	0.09	0.00	0.17
1988	0.00	0.00	0.12	0.16	0.27	0.07	0.02	0.27	0.50	0.09	0.08	0.20
1990	0.00	0.00	0.11	0.15	0.28	0.11	0.02	0.23	0.39	0.26	0.37	0.21

Funding of Each Dollar Spent by Government on Research Establishments

Table D.14c: Municipal (Dollar)

Year	Nfld	PEI	NS	NB	Que	Ont	Man	Sask	Alta	BC	Terr	Cda
1970	0.00	0.00	0.00	0.00	0.00	0.00	0.00	0.00	0.00	0.00	0.00	0.00
1975	0.00	0.00	0.00	0.00	0.00	0.00	0.00	0.00	0.00	0.00	0.00	0.00
1980	0.00	0.00	0.00	0.00	0.00	0.00	0.00	0.00	0.00	0.00	0.00	0.00
1985	0.00	0.00	0.00	0.00	0.00	0.00	0.00	0.00	0.00	0.00	0.00	0.00
1988	0.00	0.00	0.00	0.00	0.00	0.00	0.00	0.00	0.00	0.00	0.00	0.00
1990	0.00	0.00	0.00	0.00	0.00	0.00	0.00	0.00	0.00	0.00	0.00	0.00

Note: Figures may not add up due to rounding.

Funding of Each Dollar Spent by Government on Social Services

Table D.15a: Federal (Dollar)

Year	Nfld	PEI	NS	NB	Que	Ont	Man	Sask	Alta	BC	Terr	Cda
1970	0.90	0.93	0.90	0.91	0.69	0.77	0.88	0.88	0.78	0.74	0.80	0.77
1975	0.92	0.92	0.91	0.90	0.77	0.76	0.81	0.79	0.79	0.74	0.92	0.78
1980	0.91	0.91	0.87	0.89	0.74	0.70	0.78	0.69	0.70	0.71	0.87	0.74
1985	0.90	0.92	0.87	0.88	0.72	0.72	0.78	0.78	0.72	0.78	0.86	0.75
1988	0.92	0.91	0.85	0.88	0.70	0.66	0.77	0.83	0.70	0.79	0.83	0.73
1990	0.89	0.90	0.84	0.87	0.73	0.64	0.75	0.84	0.70	0.76	0.59	0.72

Table D.15b: Provincial (Dollar)

Year	Nfld	PEI	NS	NB	Que	Ont	Man	Sask	Alta	BC	Terr	Cda
1970	0.10	0.07	0.07	0.09	0.31	0.19	0.12	0.11	0.22	0.23	0.20	0.21
1975	0.08	0.08	0.06	0.10	0.23	0.20	0.19	0.20	0.21	0.25	0.08	0.20
1980	0.09	0.09	0.11	0.11	0.26	0.28	0.22	0.30	0.29	0.28	0.13	0.25
1985	0.10	0.08	0.11	0.12	0.28	0.26	0.22	0.21	0.27	0.22	0.13	0.24
1988	0.08	0.09	0.10	0.12	0.30	0.31	0.22	0.16	0.29	0.21	0.16	0.26
1990	0.11	0.10	0.11	0.13	0.27	0.35	0.25	0.15	0.30	0.24	0.41	0.28

Funding of Each Dollar Spent by Government on Social Services

Table D.15c: Municipal (Dollar)

Year	Nfld	PEI	NS	NB	Que	Ont	Man	Sask	Alta	BC	Terr	Cda
1970	0.00	0.00	0.03	0.00	0.00	0.04	0.00	0.01	0.01	0.03	0.00	0.02
1975	0.00	0.00	0.03	0.00	0.00	0.04	0.00	0.01	0.01	0.01	0.00	0.02
1980	0.00	0.00	0.03	0.00	0.00	0.02	0.00	0.01	0.01	0.01	0.00	0.01
1985	0.00	0.00	0.03	0.00	0.00	0.02	0.00	0.01	0.01	0.00	0.01	0.01
1988	0.00	0.00	0.05	0.00	0.00	0.03	0.00	0.00	0.01	0.00	0.01	0.01
1990	0.00	0.00	0.05	0.00	0.00	0.02	0.00	0.01	0.00	0.00	0.00	0.01

Note: Figures may not add up due to rounding.

Funding of Each Dollar Spent by Government on Transportation and Communications

Table D.16a: Federal (Dollar)

Year	Nfld	PEI	NS	NB	Que	Ont	Man	Sask	Alta	BC	Terr	Cda
1970	0.56	0.51	0.45	0.35	0.27	0.26	0.29	0.22	0.16	0.19	0.58	0.27
1975	0.38	0.50	0.54	0.40	0.25	0.37	0.41	0.34	0.20	0.20	0.70	0.31
1980	0.47	0.52	0.59	0.46	0.30	0.37	0.40	0.27	0.14	0.22	0.75	0.32
1985	0.51	0.62	0.58	0.49	0.28	0.37	0.36	0.27	0.16	0.21	0.61	0.31
1988	0.51	0.55	0.58	0.49	0.27	0.34	0.39	0.34	0.18	0.28	0.63	0.32
1990	0.46	0.50	0.54	0.43	0.21	0.29	0.32	0.28	0.19	0.21	0.25	0.27

Table D.16b: Provincial (Dollar)

Year	Nfld	PEI	NS	NB	Que	Ont	Man	Sask	Alta	BC	Terr	Cda
1970	0.40	0.43	0.46	0.56	0.47	0.49	0.44	0.54	0.46	0.55	0.37	0.48
1975	0.52	0.45	0.34	0.45	0.50	0.42	0.33	0.41	0.50	0.60	0.17	0.46
1980	0.41	0.44	0.33	0.44	0.45	0.45	0.35	0.40	0.50	0.59	0.14	0.46
1985	0.37	0.34	0.33	0.40	0.42	0.46	0.34	0.42	0.54	0.61	0.22	0.46
1988	0.34	0.37	0.34	0.41	0.39	0.46	0.30	0.36	0.49	0.45	0.24	0.42
1990	0.40	0.45	0.35	0.47	0.37	0.52	0.36	0.38	0.48	0.53	0.62	0.46

Funding of Each Dollar Spent by Government on Transportation and Communications

Table D.16c: Municipal (Dollar)

Year	Nfld	PEI	NS	NB	Que	Ont	Man	Sask	Alta	BC	Terr	Cda
1970	0.04	0.06	0.09	0.09	0.26	0.26	0.26	0.24	0.38	0.25	0.05	0.25
1975	0.10	0.05	0.12	0.15	0.25	0.21	0.27	0.25	0.31	0.20	0.13	0.22
1980	0.12	0.04	0.07	0.10	0.25	0.18	0.25	0.32	0.36	0.19	0.11	0.22
1985	0.12	0.04	0.09	0.11	0.30	0.17	0.30	0.31	0.31	0.18	0.17	0.23
1988	0.14	0.07	0.08	0.10	0.34	0.20	0.30	0.30	0.33	0.27	0.14	0.26
1990	0.14	0.05	0.11	0.09	0.42	0.19	0.32	0.34	0.33	0.26	0.12	0.28

Note: Figures may not add up due to rounding.

Funding of Each Dollar Spent by Government

Table D.17a: Federal (Dollar)

Year	Nfld	PEI	NS	NB	Que	Ont	Man	Sask	Alta	BC	Terr	Cda
1970	0.70	0.78	0.66	0.65	0.47	0.46	0.55	0.54	0.41	0.48	0.66	0.49
1975	0.62	0.71	0.73	0.69	0.49	0.50	0.54	0.55	0.41	0.45	0.76	0.51
1980	0.64	0.72	0.74	0.74	0.48	0.52	0.57	0.48	0.33	0.43	0.75	0.50
1985	0.71	0.75	0.70	0.67	0.48	0.52	0.54	0.49	0.39	0.48	0.84	0.51
1988	0.66	0.72	0.66	0.67	0.47	0.51	0.55	0.52	0.42	0.48	0.73	0.51
1990	0.62	0.68	0.65	0.64	0.46	0.51	0.50	0.48	0.38	0.44	0.34	0.49

Table D.17b: Provincial (Dollar)

Year	Nfld	PEI	NS	NB	Que	Ont	Man	Sask	Alta	BC	Terr	Cda
1970	0.27	0.16	0.23	0.32	0.39	0.36	0.29	0.28	0.40	0.35	0.32	0.35
1975	0.34	0.26	0.19	0.26	0.40	0.37	0.31	0.32	0.41	0.41	0.18	0.37
1980	0.32	0.25	0.20	0.23	0.42	0.35	0.29	0.39	0.47	0.42	0.19	0.37
1985	0.25	0.22	0.24	0.29	0.42	0.36	0.38	0.41	0.49	0.42	0.12	0.39
1988	0.29	0.25	0.27	0.30	0.43	0.38	0.36	0.38	0.47	0.41	0.22	0.39
1990	0.34	0.30	0.28	0.33	0.43	0.37	0.40	0.42	0.49	0.45	0.62	0.41

Funding of Each Dollar Spent by Government

Table D.17c: Municipal (Dollar)

Year	Nfld	PEI	NS	NB	Que	Ont	Man	Sask	Alta	BC	Terr	Cda
1970	0.02	0.06	0.11	0.04	0.14	0.18	0.16	0.18	0.20	0.17	0.02	0.16
1975	0.04	0.03	0.08	0.05	0.11	0.14	0.15	0.13	0.18	0.14	0.06	0.13
1980	0.04	0.02	0.06	0.03	0.11	0.14	0.14	0.13	0.20	0.15	0.07	0.13
1985	0.03	0.03	0.05	0.03	0.10	0.11	0.09	0.10	0.12	0.10	0.03	0.10
1988	0.04	0.02	0.07	0.03	0.10	0.12	0.09	0.09	0.12	0.11	0.05	0.10
1990	0.04	0.02	0.07	0.03	0.11	0.12	0.10	0.10	0.12	0.11	0.05	0.11

Note: Figures may not add up due to rounding.

Bibliography

Selected Sources

Canadian Tax Foundation, *The National Finances—An Analysis of the Revenues and Expenditures of the Government of Canada, 1993*, Canadian Tax Foundation, 1993.

________, *The National Finances—An Analysis of the Revenues and Expenditures of the Government of Canada, 1992*, Canadian Tax Foundation, 1992.

________, *Provincial and Municipal Finances, 1991*, Canadian Tax Foundation, 1992.

________, *Provincial and Municipal Finances, 1989*, Canadian Tax Foundation, 1990.

Davies, James, France St-Hilaire, and John Whalley, "Some Calcultions of Lifetime Tax Incidence," *The American Economic Review*, Vol. 74, No. 4, September 1984.

Gillespie, W. Irwin, *The Redistribution of Income in Canada*, Carleton University, Ottawa, Ontario.

Horry, Isabella, Filip Palda, and Michael Walker, *Tax Facts 8* , The Fraser Institute, 1992.

Horry, Isabella, and Michael Walker, *Government Spending Facts*, The Fraser Institute, 1991.

Ip, Irene, *Big Spenders: A Survey of Provincial Government Finances in Canada*, Policy Study 15, C.D. Howe Institute, 1991.

Katsaitis, Odysseus, "On the Substitutability between Private Consumer Expenditure and Government Spending in Canada," *Canadian Journal of Economics*, Vol. 20, No. 3, August 1987.

Miyake, Joanna, and Michael Walker, "Waiting Your Turn: Hospital Waiting Lists in Canada," 3rd. edition, *Critical Issues Bulletin 1*, The Fraser Institute, 1993.

Payette, Micheline, et François Vaillancourt, "L'Incidence des Recettes et Dépenses Gouvernementales au Québec en 1981," *L'Actualité Economique, Revue d'Analyse Economique*, Vol. 62, No. 3, Septembre 1986.

Richardson, Robin, "The Public Debt of an Independent Quebec," *Fraser Forum Critical Issues Bulletin*, The Fraser Institute, August 1994.

Government Sources

Health and Welfare Canada, *National Health Expenditures in Canada, 1975-1987*, Health and Welfare Canada, Ottawa, September 1990.

________, *Green Book Tables: Provincial Government Health Expenditures and Related Federal Contributions Canada, the provinces and the territories, 1974-75 to 1990-91*, Ottawa, July 1993.

Revenue Canada Taxation, *Taxation Statistics: Analyzing the Returns for Individuals for the 1990 Taxation Year and Miscellaneous Statistics*, Minister of Supply and Services Canada, 1992.

Statistics Canada, *Census 1986*, Supply and Services Canada.

________, *1990 Survey of Family Expenditure*, Household Surveys Division, unpublished data.

________, *1991 Survey of Consumer Finances*, Household Surveys Division, unpublished data.

________, *The Daily*, catalogue no.11-001, Statistics Canada, August 24, 1993.

________, *Canadian Economic Observer*, catalogue no. 11-210, Supply and Services Canada, various issues.

________, *Canada Yearbook*, catalogue no. 11-402, annual, Supply and Services Canada, various issues.

________, *System of National Accounts: National Income and Expenditure Accounts*, catalogue no. 13-001, quarterly, Supply and Services Canada, various issues.

________, *System of National Accounts: Provincial Economic Accounts, Annual Estimates*, catalogue no. 13-213, Supply and Services Canada, various issues.

________, *Canadian Forestry Statistics*, catalogue no. 25-202, annual, Supply and Services Canada, various issues.

________, *General Review of the Mineral Industries, Mines, Quarries and Oil Wells*, catalogue no. 26-201, Supply and Services Canada, various issues.

________, *Manufacturing Industries of Canada, National and Provincial Areas*, catalogue no. 31-203, Supply and Services Canada, various issues.

________, *The System of Government Financial Management Statistics*, catalogue no. 68-507E, Supply and Services Canada, 1984.

________, *Local Government Finance, Revenue and Expenditure, Assets and Liabilities*, catalogue no. 68-204, annual, Supply and Services Canada, various issues.

________, *Provincial Government Finance, Revenue and Expenditure*, catalogue no. 68-207, annual, Supply and Services Canada, various issues.

________, *Federal Government Finance, Revenue and Expenditure, Assets and Liabilities*, catalogue no. 68-211, annual, Supply and Services Canada, various issues.

________, *Public Finance Historical Data 1965/66-1991/92*, catalogue no. 68-512, occasional, Supply and Services Canada, 1992.

________, *Public Sector Employment and Remuneration*, catalogue no. 72-209, annual, Supply and Services Canada, various issues.

________, *Financial Statistics of Education*, catalogue no. 81-208, annual, Minister of Supply and Services Canada, various issues.

________, *Education in Canada, A Statistical review*, catalogue no. 81-229, annual, Supply and Services Canada, various issues.

________, *An Analysis of Hospital Expenditures in Canada*, catalogue no. 83-522E, Minister of Supply and Services Canada, 1982.

________, *Compendium of Public Sector Statistics*, Public Institutions Division, various issues.

________, *Federal Government Revenue and Expenditure*, Public Institutions Division.

________, *Local Government Revenue and Expenditure*, Public Institutions Division.

________, *Provincial Government Revenue and Expenditue*, Public Institutions Division.